THE POPE, THE COUNCIL,

AND THE MASS

"I enjoyed reading the text of this new book by Messrs. Likoudis and White-head, and I believe that anyone who will read the development of their chapters will find a new consistency in the Church's liturgical reforms since Vatican II as well as the 'answers' to the typical criticisms that have been made of the re-formed liturgy. The authors are to be commended for their idea and a job well done."

— Most Reverend Thomas J. Welsh
Bishop of Arlington

"I have read the entire manuscript of *The Pope, the Council, and the Mass*, and find the approach of the authors to be doctrinally, historically, and theo-logically sound and exact. In this book, the entire argument over 'traditional-ism' has finally been placed on an intellectual and factual plane and the good that the book will do for the Church and the authority of the Holy See is no doubt very great."

— Rev. John A. Hardon, S.J.
Author, *The Catholic Catechism*

"[This book] is excellent and should be of the greatest utility. It is clear, moderate, and well documented. . . ."

— Hans Urs von Balthasar

"Messrs. Likoudis and Whitehead display considerable erudition and a deep understanding of Church history and law as they make their way through the . . . objections to the new Order of Mass. . . . Their replies are well reasoned, well argued, and . . . well presented."

— Charles A. Fecher,
Catholic Review

"Charges about the validity of the New Mass, Pope Paul's authority to change the Mass, and a host of other questions are answered straightforwardly. . . . This is a book full of gems. More than an *Apologia* for orthodoxy, it is a work of love, the love of the authors for Christ and His Church."

— John A. Vitello,
New Oxford Review

"The conception of writing the chapters as comprehensive responses to 24 most frequently posed questions of the Traditionalists has resulted in a coherent, easily readable format. The answers are scholarly and thorough; the documenta-tion is copious . . . a perfect commentary on a dynamic lay organization whose essence is love for the person of the Pope and unswerving adherence to his Magisterium and directives.

— Rev. Richard W. Gilsdorf, Pastor

"Likoudis and Whitehead answer convincingly doubts raised about the right of the Pope to substitute the new rite of 1970 for the Tridentine one and to impose an obligation on the faithful to follow the new. Difficulties about such matters as the 'pro multis' phrase in the Consecration are well handled. 'The Pope, the Council and the Mass' . . . remains . . . a scholarly and sensitive answer to people who are deeply hurt, and it should do something to heal the Church."

— Paul Hallett,
National Catholic Register

"This book has been sorely needed for well over a decade . . . superb both in terms of scholarship and catechesis."

— Russell Hittinger,
L'Osservatore Romano

THE POPE, THE COUNCIL, AND THE MASS

Answers to the Questions the "Traditionalists"
Are Asking

By

JAMES LIKOUDIS

and

KENNETH D. WHITEHEAD

Preface By

H. Lyman Stebbins

". . . Remove every obstruction from
my people's way. . ." (Isaiah 57:14).

THE CHRISTOPHER PUBLISHING HOUSE
W. HANOVER, MASSACHUSETTS
02339

Imprimatur:	Joseph T. O'Keefe Vicar General Archdiocese of New York
Nihil Obstat:	James T. O'Connor, S.T.D. Censor Librorum January 4, 1982

The nihil obstat and imprimatur are official declarations that a book or pamphlet is free of doctrinal or moral error. No implication is contained therein that those who have granted the nihil obstat and imprimatur agree with the contents, opinions or statements expressed.

Library of Congress Catalog Card Number 80-68728

ISBN: 0—8158—0400—8

Revised Edition 1982

PRINTED IN

THE UNITED STATES OF AMERICA

ACKNOWLEDGMENTS AND DEDICATION

Rarely have authors enjoyed as much help and encouragement as the present authors have enjoyed. Two persons who have supplied us with both essential facts and telling arguments, so as almost to qualify as co-collaborators in the work itself, are Mrs. Madeleine F. Stebbins and Mr. E. William Sockey, III. Those who have read the manuscript and offered comments, sometimes absolutely essential comments, as it turned out, include: Most Reverend Thomas J. Welsh, Bishop of Arlington; Rev. John A. Hardon, S.J.; Rev. Robert I. Bradley, S.J.; Rev. Edward F. Hanahoe, S.A.; Rev. Msgr. Eugene Kevane; Mr. H. Lyman Stebbins; Mr. William S. Lawton, Jr.; and Mr. Gregory Pesely. Naturally the authors have to take full responsibility for any errors, omissions or other shortcomings. Mrs. Clare L. Fitzpatrick and Miss Henrietta Schwartz have proved to be a good deal more than typists through the several stages of composition but have also enthusiastically supported the work itself and have offered comments and suggestions. To all of these the authors respectfully dedicate the book, therefore, as well as to all of the members of Catholics United for the Faith everywhere in the hope of the true renewal in the faith of our Lord Jesus Christ which is still urgently called for.

J. L.
K. D. W.

PREFACE

In presenting this book to its readers it is necessary to discharge two preliminary obligations, first, to affirm that it is indeed *this* book that is being presented, and not some other book, not a "book of horrors" which would document all the abuses and errors which surround us and which sometimes fill our nostrils like the smoke of Satan. And secondly, it is necessary to answer charges of dereliction on the part of the authors for not having written that other book instead.

It is evident to everyone who is not wilfully blind that frivolous liberties in the celebration of the Holy Sacrifice of the Mass and in theological speculation have been and are causing deep anguish among the People of God, and have even provided serious temptations against the faith itself. With all our hearts we wish that such things would stop.

With all our hearts we share the grief of those who often call themselves traditionalist Catholics; we too are often brought close to tears by the frequent desacralization of the Holy Liturgy and by the misrepresentation of Vatican II and of Church teaching in other realms as well. That is why it is for these traditionalist Catholics that this book has primarily been written. By offering what they believe to be correct answers to the questions most frequently asked, the authors hope to help in healing many wounds which have been opened by incorrect answers. In seeking correct answers, they have not rummaged around in their own subjective feelings or offered at length their own opinions. What could be of less interest? They have in nearly every case sought to give only the true and ascertainable teaching of the Church.

We may believe that many who call themselves traditionalist Catholics have thought along the following lines:

1. "The desacralization of the liturgy, the misrepresentation and denial of doctrine, the forces of auto-destruction within the Church are surely displeasing to God." True.

2. "Since it all seems to have happened after the Council, we are safe in assuming that it has all happened because of the Council." False.

3. "Therefore it must be possible to show that the conciliar changes themselves are illegitimate."   False: as being based on #2 which is false.

Some such line of thought has caused some leading traditionalist Catholics to zero in on #3 above. In a massive display of the paraphernalia of scholarship (including a good deal of "in-breeding," i.e., repeating each other's arguments without recourse to primary sources), some of the more extreme traditionalists have built what looks like a huge fortress of argumentation to prove that the authoritative conciliar and post-conciliar changes are either suspect or illegitimate or both, and that true Catholics have a duty to reject them. That fortress turns out, however, to be a house of cards, as this study will show.

Many individual traditionalists are not extreme but are, rather, saddened and confused. The purpose of this book is to give a true answer—to the extent possible, the Church's answer—to their genuine difficulties, to help heal the scars of the Mystical Body of Christ, to help repair the breaches of unity by bringing to them the light of truth, certain that the truth will prevail and will make us free and bring us peace.

If this book should also help some of those in authority to take these difficulties more seriously, to understand the hearts of their flock more tenderly, and to take steps towards removing the thorns, that would be an added gift of God—and a very great one.

H. Lyman Stebbins, President
Catholics United for the Faith, Inc.
222 North Avenue
New Rochelle, New York 10801

TABLE OF CONTENTS

INTRODUCTION

Following the close of the Second Vatican Council in 1965, the Catholic Church embarked on a series of reforms and changes in her official worship and practices which have scarcely left a single Catholic unaffected; and which, in many respects, have changed the external image of the Church over the past decade.

Not all of the "changes" which the average Catholic in the pew has experienced over the past decade and more were necessarily decreed, or even desired, by the Council or by the Holy See, as far as we can judge by their official acts. Some of the most characteristic and best known of the post-conciliar changes — "the guitar Mass, the handshake of peace, nuns wearing lay garb," as one post-conciliar survey, superficially, has described them[1] — really seem to have arisen out of what many Catholics evidently *thought* Vatican II called for or meant. Too few people have yet grasped that the Council was not supposed to have been the pretext for novel and often purely external changes; it was supposed to have been the basis for a profound renewal of the Catholic faith itself in the hearts of the Catholic faithful, a renewal of faith which would enable them to evangelize the whole world once they had "turned again" (*Lk.* 22:31) and truly renewed their own faith. Anyone willing to take the trouble to peruse the Council's own documents and the principal post-conciliar documents which have issued from it can ascertain for himself the true meaning and purpose of the Council.[2] The fact that this profound renewal of the faith has evidently not yet come about does not alter the fact that this *was* the original purpose of the Council.

The Church held a general council. Many changes in the worship and practice of the Church were decided upon in a missionary spirit in order to renew the faith of the Church and enable her more effectively to meet the challenge of the modern world. Meanwhile, however, inextricably mixed up with what the Church herself actually ordained in the way of change, there have been other changes brought about, as it were, "from below"; while officially decreed "change" was being sanctioned by the authority of the

11

Church, in other words, a good many other people seem to have been able to get introduced *their* idea of what the Vatican II changes *should* have been.

What we are saying here is really well known though not too often candidly discussed. Perhaps people do not know what to make of it; or perhaps they do not consider it a very serious problem. But it is surely now indisputable that many changes have been adopted or imposed in the Church which Vatican II in no way called for and, on the evidence of what it *did* call for in its official documents, it could in no way be supposed to have wanted or sanctioned.

At the time of the election of Pope John Paul I, the world press circulated widely a quotation from the French Dominican Yves Congar which the beloved "September Pope" had used and endorsed when he was the Cardinal Patriarch of Venice:

> "The greater part of the ideas that are attributed to the Council today are not at all from the Council. For many the Council simply means change. Some things that we had believed or done before, according to them, are now no longer to be done, no longer to be believed. This has become the meaning of the Council."[3]

What the average Catholic in the pews has experienced since Vatican II, then, has been an extensive series of changes in the practice or worship of the Church, the reasons for which have often not been adequately explained, and which now, it sometimes seems, will never come to an end; for one of the most significant of all the changes which contrasts the Church of today with the Church in the days before the Council, has been the establishment of a veritable Cult of Continuing Change; almost everybody has come to expect things to keep on changing; change has come to seem the new norm.

And an average Catholic is very little able to judge of the legitimacy of all these changes, beyond knowing which ones he may personally like or dislike, *because* the official ones, and the reasons for them, have so often not really been explained. Thus, he may tend to consider to be on the same level:

> 1. legitimate changes called for by the Council, officially decreed by the Holy See in one of its official enactments, and subsequently applied by the National Conference of Catholic Bishops;

2. changes which seem to have been introduced for no other reason than that it suddenly seemed to some experts or committees a good idea to introduce them, whether or not they were in harmony with the desires of the Council—examples would be the famous "guitar Mass," or standing for communion, which, though permitted by the Church as a "custom," almost nowhere *was* a custom in the U.S. until it was apparently thought to have been called for by Vatican II; and:

3. things which have actually been forbidden, as well as unauthorized abuses of existing liturgical prescriptions, examples of which would be the use of altar girls, the indiscriminate use of extraordinary lay ministers, "self-service" from the chalice, the insertion of extraneous words and formulations into the liturgy, etc.

What we have had in the way of change since Vatican II, in other words, seems to have proceeded as much from "the spirit of the times"—a radically secularized, this-worldly spirit, lacking in a real sense of the sacred—as it has proceeded from the actual enactments of the Council.

The Council still can, in the providence of God, bear fruit, if Catholics will finally begin responding to it properly. It was many years before the Council of Trent was fully and finally implemented, for example. But meanwhile it would be unrealistic not to realize the great harm that has been done to the Church, indeed to the future of the true renewal desired by the Council, by the admixture of *false* renewal which has been flourishing so confidently since the Council under the name of "the spirit of Vatican II."

Now the "spirit" of anything is always of essential importance since it "gives life" (II *Cor.* 3:6), but there are times when we also need to go back to take a look at the letter, and Vatican II is surely one of them. In considering some of the harm that false renewal has done to the Church, we must also consider how, during the same period when some of his old habits of worship were being more or less rudely upset and changed, the average Catholic in the pew has also been exposed to a spectacle of dissent and disobedience unheard of in recent centuries. The average Catholic cannot have failed to notice, especially if he reads the Catholic press, that not only theologians, and "modern" married couples, but apparently even some bishops now reserve the right to differ from the Vicar of Christ, as in the famous case of the encyclical *Humanae Vitae*.

In the United States, the Catholic Theological Society—no less—commissions studies which publicly advocate views at variance with what the Holy See and the U.S. bishops have recently and expressly declared with regard to sexual ethics and the ordination of women. Nor are the theologians engaged in polite debates or discussions among scholars in arcane journals; rather, doctrinal and moral views patently at variance with the authentic teaching of the Church are widely and openly propagandized for, in the media, in the public forum, and in the marketplace, as being now acceptable for Catholics. This was the case, for example, with all the well-known theologians who publicly leaped to the defense of Fathers Hans Küng and Edward Schillebeeckx when the Holy See announced its investigation of the latter and issued its Declaration that the former could no longer function as a Catholic theologian. And, although Church authorities have moved in the case of such well-known dissenters as Fathers Küng and Schillebeeckx, others with views not so dissimilar to theirs continue to hold official positions in the Church even as they openly undermine her official Magisterium in the minds of the faithful.

The average Catholic, if he happens to be a parent, has also had to cope with the quite inexplicable fact that the solid authentic doctrinal content of the faith—still guaranteed by the Magisterium of the Church, for instance, by the 1971 General Catechetical Directory issued by the Holy See, by Pope John Paul II's outstanding 1979 Apostolic Exhortation *Catechesi Tradendae*, and indeed by the U.S. bishops' own National Catechetical Directory, *Sharing the Light of Faith*, approved in 1978—has in varying degrees simply disappeared from out of many of the slick, attractive new religion books which have been the favored means of teaching religion in Catholic schools and CCD classes in recent years. This average Catholic parent has also learned to his sorrow that there often exists little interest at any official level in the United States in correcting the deficiencies in Catholic religious education which have been patent for years to anyone seriously looking at 1) what is actually being taught in Catholic religious education as evidenced by current religion books and "methodologies," or 2) how little the present generation of Catholic-educated children actually knows about its faith.

If what we are saying seems exaggerated or extreme, perhaps we should simply yield the floor for a moment to the editor of *Sacred*

Music magazine whose testimony about the post-conciliar years runs parallel to what we have said here:

". . . priests with the care of souls hailed the council and the possibilities it held for great pastoral achievement.

"But then came the post-conciliar interpreters and implementors who invented the 'spirit of the council.' They introduced practices never dreamed of by the council fathers; they did away with Catholic traditions and customs never intended to be disturbed; they changed for the sake of change; they upset the sheep and terrified the shepherds.

"With carefully orchestrated propaganda they deceived pastors into thinking that what they were proposing was the will of the Church, the directives of the council, and the Pope. They turned around the altars; they abolished Latin; they threw out the choirs; they destroyed statues and much ecclesiastical furniture; they even discouraged the Rosary and Benediction of the Blessed Sacrament, processions, novenas, and devotions. Instead of attracting those who were outside the fold, they drove away many of those who had been born and lived their lives within the Church. Pastors became worried when attendance at Sunday Mass began to decline; numbers at confession grew fewer; the young said they did not need the Church or her Sacraments. What happened to converts to the Faith? A false ecumenism cut off the former steady stream of people entering the Church.

"Worse yet, a new theology disturbed the pastors. What was being taught by these new theologians about the Incarnation and the Redemption? What indeed is the role of the Blessed Virgin and the saints? Were *de fide* truths still to be upheld? Some who claimed to know what the Vatican Council had taught denied even these basic truths. In matters of morality 'theologians' were teaching new ideas about the commandments, if indeed they still existed at all, especially in matters of sexual conduct. And all this came into the parish and the parochial school with new catechetical materials. Parents grew disturbed along with their pastors. . . ."[4]

Thus the editor of *Sacred Music*. We do not endorse everything he says; we only cite him as a concurring witness to what we are asserting, namely, that, regardless of the intentions of the legitimate authorities in the Church, there has been a great deal of confusion in the liturgy in the post-conciliar years and that many of the faithful have become upset as a result of that confusion.

Is it really any wonder, indeed, in the face of such confusion, dissent and disobedience within the Church, even evident loss of faith, if some Catholics have actually been *affected* by it all? Is it really surprising if the faith of some Catholics in the Church might actually be *shaken* by all that has been going on? Hasn't it really been inevitable that some Catholics would have connected the current disarray they see in the Church with the Second Vatican Council and with the changes that have been instituted since? We do not assert that there was anything wrong with the Council or with the legitimate post-conciliar changes. We only point to the evident fact that some of the faithful have unfortunately drawn this conclusion.

It should now be widely known—although almost nobody has cared to talk about it—that disaffection with the state of the Church is, in fact, spreading among some of the very Catholics perhaps formerly most concerned about their faith and their Church. Independent "chapels" are increasingly being set up by Catholics who believe they must be faithful to Catholic "Tradition," as they understand it. More and more unauthorized "motel Masses" are being said by roving priests who reject the new revised Roman Missal and say only the Latin Tridentine Mass celebrated everywhere in the Roman rite prior to Pope Paul VI's 1969 revision of the Roman Missal.

The disaffection and disillusionment with the Church that currently exists among these Catholics calling themselves "traditionalists" has most commonly expressed itself through resentment of the reforming acts since Vatican II of the Holy See (and the Conferences of Catholic Bishops).

It has especially expressed itself through pointedly voiced doubts about the validity or suitability of the New Order of the Mass. Many Catholics, confused or distressed by the apparent unraveling of what they regarded as the essential fabric of their Catholic faith, have congregated in a number of "little churches" where the "Tridentine" Mass is still celebrated. It is not only the followers of French Archbishop Marcel Lefebvre who are doing this; a number of groups in addition to his Society of St. Pius X now operate. They are composed of Catholics who have been alienated by all the famous "changes" which seemed to crop up helter skelter, which they could not understand and which they came to believe, or were brought to believe, were changes in "essentials" of the Catholic faith that by definition they knew could never change, since Jesus had committed certain eternal truths into the keeping of His Church.

If the Church was not "holding fast," as, in the opinion of some, she was not doing, then it meant for some either that Antichrist had come, or that the "true Church" was henceforth to be found somewhere else than in the visible contemporary hierarchical Church which at another apparent "robber Council"* *seemed* to have betrayed Catholic Tradition.

Because of this some conscientious Catholics have felt obliged to attach themselves to a priest who seemed to them to be true to what they considered authentic Catholic Tradition, or to attend Mass at a chapel where the old, familiar Latin was intoned in an atmosphere of hushed reverence. Hence all the new "little churches" which are springing up.

Moreover, all these new traditionalist "little churches" are not phenomena which unhappily sprang up some time back owing to unfortunate misunderstandings now over and done with: every day there are more Catholics losing their faith in the Church and deciding to abandon their parishes in favor of Mass at one of these independent "chapels," no longer in communion with the local Catholic bishop or with the Pope. Sometimes people will drive miles on Sundays to reach their chapels, but they will do it because they still find there the externals of what they had once learned to regard as "the Church."

It is worthy of note that the phenomenon is not confined to older Catholics "shell-shocked" by all the changes; Archbishop Lefebvre's seminarians, for example, are all young men.

To be sure, energetic recruitment campaigns are also being directed by those traditionalists who have already "gone over," towards confused and baffled Catholics who cannot understand what has happened to the Catholic Church since the Council.

A vast "underground" literature now circulates "proving" such things as that Pope Paul VI did not truly abrogate the Tridentine Mass, that the New Order of the Mass is invalid and sacrilegious or at the very least ambiguous, that certain officials of the Roman Curia have really been secret Masons all along, that the Second Vatican

---

*A phrase of Pope St. Leo the Great applied to the false council held by a number of bishops at Ephesus a few years before the true Council of Chalcedon in 451.

Council taught certain things contrary to Tradition, that Protestants were allowed to infiltrate the Church at Vatican II, and that Pope Paul himself, whether consciously or unconsciously, was an accomplice in dismantling the Church during the post-conciliar years.

A more serious and nuanced traditionalist literature is also now being produced—which employs all the trappings of scholarship and is sometimes published by regular publishing houses. It is interesting how plausible and persuasive such literature can be within its own terms of reference. Once certain traditionalist premises are accepted, the case that can be built is quite imposing, and it would be a mistake for anyone who cares about the Church to dismiss it. We cannot regard the widespread circulation of such literature as anything but a serious *malaise* in the post-conciliar Church. A funny thing *has* happened on the smooth road to renewal.

And it seems beyond doubt that the principal cause of the traditionalist revolt is to be found in the proliferation of errors and abuses, as well as in the generalized confusion, in the post-conciliar Church. An international theologian of the stature of Hans Urs von Balthasar has been willing to subscribe to this thesis. In a 1977 speech in St. Gall, Switzerland, he said that "a systematic destruction of the faith is taking place. I could give you massive evidence of this. . . . This is the real background which has provoked the tiresome history of Archbishop Lefebvre. . . . Very few understand who the true culprits are."[5]

Indeed the authority of Pope John Paul I can be invoked for the thesis that abuses by liberals or progressives have provoked the traditionalist reaction. In the homily he delivered when taking possession of his Cathedral of St. John Lateran, John Paul I declared: "Certain abuses in liturgical matters have succeeded, through reaction, in favoring attitudes that have led to a taking up of positions that in themselves cannot be upheld and are in contrast with the Gospel."

Thus John Paul I didn't think the traditionalist reaction was *justified*, but he did see that it *was* a reaction to other things that had been going on in the post-conciliar Church. However mistaken the traditionalists may have turned out to be in the answers they have found to the questions that perplexed them, the fact is that they did have questions about the state of the Church which, for them, were both serious and honest questions; some of these Catholics have migrated over into one of the "little churches" only when they couldn't get any answers to their questions.

It is thus the intention of the two authors in this volume to consider the major questions that have been raised by many Catholic traditionalists about the Pope, the Council, and the Mass—and, to the best of our ability, to try to provide to these questions satisfactory answers which accord with the true faith and discipline of the Church. We believe that the position of the traditionalists is intrinsically untenable; we hope to be able to show that this is so primarily from official teachings of the Catholic Church, principally those dating from before the Second Vatican Council. But we do believe that the traditional questions are serious questions that deserve serious answers and that is what we have tried to provide. We sympathize in some measure with the grief and outrage that have sometimes afflicted Catholics in the present desacralized age; but we believe that the ultimate restoration of values which we share with some traditionalists depends upon continuing *sentire cum ecclesia,* "to think with the Church."

The authors have both frequently written and spoken in defense of the authentic Catholic faith, against those we may term the "modernists" in the Church, regarding such subjects as abortion, contraception, sex education, catechetics, etc. We are far from being unaware or naive about the problems in this area. But it must be emphasized that we are not writing about any of these subjects in this particular book.

The authors are also both national Vice-Presidents of a lay association, Catholics United for the Faith, which at its founding pledged "unshakeable loyalty to the Pope, and thus to the Church, and thus to Christ," and which unhesitatingly accepts and submits to all the enactments of legitimate authority in the Church, whether in the liturgical sphere or in any other sphere. As the following pages will demonstrate, both authors unreservedly accept the enactments and reforms of Vatican Council II—indeed, even enthusiastically so, as we read and understand the Council's official documents. We likewise accept all the authentic enactments and decisions of Popes John Paul II, John Paul I, Paul VI and John XXIII, *and* of the U.S. bishops acting within their sphere of competence, since the Council.

By virtue of our work as national officers of CUF over the past years we believe we have achieved some understanding of the questions the traditionalists are asking. We have achieved this primarily through a rather extensive correspondence with people who have directed their questions at CUF (or have sometimes challenged CUF for its loyalty to the Pope and the bishops). Hence, in the absence of a more "official" answer from the Church herself, through duly constituted authorities, to the questions many traditionalists are asking, we are essaying, as Catholic laymen bearing witness and subject to correction by the authority of the Church, the answers given in this volume, relying as far as possible on official Church documents, in the hope that many who might be tempted to despair of the Church in the middle of the present confusion will realize that God did not guide His Church down through all the centuries only to abandon her now, in the second half of the secularized twentieth century. The Church enjoys a promise from Christ himself that she will never fail; the successor of Peter, in particular, enjoys a promise that his faith will never fail and that he will confirm his brethren.

Hence, we average Catholics, men and women in the pews, must remember, in spite of whatever degree of confusion, disarray, or false renewal we may witness, that Christ still asks us to have *faith* in His Church. The Church still does go on. The true faith has not endured for nearly twenty centuries only to be put out of business by such things as "dissent," "altar girls," the "rock Mass" and the like. The true faith still is very widely preached and practiced, often edifyingly so. Exemplary Catholics in all walks of life and in all degrees in the Church do still let their light shine among men, as Our Savior asked; and not even the distortions of today's mass media can entirely obscure the clear teaching voice of the Successor of Peter, who regardless of his personal identity and regardless of the difficulties with which he has had to cope in the past few difficult years, *has* continued to teach "in season and out of season" (II *Tim.* 4:2). We have recently seen confirmed in a dramatic way by the attention focused by the whole world on the twin elections of Popes John Paul I and John Paul II, and on the spectacular pilgrimages of Pope John Paul II to Mexico, Poland and the United States, how the whole world has been obliged to "confess," as it were, that the Bishop of Rome is indeed not only the visible head of the Catholic Church but also the obvious world leader of all who profess the name of Christ.

And Pope John Paul II has not otherwise been slow to provide us new hope for a new era in which we will surely witness renewed respect and reverence for the central mystery of our holy faith, the Mass. In his first encyclical *Redemptor Hominis*, John Paul II declared (#20):

"... it is not permissible for us, in thought, life or action, to take away from this truly most holy sacrament its full magnitude and its essential meaning. It is at one and the same time a sacrifice-sacrament, a communion-sacrament, and a presence-sacrament. And, although it is true that the Eucharist always was and must continue to be the most profound revelation of the human brotherhood of Christ's disciples and confessors, it cannot be treated merely as an 'occasion' for manifesting this brotherhood. When celebrating the sacrament of the body and blood of the Lord, the full magnitude of the divine mystery must be respected, as must the full meaning of this sacramental sign in which Christ is really present and is received, the soul is filled with grace and the pledge of future glory is given. This is the source of the duty to carry out rigorously the liturgical rules and everything that is a manifestation of community worship offered to God Himself, all the more so because in this sacramental sign He entrusts Himself to us with limitless trust, as if not taking into consideration our human weakness, our unworthiness, the force of habit, routine, or even the possibility of insult. Every member of the Church, especially bishops and priests, must be vigilant in seeing that this sacrament of love shall be at the center of the life of the People of God, so that through all the manifestations of worship due to it Christ shall be given back 'love for love' and truly become 'the life of our souls.'"

Pope John Paul II also delivered the same message to the U.S. bishops when he spoke to them in Chicago on October 6, 1979:

"As chosen leaders in a community of praise and prayer, it is our special joy to offer the Eucharist and to give our people a sense of their vocation as an Easter people, with the 'Alleluia' as their song. And let us always recall that the validity of all liturgical development and the effectiveness of every liturgical sign presupposes the great principle that the Catholic liturgy is theocentric and that it is above all 'the worship of Divine Majesty' in union with Jesus Christ.

"Our People have a supernatural sense whereby they look for reverence in all liturgy, especially in what touches the Mystery of the Eucharist. With deep faith our people understand that the Eucharist—in the Mass and outside the Mass—is the Body and Blood of Jesus Christ, and therefore deserves the worship that is given to the living God and to Him alone."

Rejoicing in the hope of the new era inaugurated by the Pope from Poland, but also "patient in tribulation" as St. Paul counseled (*Rom.* 12:12), we must carry on and keep the faith in spite of what may have happened in the post-conciliar years because our faith is based not on the state of the Church, in this or any other age, but rather upon "the authority of God who reveals, and who can neither deceive nor be deceived" (Vatican Council I, Dogmatic Constitution of the Catholic Faith *Dei Filius*, #3).[6]

James Likoudis
Kenneth D. Whitehead
Memorial: St. Thomas Aquinas
January 28, 1980

Question # 1

WHY WERE ALL THE CHANGES MADE WHEN EVERY-THING WAS GOING SO WELL FOR THE CHURCH? CONVERSIONS WERE UP, VOCATIONS WERE UP, AND WE HAD A BEAUTIFUL TRADITIONAL MASS WHICH COMMUNICATED THE SENSE OF THE SACRED. WHY WAS ALL THAT ABRUPTLY CHANGED?

It would be foolish to deny that in some respects older Catholics can look back upon a "golden age" of the Church which witnessed extraordinary developments in piety, devotion, conversions, mission-ary conquests, and a remarkable material flourishing, especially in the United States, indeed, throughout North America. A truly impressive network of seminaries, convents, houses of study, and schools (from elementary schools to colleges and universities) re-flected heroic labors by bishops, priests, religious and laity to estab-lish the Church in a cultural environment in many ways hostile to Catholicism. The holy lives and wise policies of the Popes from Leo XIII to Pius XII contributed enormously to the prestige of the Church in a world growing increasingly secular.

Nevertheless, it is also undeniable that there were some weaknesses underlying the imposing external facade of twentieth-century Cath-olicism. Pope Leo XIII had prophetically diagnosed the major weak-nesses of the Church in the United States as early as 1899 in his Apostolic Letter *Testem Benevolentiae*, sent to James Cardinal Gibbons, Archbishop of Baltimore. In this letter Pope Leo spoke of "followers of . . . novelties [who] judge that a certain liberty ought to be introduced into the Church so that, limiting the exercise of its powers, each one of the faithful may act more freely in pursuance of his own natural bent and capacity."[1] What the great Pontiff describes here as a danger to the Church resembles more than a little what some today now consider the church to be, a "do-as-you-please" Church; the fact that Leo XIII was warning Catholics in

America about the *danger* of this way back before the turn of the
century means that the *seeds* of it already existed before then. We
have seen the danger grow abundantly since.

It is also worthy of remark that serious deficiencies in the life of
the Church prior to the Council were commented upon at great
length by various converts to the Church, many of whom were disturbed at the apathy, indifference, conformism, and lack of apostolic
zeal and ardor evident in the lives of all too many Catholics. The
appearance of a liturgical movement among American Catholics (in
addition to a renewed interest in biblical and theological scholarship,
as well as in Thomistic philosophy) also indicated the existence of
further efforts to bring a greater understanding of liturgy to the
people, some of whom were ill-instructed in the faith. For the gap
between awareness of the meaning of faith in one's personal life and
the steadily increasing secularization of public and social life was
growing ever wider as the century progressed, and Catholics were
affected by the secularization and materialism around them more
deeply than they always realized.

No greater proof of the weakness underlying much traditional
Catholic observance and practice can be found than in the amazingly
quick collapse of the formerly imposing facade of American Catholicism that has been manifested since the Second Vatican Council
and the rapid changes which followed in its wake. The faith of countless numbers of the faithful proved unable to withstand the sharp
challenge or the confusion of today. Whether the issue was birth
control or liturgical change, too many Catholics proved to be not
very Catholic, in the sense of being willing to follow the hierarchical
Church, when the crunch came. This is a continuing phenomenon.
A beautiful Latin liturgy proved to be no barrier to such widespread
spiritual collapse, incidentally; and we must not, moreover, romanti-
cize the matter; for the liturgy was often *not* celebrated with that
much care, reverence, beauty and splendor.

Much responsibility for the confusion which has followed the
Council in the United States and Canada can undoubtedly be laid at
the door of the clergy, and this because of the sometimes mindless
way in which the Council liturgical reforms were carried out in the
experience of most Catholics; yet what can one say about the kind of
supernatural *faith* in Christ and His promises which *could* actually
be shaken because the Mass began to be said in English translation,
for example? Or merely because of liturgical scandals? This is not to
minimize the consequences of such scandals in the lives of those who

have found the very sense of the sacred eliminated in their parish's liturgical life. But *Christ* must always remain the proper object of our faith, and never the externals of liturgical practice which admittedly have been confusing over the past few years; *any* change in deep-rooted habits can cause confusion; certainly this is especially true when habits of worship are concerned. But allowing the fact of confusion to drive one from the Church is a much more unfortunate thing than the liturgical chaos itself. And the fact is that, whatever the justification, the Church did determine through the Second Vatican Council to make far-reaching changes in her worship and practices; the calling of the Council by Pope John XXIII was a perfectly legitimate exercise of the supreme authority in the Church which, as we shall see in the answers to later questions, he possessed. The convocation of a council by the Pope to help him deal with the current problems which the Church had to face was also an eminently traditional act. Popes have many times called councils to deal with problems and, almost without exception, councils have introduced modifications in the Church's discipline.

Pope Leo XIII, in his letter on Americanism quoted above, even remarked how fitting it is for the Church "to admit modifications" in her discipline (though never in her doctrine) "according to the diversity of time and place." "The Church, indeed," Pope Leo continued:

"posseses what her Author has bestowed on her, a kind and merciful disposition; for which reason from the very beginning she willingly showed herself to be what Paul proclaimed in his own regard: 'I became all things to all men, that I might save all' (I *Cor.* 9:22). The history of all past ages is witness that the Apostolic See, to which not only the office of teaching but also the supreme government of the whole Church was committed, has constantly adhered to the same doctrine, in the same sense and in the same mind (First Vatican Council): but it has always been accustomed to so modify the rule of life that, while keeping the divine right inviolate, it has never disregarded the manners and customs of the various nations which it embraces. If required for the salvation of souls, who will doubt that it is ready to do so at the present time? But this is not to be determined by the will of private individuals, who are mostly deceived by the appearance of right, but ought to be left to the judgment of the Church."[2]

When Pope John XXIII convoked a general council to deal with the actual "manners and customs" of the modern world, he was only demonstrating what his predecessor had indicated, namely, that the Church was ready to change "if required for the salvation of souls." And what Pope John actually saw—one of the principal reasons he gave for calling the Second Vatican Council—were the souls of countless modern men in need of Christ but without Christ. "It is a source of considerable sorrow," Pope John said in his opening speech to the Council, "to see that the greater part of the human race ... does not yet participate in those sources of divine grace which exist in the Catholic Church." It was in order, therefore, that the Church's doctrine might "influence the numerous fields of human activity" that Pope John thought a council was necessary so that the Church could better "look to the present, to the new conditions and new forms of life introduced into the modern world which have opened new avenues to the Catholic apostolate."[3]

This remains true today; the Council was called for a legitimate reason, and the program of the Council still remains to be carried out.

"What the Spirit said to the Church through the Council of our time," Pope John Paul II wrote in his first encyclical *Redemptor Hominis* (#3), ". . . cannot lead to anything else—in spite of momentary uneasiness—but a still more mature solidity of the whole People of God, aware of their salvific mission."

In an address to a special plenary session of the College of Cardinals held between November 5 and 11, 1979, Pope John Paul II went even further in speaking of the central importance of the Second Vatican Council in spite of some of the deformations that have followed it. The Pope said:

> ". . . Obedience to the teaching of the Second Vatican Council is obedience to the Holy Spirit, who is given to the Church in order to remind her at every stage of history of everything that Christ said, in order to teach the Church all things (cf. *Jn.* 14: 26). Obedience to the Holy Spirit is expressed in the authentic carrying out of the tasks indicated by the council, in full accordance with the teaching set forth therein.
>
> "These tasks cannot be treated as though they did not exist. It is not possible to claim to make the Church go back, so to speak, along the path of human history. But neither is it possible to rush presumptuously ahead, toward ways of living, thinking and preaching Christian truth, and finally to ways of

being a Christian, a priest, a religious that are not envisioned in the integral teaching of the council — 'integral,' that is to say, understood in the light of the whole of sacred Tradition and on the basis of the constant Magisterium of the Church herself."

It was providential, then, that the Council later under the guidance of Pope John XXIII and Pope Paul VI clearly addressed itself to the removal of some of the past Church patterns of externalism, legalism, and formalism which in some ways had served to paralyze the evangelizing energies of priests, religious and lay people in spreading the Gospel among the peoples of the modern world already undergoing vast cultural and technological changes. Anyone who remembers the pre-conciliar Church remembers how common was the attitude of the Catholic laity that it it was not their responsibility to spread the faith; religion was the business of the priests and religious. That was the attitude of the clergy too! It is an attitude that must now be changed. In a de-Christianized world, religion *is* the business of the believing laity too, even while it remains the business also of the clergy.

Just as the Council of Trent itself was a "reforming Council" preparing the Church to meet effectively the challenges of a Post-Reformation Europe, so the Second Vatican Council was similarly intended to be a reforming Council designed by God's Providence to meet the new challenge of contemporary unbelief which calls for *evangelization* in our day. In the words of Pope Paul VI, "the objectives [of the Council] are definitely summed up in this single one: to make the Church of the Twentieth Century ever better fitted for proclaiming the Gospel to the people of the Twentieth Century" (Pope Paul VI, Apostolic Exhortation on Evangelization in the Modern World *Evangelii Nuntiandi*, #2).

Pope John Paul II echoed this when he wrote in *Redemptor Hominis* (#4) that "the Church's consciousness must go with universal openness, in order that all may be able to find in her 'the unsearchable riches of Christ' (*Eph.* 3:8) spoken of by the Apostle of the Gentiles. Such openness, organically joined with the awareness of her own nature and certainty of her own truth, of which Christ said, 'The word which you hear is not mine but the Father's who sent me' (*Jn.* 14:24), is what gives the Church her apostolic or in other words her missionary dynamism professing and proclaiming in its integrity the whole of the truth transmitted by Christ."

This does not mean that the Church since the Council has not been beset with problems. Pope John Paul II admitted that "the Church that I . . . have had entrusted to me is not free of internal difficulties and tension" (*Redemptor Hominis*, #4); but he insisted in this encyclical that Catholics must now move ahead in spite of these difficulties because God "desires all men to be saved and to come to the knowledge of the truth" (*Tim.* 2:4), and who but those in what Vatican II reiterated is "the true Church" (Constitution on the Sacred Liturgy *Sacrosanctum Concilium*, #2) can better help bring men to the knowledge of the truth which resides in the Catholic Church?

If we will make the effort to look at recent Church history from the long-range perspective of God's dealings with His People, we must realize how possible and even likely it was that no one would have ever paid the slightest attention to any of the things the Second Vatican Council *really* said, or that the Popes have said subsequently, if we had not had the thorough shaking up that in fact we have had. "Why are you afraid, O men of little faith?" (*Mt.* 8:26). As St. Anthony of Padua said long ago, and as is true today, "Only when the proud house of earthly comfort is reduced to a ruin, can the Lord prepare a dwelling place for His inward comforting." It should be clear by now to any thinking Catholic that we no longer have any alternative to looking once again more carefully at the actual teachings of the Council, and trying, finally, to go forward to put the injunctions of the Council into practice. We certainly cannot go back into the past, however glorious its successes were. It is towards the long-awaited "second spring" in the life of the Church (foreshadowed in the writings of Pius XII and more recently by the Second Vatican Council) that we must now head under the guidance of the Successor of Peter, Chief Shepherd of the flock.

What John Paul II has said on this subject is unmistakable:

"The Pope . . . expects a noble and generous effort on your part to always know better your Church. The Second Vatican Council wanted to be a Council about the Church. Take the documents of the Council, especially *Lumen Gentium*, and study them. With loving attention. Then you will discover that there is not a 'new Church!' The Council has revealed with more clarity the one Church of Christ, one having new dimensions but the same in essence.

"The Pope expects from you a loyal acceptance of the Church. You cannot be faithful and remain attached to secondary things, valid in the past but already outdated. You will not be faithful either if you try to build the so-called Church of the future, unrelated to the present.

"We must be faithful to the Church born once and for all from the plan of God: at the cross, the empty tomb and at Pentecost, which is born not of the people or from reason, but from God." (Homily delivered in Mexico City, January 29, 1979).

With respect to the liturgical abuses which have scandalized many Catholics, and caused some to doubt the Church, a further observation is perhaps in order. These scandals have *not* flowed from the genuine reform of the Mass decreed by the Council, but from *disobedience* to the decrees of the Council and to the subsequent liturgical enactments of the Holy See. It is no remedy to these abuses and scandals to engage in disobedience oneself by rejecting or criticizing the authority of a Pope or an ecumenical council convoked and presided over by a Pope. There is nothing traditionally Catholic about that at all; the very idea of Catholics opposing a Pope or an ecumenical council would surely have scandalized any earlier generation of Catholics as much as the liturgical aberrations have scandalized some today.

If we imagine that the course the Church has taken since the Council is going to be reversed—again we are talking about the official changes, not unauthorized abuses that individuals may have introduced—we should reflect prayerfully on the fact that both of the Roman Pontiffs elected since the end of the Council, Popes John Paul I and John Paul II, declared decisively at the outset that their pontificates would be dedicated to carrying out the official decrees of the Council. Pope John Paul I inaugurated his brief reign by saying:

". . .We wish to continue implementing without interruption the legacy left us by the Second Vatican Council. Its wise norms must be applied. Here we must be on guard lest impulses that arise perhaps from generosity but are nonetheless imprudent, should distort the teaching and meaning of the council. We need also to be vigilant lest, on the other hand, efforts at restraint that are inspired by timidity should dampen the stimulus to renewed life which the council gave." (To the Cardinals and to the World, August 27, 1978).

Upon his election to the office of Peter, Pope John Paul II similarly declared:

"First of all, we wish to point out the unceasing importance of the Second Vatican Ecumenical Council, and we accept the definite duty of assiduously bringing it into effect. Indeed, is not that universal Council a kind of milestone as it were, an event of the utmost importance in the almost two thousand year history of the Church, and consequently in the religious and cultural history of the world?" (To the Cardinals and to the World, October 17, 1978).

It seems clear that, whatever we may be obliged to think of some of the gusts that blew in when good Pope John opened up those famous windows, we are nevertheless now equally obliged to go forward *from* the fact of the Council and what it decreed. If mistakes have been made in the implementation of its decrees —and they have —if errors and abuses have cropped up —and they have —the remedy for them is nevertheless now to be found in a more careful implementation of the official reforms of the Council. The Church has to move forward, not back. The revised Roman Missal containing the New Order of Mass is now an integral part of what is today "given" for loyal Catholics. To continue to protest about the *Novus Ordo* and to call for a return of the "Tridentine Mass" is to distract attention from more important issues of concern to Catholics —the integrity of Catholic doctrine in the face of the unprecedented assault against it by the forces of the modern world, for example. Possible further revisions of the Roman Missal to help enhance or restore greater reverence and a more profound sense of the sacred, the possible revival of Latin as a liturgical language alongside the vernacular, better (and perhaps more accurate) vernacular translations of the Mass and the other sacraments —all these aims will only be achieved in loyal submission to and docile partnership with legitimate Church authority, not in acrimonious conflict with that authority because of the changes which have already been made and which unfortunately haven't always turned out as well as they could.

When the New Order of Mass is celebrated as it ought to be — with reverence and dignity and splendor and solemnity, all called for by the rubrics for the *Novus Ordo Missae* —the average Catholic would really find it difficult to distinguish between the "Mass of St. Pius V" and the "Mass of Paul VI" using the Roman Canon. The latter, as we will show in some of the answers to questions which follow, is really the same as always, and continues to give us the living Christ as sacrifice and sacrament. Then too we should remember that even if the traditional liturgy as decreed by St. Pius V had never been changed, infidelity, modernism and secular humanism would still be with us, as they were with us before the changes came about, and *they* would still constitute the main dangers to the faith today.

We of the laity may sometimes have much to suffer these days. But we cannot complain about the disobedience of modernists and secularizers in the Church if we become disobedient ourselves to the legitimate authority of the Church.

And, in considering the whole question of the extent to which the Church can change the externals of the liturgy or the administration of the sacraments, a matter which will be discussed in detail in the sections which follow, we would consider the wise words of Pope Pius XII, who said:

> ". . . as our Lord Jesus Christ gave the Church only one government under the authority of the Prince of the Apostles, one single faith, one single sacrifice, so He gave only one single treasury of signs producing grace, namely, the sacraments. Nor has the Church in the course of centuries substituted other sacraments for those sacraments instituted by Christ, nor has she the power to make this substitution, for, according to the teaching of the Council of Trent, the seven sacraments of the New Law were instituted by our Lord Jesus Christ, and the Church has no power over 'the substance of the sacraments,' that is, over those things which, according to the source of divine revelation, Christ the Lord Himself prescribed must be maintained in the sacramental signs. . . .

> "But if, by the will and prescription of the Church, these rites were at one time necessary for the validity [of the sacrament], everyone knows that *what the Church has decreed she has also the power to change or to abrogate*" (Emphasis added).[4]

Thus the Third General Council of the Church, at Ephesus in Asia Minor, decreed in 431 A.D. that "it should not be lawful to publish another faith or Creed than that which was defined by the Nicene Council"; the Fourth General Council at Chalcedon twenty years later explicitly confirmed this decree; yet the great Council of Trent in the sixteenth century decreed that a new Creed did have to be published—what has since been most commonly called the Creed, or Profession of Faith, of Pope Pius IV.[5] What the Church has herself decreed she also has the power to change or abrogate through proper Church authority.

Similarly, among the large number of decrees issued by the Fourth General Council of the Lateran, convened by Pope Innocent III in 1215 A.D., was a canon forbidding the foundation of any new religious orders.[6] Considering all the new religious orders that have been founded since 1215—including the great Dominican order which dates its foundation to within a decade after this Lateran decree forbidding any new religious orders—it is clear that the Church has the authority to change her own Church laws (not divine laws) for reasons which seem to her good and sufficient; and, in the past, she has made changes in Church law or discipline which may have seemed to some to affect unchangeable essentials — but the Church herself was the judge that they were not changes in essentials.

We shall demonstrate in the course of subsequent answers to specific questions raised by those concerned about the post-Vatican II changes that the principal changes which have most disturbed or distressed people do *not* affect what Pope Pius XII above calls "the substance of the sacraments"—insofar, of course, as these disturbing changes are really official changes decreed by the authority of the Church and not aberrations introduced by individuals on their own. We shall also show that the changes which the Church herself has made she had the authority to make in exactly the sense understood by Pope Pius XII—and exercised by the Council of Trent when it modified decrees of the Councils of Ephesus and Chalcedon and by the medieval Popes when they approved the foundation of new religious orders in the face of the decree prohibiting their foundation enacted by the Fourth General Council of the Lateran.

BUT WASN'T VATICAN II MERELY A "PASTORAL COUNCIL"? ARE THE FAITHFUL OBLIGED TO FOLLOW SUCH A COUNCIL, ESPECIALLY WHEN ITS "FRUITS" HAVE PROVED TO BE SO BITTER?

The term "pastoral council" as applied to Vatican II is merely a popular description and does not refer to any specific type of council recognized by the authority of the Catholic Church (the teachings and decisions of which would presumably somehow not be as binding upon members of the Church as those of a "dogmatic" council). In the Church there are traditionally councils, or synods, which are styled "national councils," "provincial councils," or "general (ecumenical) councils," but none styled specifically a "pastoral council."

Pope John XXIII, in calling the Council, stated that the reasons he was doing so were of a character that could be broadly termed "pastoral," although Pope John himself, in using the word, merely spoke of the need today of a Church Magisterium "which is predominantly pastoral in character." Pope Paul VI similarly spoke of the "pastoral nature of the Council" in his Weekly General Audience of January 12, 1966, but he didn't call it a "pastoral council" as if this were some new species of Church gathering which the faithful might go along with or not, as they chose.

To convene a general council with a pastoral purpose, in short, was *not* to convene a new kind of Church council not binding on the faithful. What Pope John XXIII really said with regard to his reasons for convoking the Council was that "a Council was not necessary. . . as a discussion of one article or another of the fundamental doctrine of the Church which has repeatedly been taught. . . and which is presumed to be well known and familiar to all" (Opening Speech to the Council).

This did not mean, however, that doctrine—Catholic truth—was to be of no importance at the Council. On the contrary, Pope John XXIII said that the "*greatest* concern of the Ecumenical Council is this: that the sacred deposit of Christian doctrine should be guarded and taught more efficaciously" (*Ibid.*; emphasis added). And this concern of Pope John that doctrine be, at least in a sense, the greatest concern of the Council is entirely in keeping with the real meaning of the word "pastoral."

For the word "pastoral" refers to the work of a shepherd; and Jesus, the Good Shepherd, taught plainly that "for this I was born and for this I have come into the world, to bear witness to the *truth*" (*Jn.* 18:37). Our Lord remarks in one place that "the sheep follow Him for they know His voice" (*Jn.* 10:4) and in another place He makes clear that those who do hear His voice are those who are "of the truth" (*Jn.* 18:38). When Our Lord solemnly commissioned Simon Peter and said, "Feed My sheep" (*Jn.* 21:17), He meant that in the first place Peter was to feed them with the truths of the faith; and thus to be "pastoral" is, precisely, to be "doctrinal" first of all. The two words are in no way opposed.

Hence in calling a council for a pastoral purpose, Pope John XXIII was in no way downgrading doctrine. What Pope John wanted was rather a re-ordering of the Church's priorities so that the truths entrusted to her by Christ could be more effectively communicated to the world for the benefit of the latter. The Pope wanted to call all the bishops of the world together to help him decide how the Church should present herself to the world over the next several generations in order to meet the challenges of modern times. In order to bring "the modern world into contact with the vivifying and perennial energies of the gospel," Pope John said, "the Church finds very alive the desire to fortify its faith and . . . to promote the sanctification of its members, the diffusion of revealed truth, the consolidation of its agencies" (Apostolic Constitution convoking the Council *Humanae Salutis*).[1]

What Pope John meant by that "renewal" which he ardently hoped would be the principal result of the Council was that "by bringing herself up to date where required, and by the wise organization of mutual cooperation, the Church will make men, families and peoples really turn their minds to heavenly things" (Opening Speech to the Council). In other words, far from not being concerned with doctrine, or the truths of the faith, the Council was originally intended to result in precisely the widest possible diffusion of that Catholic truth so desperately needed by the whole world.

Even if good Pope John's fond hopes for the Council still remain largely to be realized, nobody can thereby argue that the purposes for which he called the Council were not legitimate purposes of the Church which God placed in the world to sanctify and save all mankind.

In fact, however, it has never been the case that general or ecumenical councils have been assembled merely to "define doctrine," as would seem to be assumed by those who want to downgrade the importance of Vatican II by calling it "merely" a "pastoral council."

When convoking the First Vatican Council back in 1868, for example, Pope Pius IX also included among his reasons for doing so, in addition to defining and defending doctrine, "the maintenance and establishment of ecclesiastical discipline, and moral reform among peoples overtaken by corruption"—reasons, surely, entirely in harmony with those adduced by Pope John XXIII for bringing together all the bishops of the world for the Second Vatican Council nearly a century after the First had met under Pius IX. Indeed, Pius IX's general description of why general councils are brought together at all could have been equally used by Pope John XXIII: "When they have judged it timely and, above all, during the most troubled eras when our holy religion and civil society are prey to disaster, [the] . . . Pontiffs have not neglected to convoke general councils in order to act with and unite their strength to the strength of the bishops of the whole Catholic world. . . ."[2] Pius IX's description here surely applies to our own times as much as to his.

And some of the fruits which the First Vatican Council ascribed to the great Council of Trent were similarly not unlike those which Pope John hoped would come out of Vatican II: ". . . closer communion of members with the visible head of the Church, and increased vitality in the entire Mystical Body of Christ; a multiplication in the number of religious congregations and other institutions of Christian piety; and a zeal in spreading the Kingdom of Christ throughout the world that was unremitting and steadfast even to the shedding of blood" (Vatican Council I, Dogmatic Constitution of the Catholic Faith *Dei Filius*, Introduction).[3] In the event, the Council of Trent gave the Church an immense body of pastoral directives. No ecumenical council in the history of the Church defined more doctrines than Trent; yet most of Trent's work was nevertheless "pastoral."

The very first general council of the Church, the Council of

Nicaea, which met in 325, in addition to dealing with the Arian
heresy, was also involved with disciplinary matters concerning disputed bishoprics and the disputed date of Easter, and actually promulgated twenty disciplinary canons[4] —so far from "defining doctrine" being the only purpose of a general council!

Another early council, the Fourth General Council of Constantinople, which took place in 869-870, was not even called to deal
with doctrine at all, but merely to deal with disciplinary matters,
and thus, like Vatican II, was certainly "pastoral" in nature as Popes
Paul and John styled Vatican II. The great Catholic historian Msgr.
Philip Hughes has described Constantinople IV, the Eighth General
Council of the Catholic Church, as "a matter of personalities in
conflict, and not ideas, still less, doctrines." The same historian has
recorded how the Second General Council of Lyons in 1274 A.D.
was also a Council predominantly "pastoral" in nature, summoned
by Pope Gregory X "to inaugurate a real restoration of religious
fervor" to offset what Msgr. Hughes described as "the miserable
degradation of Christian life throughout the West" at the time.[5]

Yet even these councils, "pastoral" as their nature was, ended up
teaching some doctrine: besides all its disciplinary canons, the Fourth
General Council of Constantinople issued a dogmatic pronouncement
condemning a contemporary heretical theory that man had two
souls; and, in addition to thirty disciplinary canons, the second
General Council of Lyons issued a Constitution on the Blessed Trinity and the Catholic faith defining the procession of the Holy Spirit.[6]

This brings us to the very important point that Vatican II, although convoked by Pope John XXIII for the "pastoral" reasons
quoted above, also did end up teaching Catholic doctrine, like the
earlier Church "pastoral" councils. Vatican II issued two dogmatic
Constitutions: *Lumen Gentium* on the Church, and *Dei Verbum*
on Divine Revelation, exactly the same number of dogmatic Constitutions as issued, for example, by Vatican Council I.

These two Dogmatic Constitutions from Vatican II do not contain canons with anathemas attached ("If anyone say . . . let him be
anathema"), as has been the case with some other ecumenical
councils; but Catholic doctrine need not be framed in a dogmatic
canon with an anathema attached in order to be true—in order to
qualify as authentic Catholic doctrine which the Catholic faithful
are obliged to believe. When Jesus Christ taught that "I am the Way,
the Truth, and the Life" (*Jn.* 14:6) and "The Bread which I shall

give for the life of the world is My flesh" (*Jn.* 6:51), these doctrines are not drawn up in dogmatic canons with anathemas attached; but they remain no less true for all of that—and no less binding on the belief of Catholics. The Church has no requirement that her doctrine always be expressed in a particular way. The fact that Vatican II's two Dogmatic Constitutions, as well as, in varying degrees, the fourteen other documents of the Council, contain considerable authentic doctrine to which assent by the faithful is required, should be obvious to any instructed Catholic who will read through the Vatican II documents.

Indeed a note to Vatican II's Pastoral Constitution on the Church in the Modern World *Gaudium et Spes* explicitly says that in this "pastoral" document the Church: 1) develops her *teaching* and also: 2) applies it to some of the pressing problems of today—the latter of which, the note says, are "contingent"; but this certainly does not mean that the basic doctrinal teachings as such are also contingent, only that the application of them might change. The whole point of bringing together at a Council all the Catholic bishops from all over the world was, precisely, to teach and where necessary to apply those teachings to the problems Catholics and the Church face today. It would have been strictly nonsensical to convene a Council the results of which would somehow be disregardable at the option of the faithful. What would be the point of having a teaching Church at all if, in a solemn general council, she doesn't necessarily teach? Or, how could it be said that the Church really ruled in Christ's stead if the disciplinary enactments of her Twenty-First General Council of the Church were similarly to be considered optional for the faithful?

In fact, of course, the Vatican II documents resemble the acts of all the other twenty ecumenical councils in the history of the Church in containing *both* doctrinal *and* disciplinary matters — the former of which require the assent of our intellects and the latter of which require the obedience of our wills.

In his book *Sources of Renewal* Karol Cardinal Wojtyla (Pope John Paul II) wrote:

"It may be said that every Council in the Church's history has been a pastoral one, if only because the assembled bishops, under the Pope's guidance, are pastors of the Church. At the same time every Council is an act of the supreme magisterium of the Church. Magisterium signifies teaching based on authority, a teaching which is the mission of the Apostles and their successors, it is part of their function and an essential task. This teaching is concerned essentially with questions of faith and morals: what men and women should believe in and in what manner, and hence how they should live according to their faith. The doctrine of faith and morals *(doctrina fidei et morum)* is the content of the teaching of the pastors of the Church, so that on the one hand doctrinal acts of the magisterium have a pastoral sense, while on the other pastoral acts have a doctrinal significance, deeply rooted as they are in faith and morals. These pastoral acts contain the doctrine that the Church proclaims; they often make it clearer and more precise, striving incessantly to achieve the fulness of the divine truth" (cf. John 16:13).

All this has been signally confirmed by Vatican II, which, while preserving its pastoral character and mindful of the purpose for which is was called, profoundly developed the doctrine of faith and thus provided a basis for its enrichment.[7]

To what extent have Catholics always been required to give their assent and obedience to the teaching and enactments of a general council—according to the Tradition of the Church?

Pope Pius IX taught on this subject in a letter to the Abbott of Solesmes: ". . . the Ecumenical Council is governed by the Holy Spirit . . . it is solely by the impulse of this Divine Spirit that the Council defines and proposes what must be believed. . . ." Not only what the Council "defines"—it should be noted—but what it "proposes." In another letter, the same Pontiff inveighed against those who had dared "to state in most pernicious writings that in the definition and the promulgation of the decrees of the [First Vatican] Council. . .there was something lacking to the full value and the full authority of an Ecumenical Council." The Pope sadly recalled what he termed "the well-known calumnies spread against other Councils, and, especially, the Councils of Florence and of Trent, by the schismatics and heretics of the age, to their own loss and the spiritual ruin of a great number."[8]

Pope Leo XIII similarly taught on the subject of the assent and obedience owed by Catholics to the enactments of a general council: "There can be no doubt that the decisions of the Holy See or those of the General Councils, above all in matters of faith, are by themselves and by their very nature obligatory on all the faithful."[9] Let us note well that Leo XIII says not "only" or "uniquely" in matters of faith but "above all" in matters of faith—thus not excluding those things in the *acta* of a council which are not, strictly speaking, matters of faith.

This, then, is the traditional teaching of the Church: the teachings of an ecumenical council are protected from error and their decisions are binding on all Catholics. Ludwig Ott says: "It has been the constant teaching of the Church from the earliest times that the resolutions of General Councils are infallible."[10] St. Athanasius wrote of the First General Council of the Church that "the word of the Lord, put forth by the Ecumenical Council at Nicaea, is an eternal word, enduring forever."[11] What the ecumenical councils "teach as the truth," Msgr. Philip Hughes remarks, speaking as an historian summing up the Tradition, "is taken to be as true as though it were a statement of Scripture itself."[12] Cardinal Newman is not afraid to say that what a "General Council speaks is the word of God."[13] And all those testimonials reflect the view the apostles themselves took of their own decisions at the Council of Jerusalem described in the *Acts of the Apostles*: ". . . it has seemed good to the Holy Spirit and to us . . ." (*Acts* 15:28).

And let us bear in mind that this view of Church councils acting in the place of God Himself was not limited to what these councils taught as doctrine; it extended also to what they decided in disciplinary matters. At the Council of Jerusalem itself the thing which it "seemed good to the Holy Spirit" and to the apostles present to decide was the disciplinary question of whether gentile converts to Christianity were subject to Jewish ritual laws. In the fifth century, at the Council of Chalcedon, the bishops attending decreed the deposition of the Archbishop of Alexandria, Dioscorus. Having deposed him, the bishops in council who had made the decision then cried out, "God has deposed Dioscorus! Dioscorus has been justly deposed. It is Christ Who has deposed him."

Similarly, at the Council of Ephesus, earlier in the fifth century, the fathers acclaimed with regard to their disciplinary judgment deposing Nestorius as the Archbishop of Constantinople: "Our Lord Jesus Christ, Whom Nestorius has blasphemed, declares Nestorius to be deposed as bishop and excluded from the entire sacerdotal college."[14] Christ Himself was understood to be acting through this general council; and in a purely disciplinary matter.

The view of the fathers of Chalcedon and Ephesus of what they believed they were doing when acting together in general council naturally has to be understood today in the light of the developed doctrine that acts of a general council have to be ratified by the Pope. "There is never an ecumenical council," Vatican II taught, summing up the Tradition, "which is not confirmed or at least recognized as such by Peter's successor" (Dogmatic Constitution on the Church *Lumen Gentium*, #22). Nevertheless the Catholic Tradition concerning the importance of the acts of a general council, whether in doctrine or in discipline, is very clear, as the Council of Trent too recognized in its explicit teaching that the Catholic bishops are the successors of those apostles who at the Council of Jerusalem presumed to speak in the name of the Holy Spirit.

Indeed, the Profession of Faith of the Council of Trent—also known as the Profession of Faith of Pius IV since it was issued in 1564 by this Pope in response to Trent's decree (1563) that all prelates in the Church would have to make a specific act of faith and obedience to the Holy See—specifically required acceptance of and belief in everything "transmitted, defined *and declared* by the sacred canons and the ecumenical councils" (emphasis added).[15] In other words, what Catholics must hold with regard to the decisions of general councils of the Church is *not* limited, according to this Tridentine Profession of Faith, only to what is strictly "defined."

Vatican Council II, convoked, presided over, and ratified by a Vicar of Christ, definitely falls within the category of ecumenical or general councils—we use these terms synonymously—to which these traditional Church teachings certainly apply. We must, as Catholics, accept and obey the decisions and decrees of this Council (as of all the other twenty general councils of the Church that preceded it) as interpreted by the continuous living authority of the Church.

To be able to hold any other position about Vatican II, whether with regard to its teaching or its disciplinary enactments (as, for instance, when the Council says in its Constitution on the Sacred Liturgy *Sacrosanctum Concilium*, #25, that the Church's "liturgical books are to be revised as soon as possible"), it would be necessary to prove that Vatican II was not a general council of the Church. This, needless to say, cannot be proved. Merely styling Vatican II a "pastoral council" does not constitute a proof that the documents of this particular Council are not just as binding upon the faithful as those of any of the other twenty ecumenical councils which preceded it. A general council is a general council. There is no support in Catholic Tradition for the idea that the faithful may elect not to follow the enactments of a general council of the Church.

As Joseph Cardinal Hoeffner, the Archbishop of Cologne, declared in a Pastoral Letter on August 10, 1975:

"Decisions [of general councils] concerning disciplinary and liturgical questions are also under the guidance of the Holy Spirit. When the apostles held their so-called apostolic council, they promulgated their disciplinary decisions with the solemn words: 'the Holy Spirit and we have decided' (*Acts* 15:28)."

We may safely conclude that the Catholic faithful are obliged to follow Vatican II; its pastoral nature exempted no one from the obligation to follow its directives.

Above all, and finally, we should not confuse the question of the obligation of Catholics to obey the Council's disciplinary enactments with the question of whether or not what it taught was "infallible." As we have already seen, the Catholic Tradition is that general councils are protected from doctrinal error by the Holy Spirit even when they are not engaged in making dogmatic pronouncements.

Some try to reason, erroneously: "The Council was not infallible (meaning it did not solemnly define any new dogmas of faith); *therefore* we need not follow it." This is a fallacy. As Pope Paul VI said: the Council's teachings always have at least "the authority of the supreme ordinary Magisterium. This ordinary Magisterium, which is so obviously official, has to be accepted with docility and sincerity by all the faithful, in accordance with the mind of the Council on the nature and aims of the individual documents" (General Audience of January 12, 1966).

Pope Paul VI was propounding nothing new to the Catholic Tradition here. Pope Pius IX as far back as 1863 had already made clear that Catholics owe the submission of internal assent not only to defined dogmas but to the decisions of the ordinary Magisterium as well. Writing to the Archbishop of Munich about a theological Congress being held in the latter's diocese, Pope Pius IX said:

"We address to the members of this Congress well-merited praise, because, rejecting, as We expected they would, this false distinction between the philosopher and the philosophy of which We have spoken in earlier letters, they have recognized and accepted that all Catholics are obliged in conscience in their writings to obey the dogmatic decrees of the Catholic Church,

which is infallible. In giving them the praise which is their due
for confessing a truth which flows necessarily from the obligation of the Catholic faith, We love to think that they have not
intended to restrict this obligation of obedience, which is strictly binding on Catholic professors and writers, solely to the
points defined by the infallible judgment of the Church as
dogmas of faith which all men must believe. And We are persuaded that they have not intended to declare that this perfect
adhesion to revealed truths, which they have recognized to be
absolutely necessary to the true progress of science and the re-
futation of error, could be theirs if faith and obedience were
only accorded to dogmas expressly defined by the Church.
Even when it is only a question of the submission owed to
divine faith, this cannot be limited merely to points defined by
the express decrees of the Ecumenical Councils, or of the
Roman Pontiffs and of this Apostolic See; this submission must
also be extended to all that has been handed down as divinely
revealed by the ordinary teaching authority of the entire
Church spread over the whole world."[16]

What all this means is that teachings of the Church do not have to
be expressed as solemnly defined dogmas before they have to be believed with "loyal submission of the will and intellect," as Vatican II
phrased it (Dogmatic Constitution on the Church *Lumen Gentium,*
25). Nor do the disciplinary enactments have to involve "infal-
lible" pronouncements in order to oblige us to obey them. This
issue has sometimes been confused in some traditionalist writing
and argument when it has been asserted on the one hand that council
(or papal) decisions need not be followed because they do not
enjoy the note of infallibility, and that, on the other hand, opposition to, say, the New Order of the Mass is not a doctrinal but a disciplinary matter "only."

All this is to argue inconsistently. It cannot be shown from Catholic Tradition either that Catholics may dissent from non-infallible
Church teachings *or* that they may disobey or disregard authentic
Church disciplinary enactments. The contrary is rather the case, as
we have demonstrated above as far as the Second Vatican Council
is concerned.

Question # 3

DID POPE PAUL VI HAVE THE AUTHORITY TO REVISE THE ROMAN MISSAL AND MAKE THE NEW ORDER OF THE MASS NORMATIVE FOR CATHOLICS OF THE ROMAN RITE IN PLACE OF THE "TRIDENTINE MASS"?

The Pope's authority over the regulation of the liturgy and the administration of the sacraments stems from his supreme authority over the Church in general; it stems, in other words, from what is called his primacy (supremacy in governing the Church), which the First Vatican Council *defined*, every bit as definitely as it defined the Pope's infallibility (divine protection against the possibility of teaching error when defining matters of faith and morals in his capacity as supreme Pastor in the Church).

This primacy, which the successors of the Apostle Peter have always possessed over the Church, was promised by Jesus Christ Himself in the famous incident at Caesarea Philippi when, after Simon Bar Jonah's profession of faith in Christ as the Son of the living God, the same Christ renamed him Peter, "the Rock," declared He would build His Church on him, and further committed specific powers into his hands to be passed on to his successors after His own death, resurrection, and ascension, and the descent of the Holy Spirit: Peter was given "the keys of the kingdom of heaven" and the power of "binding" and "loosing" on earth (Cf. *Mt.* 16:13-20).

From the earliest times the successors of Peter as bishop of Rome, where the Prince of the Apostles had installed himself and where he was martyred, exercised this primacy over the other "Churches" established by the other apostles and their helpers. Before the end of the first century, we already find Pope Clement I intervening in the affairs of the Church at Corinth where some of the laity, dissatisfied with their bishops, had taken it upon themselves to try to depose them from office![1]

At the great ecumenical council held at Ephesus, in Asia Minor, in the year 431, Philip, the Papal Legate at the Council, spoke of the Roman primacy over the Church to the great assembly of bishops as if the fact of this primacy were already the most familiar of facts about the Catholic Church that might ever occur to anyone:

"No one doubts, nay it is a thing known for centuries, that the holy and most blessed Peter, the prince and head of the Apostles, the pillar of faith and the foundation on which the Catholic Church is built, received from Our Lord Jesus Christ, the saviour and redeemer of the human race, the keys of the kingdom, and that to him there was given the power of binding and of loosing from sin; who, down to this day, and for evermore, lives and exercises judgment in his successors."[2]

We might add to this that the same thing has been true down to *this* day; it would be hard to improve, even today, upon this formulation of the papal primacy by this Papal Legate, Philip. Nevertheless, nearly fifteen hundred years after the Council of Ephesus, the Fathers of the First Vatican Council in 1870 saw fit to define dogmatically the papal primacy over the Church:

"We teach and declare. . .that by the disposition of the Lord, the Roman Church possesses preeminence of ordinary power above all the Churches; and that this power of jurisdiction of the Roman Pontiff, which is truly episcopal, is immediate. This power obligates shepherds and faithful of every rite and dignity, both individually and collectively, to hierarchical subordination and true obedience, *not only in matters pertaining to faith and morals, but also in those pertaining to the discipline and government of the Church throughout the world*; so that by maintaining with the Roman Pontiff unity of communion and unity in the profession of the same faith, the Church of Christ may be one flock under one supreme Shepherd. This is the teaching of Catholic truth. No one can deviate from it without danger to faith" (Emphasis added).

Further along, the Fathers of Vatican I declare that "a decision of the Apostolic See, whose authority has no superior, may be revised by no one, nor may anyone examine judicially its decision." Finally, the Council Fathers also decided to formulate the whole doctrine in a canon with anathema attached:

"If anyone should say that the Roman Pontiff has merely the function of inspection or direction but not full and supreme power of jurisdiction over the whole Church, *not only in matters pertaining to faith and morals, but also in matters pertaining to the discipline and government of the Church throughout the entire world,* or that he has only the principal share, but not the full plenitude of this supreme power; or that this power of his is not ordinary and immediate over all Churches and over each individual Church, over all shepherds and all the faithful, and over each individual one of these: let him be anathema" (Vatican Council I, Dogmatic Constitution of the Church of Christ *Pastor Aeternus,* #3; Emphasis added).[3]

This teaching of Vatican Council I on the papal primacy, less well known and understood than the same Council's definition of papal infallibility, may come as a surprise especially to those who hold that while Catholics have to follow the teaching of the Pope in faith and morals ("because he is infallible"), we don't necessarily have to follow his merely disciplinary decisions and enactments. We have seen, in the answer to Question #2, that such a view is wrong with regard to the decrees of a general council. The language of Vatican I quoted here shows that it is wrong with regard to the decrees of a Pontiff too.

Vatican II, incidentally, both repeats the same teaching on the supreme power of the Pope to govern the whole Church, and amplifies the teaching, especially with respect to how the Roman primacy over the Church is exercised in conjunction with the authority of the bishops throughout the world (Cf. Vatican Council II, Dogmatic Constitution on the Church *Lumen Gentium,* #18, #22). The consistency with which this same idea recurs in Church documents reinforces the conclusion that it represents the authentic Catholic Tradition in the matter.

The Pope has general authority over the whole Church, then, but does that mean, specifically, that he could revise the Roman Missal to substitute the New Order of the Mass for the Tridentine Mass? That, after all, is the specific question under review here.

We shall deal in later sections (Questions #4 and #5) with specific objections that have been raised about the authority of the Pope to establish the New Order of the Mass in place of the old Tridentine Mass. Here we have to establish that: 1) the Church does have the authority and can indeed "change" certain externals in the form or manner of the liturgy or the sacraments including the Mass (and such externals are all that have been changed in the New Order of the Mass); and that: 2) the Pope, possessing supreme authority over the whole Church, as we have already seen, also possesses supreme authority over the manner in which the Mass and the other sacraments are to be celebrated or administered, changed in their externals, or retained intact.

What, then, is the traditional teaching of the Church on these two points?

The great Council of Trent explicitly recognized that the Church can, for the good of the faithful, make changes in the liturgy or sacraments, provided their substance is preserved. In the Council's exact words:

> ". . .in the dispensation of the sacraments, provided their substance is preserved, the Church has always had the power to determine or change, according to circumstances, times and places, what she judges more expedient for the benefit of those receiving them or for the veneration of the sacraments" (Council of Trent, Twenty-First Session).[4]

In his 1947 encyclical *Mediator Dei*, Pope Pius XII also explicitly recognized that "as circumstances and the needs of Christians warrant, public worship is organized, developed and enriched by *new* rites, ceremonies and regulations" (#22; emphasis added). According to Pius XII, the hierarchy of the Church "has not been slow — keeping the substance of the Mass and sacraments carefully intact — to modify what it deemed not altogether fitting, and to add what appeared more likely to increase the honor paid to Jesus Christ and the august Trinity, and to instruct and stimulate the Christian people to greater advantage" (#49).

It is clear, then, that the Church possesses from God the authority to make the changes she deems fitting in the externals, or human components, of the liturgy and the sacraments. When Vatican II decided to recommend the changes in the Mass that later became the New Order of the Mass as contained in the current revised Roman Missal, therefore, the Council was in no way departing from the Tradition of the Church as explicitly recognized by the Council of Trent and by Pope Pius XII, long before Vatican II ever assembled.

Moreover, in revising the Roman Missal at the behest of the Council, thereby substituting the New Order of the Mass for the

Tridentine Mass, Pope Paul VI was simply exercising a power which Pope Pius XII also expressly recognized further on in *Mediator Dei* as indeed being vested in the Pope alone: ". . .the Sovereign Pontiff alone enjoys the right to recognize and establish any practice touching the worship of God, to introduce and approve new rites, as also to modify those he judges to require modifications," (Pope Pius XII, Encyclical *Mediator Dei,* #58).

We may surely conclude from all this that it was in the legitimate exercise of his supreme authority as the successor of Peter that Pope Paul VI issued, on April 3, 1969, his Apostolic Constitution on the Roman Missal *Missale Romanum,* replacing the Tridentine Mass celebrated up to that time out of the older Roman Missal with the New Order of the Mass contained in the current Roman Missal. In this Apostolic Constitution, Paul VI himself notes that, in revising the Roman Missal at the request of Vatican II, he is doing exactly what Pope St. Pius V did when he revised the Roman Missal at the request of the Council of Trent. Because of the central importance of this Apostolic Constitution of Pope Paul VI, we are publishing the full text of it in Appendix I.

In a General Audience on November 19, 1969, the Pope further carefully explained to the world what he was doing in issuing his Apostolic Constitution *Missale Romanum*, and emphasized the obligatory nature of it for all the faithful. In this General Audience, the Holy Father made clear that the changes in no way affected the substance of the holy sacrifice—which the Church had no power to change—but consisted of "new directions for celebrating the rites." He called his address, significantly, "The Mass is the Same."

How much grief could have been avoided if only more attention had been paid at the time to what the Pope himself was actually saying. Arguments continued to rage for nearly a decade about whether in fact the Tridentine Mass had been replaced or whether the New Order as established was binding on the faithful; but then it was one of the tragedies of the pontificate of Pope Paul VI that some of the words of this Pope were so little heeded, on all sides. Nevertheless it is still worth quoting excerpts of what he did say himself about why he was changing some of the externals which surrounded the celebration of the Mass and about how "binding" this change was upon the faithful.

In his General Audience of November 19, 1969, then, the Holy Father declared that:

"We wish to draw your attention to an event about to occur in the Latin Catholic Church: the introduction of the liturgy of the new rite of the Mass. . . . The Mass will be celebrated in a rather different manner from that in which we have been accustomed to celebrate it in the last four centuries, from the reign of St. Pius V, after the Council of Trent, down to the present. . . .

"How could such a change be made? Answer: It is due to the will expressed by the Ecumenical Council held not long ago. The Council decreed: 'The rite of the Mass is to be revised in such a way that the intrinsic nature and purpose of its several parts, as also the connection between them, can be more clearly manifested, and that devout and active participation by the faithful can be more easily accomplished. For this purpose the rites are to be simplified, while due care is taken to preserve their substance. Elements which, with the passage of time, came to be duplicated, or were added with but little advantage, are now to be discarded. Where opportunity allows or necessity demands, other elements which have suffered injury through accidents of history are now to be restored to the earlier norm of the holy Fathers.' (Vatican Council II, Constitution on the Sacred Liturgy *Sacrosanctum Concilium*, #50). The reform which is about to be brought into being is therefore a response to an authoritative mandate from the Church. . .

"It is not an arbitrary act. It is not a transitory or optional experiment. It is not some dilettante's improvisation. *It is a law*. . ." (Emphasis added).

Because of the importance of the Pope's own explanation of what he was doing in revising the Roman Missal to establish the New Order of the Mass as obligatory for all the faithful, and why he was doing it, we are reprinting in full in Appendix II, in addition to the Apostolic Constitution *Missale Romanum* found in Appendix I, both the Pope's General Audience of November 19, 1969, quoted here, and his subsequent General Audience of November 26, 1969, in which he further spoke about the liturgical reform the Church was instituting following the recommendations of Vatican II.

In summary, it seems that Pope Paul VI did have the authority to revise the Roman Missal and thus to replace the Tridentine Mass with the *Novus Ordo* in the Roman rite. He had the authority to do this; it was his intention to do it; and he did do it — as we shall see further in answering other questions that have been raised on this subject.

The only question that remains, and must puzzle well-instructed Catholics who understand what legitimate authority in the Church entails and what our obligations are towards it, is the question of why so many continue to believe that they may remain Catholics in good standing while rejecting the Pope's revision of the Roman Missal. Some argue that the infallibility of the Pope was not involved in the replacement of the Tridentine Mass by the *Novus Ordo* and therefore they need not accept the change. Others claim that the whole thing involves discipline only and does not touch upon faith and morals and hence for this reason they need not obey the Pope. Some, inconsistently, attempt to combine elements of both of those arguments.

We have already treated essentially this same question with regard to the assent and obedience owed by the Catholic faithful to the enactments of a general council (Question #2); the answer found there is the same as regards the assent and obedience required of the faithful to the teachings and directives of a Pope. The faithful may not reject authentic Church teachings or disciplinary measures even though they may honestly judge them to be detrimental to the best interests of the Church.

In his famous 1864 encyclical *Quanta Cura*, Pope Pius IX actually censured the idea that the faithful could disregard Church discipline on the grounds that it did not concern "faith and morals"; this is the exact proposition the great nineteenth-century Pontiff censured:

> "It is possible, without sinning and without at all departing from the profession of the Catholic faith, to refuse assent and obedience to those decisions and decrees of the Apostolic See whose declared object is the general good of the Church and its rights and discipline, provided only that such decisions do not touch upon dogmas of faith and morals."

"No one can fail to see," Pius IX added in *Quanta Cura*, "that this doctrine *directly opposes Catholic dogma* according to which Christ our Lord with His divine authority gave to the Roman Pontiff the supreme power of shepherding, ruling, and governing the Church" (emphasis added).[5] We should note well that Pius IX declares that any attempt to evade Church discipline on the ground that faith and morals are not involved goes contrary to Catholic *doctrine;* it is part of Catholic "faith and morals," in other words, that disciplinary decrees of the Holy See must be obeyed by Catholics.

In 1873, the same Pope Pius IX taught that "it is as contrary to the divine constitution of the Church as it is to perpetual and constant tradition for anyone to attempt to prove the catholicity of his faith and truly call himself a Catholic when he fails in obedience to the Apostolic See."[6]

What Pope Pius IX has here placed the seal of the Magisterium upon as regards the obedience owed to the Vicar of Christ was always, of course, the common opinion of traditional Catholic theologians. St. Robert Bellarmine, for example, writes apropos of the same question "that the Pope with General Council cannot err, either in framing decrees of faith or general precepts of morality; [and] . . .that the Pope when determining anything in a doubtful matter, whether it is possible for him to err or not, is to be obeyed by all the faithful."[7]

Thus, according to St. Robert Bellarmine, no Catholic can withdraw his acceptance of the *Novus Ordo* on the grounds that the Pope was gravely mistaken in instituting it—even if this latter contention were proved to be true.

John Henry Cardinal Newman endorses the opinion of St. Robert Bellarmine in language which goes right to the heart of all the controversies today over whether Catholics are obliged to accept the New Order of the Mass. Newman writes:

"I say with Cardinal Bellarmine whether the Pope be infallible or not in any pronouncement, anyhow he is to be obeyed. No good can come from disobedience. His facts and his warnings may be all wrong; his deliberations may have been biased. He may have been misled. Imperiousness and craft, tyranny and cruelty, may be patent in the conduct of his advisers and instruments. But when he speaks formally and authoritatively he speaks as our Lord would have him speak, and all those imperfections and sins of individuals are overruled for that result which our Lord intends (just as the action of the wicked and of enemies to the Church are overruled) and therefore the Pope's word stands, and a blessing goes with obedience to it, and no blessing with disobedience."[8]

We in no way have to accept that the Pope, in revising the Roman Missal, was guilty of any of the faults Newman mentions. Newman is deliberately posing the worst possible case in order to make more forcibly his point that the Pope does have to be obeyed in his official enactments *as* Vicar of Christ.

With these characteristically definite words of the great English Cardinal we may fittingly close this section of our discussion of this question. Having established here the general proposition that the Pope has to be obeyed, we will go on in the answer to Question # 8 to show specifically the obligation of Catholics of the Roman rite to accept the replacement of the Tridentine Mass by the *Novus Ordo* Mass. Here our conclusion has to be considered firm that: 1) Pope Paul VI did have the authority to institute the New Order of the Mass through his revision of the Roman Missal and to make it normative for Catholic worship in the Roman rite; 2) the Pope did, in fact, do this; and 3) Catholics of the Roman rite are obliged to obey and follow his enactments as being the latest authoritative directives in the matter from the Holy See, implicitly accepted and continued by the two Popes who have followed him (see also Question # 8).

Finally, in any case, Pope John Paul II, after becoming Pope, specifically said the faithful must follow the liturgical discipline currently in force —the New Order of the Mass—when he declared the day after his election in his speech to the Cardinals that "fidelity . . .implies the observance of the liturgical norms laid down by ecclesiastical authority" ("To the Cardinals and the World," October 17, 1978).

Question # 4

DIDN'T POPE ST. PIUS V, IN HIS APOSTOLIC CONSTITUTION *"QUO PRIMUM,"* ISSUED IN 1570, ESTABLISH THE TRIDENTINE MASS FOR ALL TIME?

Pope St. Pius V's Apostolic Constitution *Quo Primum* has figured so prominently in all the controversies surrounding the New Order of the Mass versus the Tridentine Mass that we are reprinting this 1570 Apostolic Constitution in its entirety in Appendix III. Reading over this ecclesiastical document of the sixteenth century today, we cannot but be impressed by a number of things about it.

It is clearly a disciplinary document. Pope St. Pius V is not engaged in defining doctrine about the Mass or the sacrifice; he is concerned with establishing a uniform discipline throughout the Roman rite with regard to the manner of celebrating Mass, and not with regard to any essential element in the sacrifice.

Thus *Quo Primum* does not involve the issue of the Pope's infallibility; it is not a statement dealing with faith and morals which could never be reversed by virtue of having been issued *ex cathedra* by a Pope acting in his capacity as shepherd and teacher of all Christians or by other ways in which the Pope could express his infallibility. Rather, it is a disciplinary document in which the Pope is at pains to insure that the new revision of the Roman Missal which he is promulgating will be followed, geographically, everywhere that the Roman rite is celebrated; this is evident from the language of the text. The Pope devotes fully as much space to specifying how the new Roman Missal is to be printed and publicized throughout the Church—even getting into the difference between priests south of the Alps or beyond the Alps and the time required to transmit messages in those days—as he does to the points which some have interpreted to mean that he intended by this document to establish a particular discipline of the Mass once and for all.

That such an idea was not the Pope's intention may be deduced from the fact that he himself, assisted by his commission — "learned men of our selection"—was precisely engaged in extensively revising the discipline of celebrating Mass of his own time at the behest of the Council of Trent—just as, four hundred years later, Pope Paul VI would embark upon a similar revision of the Roman Missal at the behest of another general council, Vatican II. Pope St. Pius V could thus surely not have believed that the manner and form of Catholic worship can never be changed, for the simple reason that he was himself engaged in doing just that. In *Quo Primum* he even calls his revised Missal a "new rite"; he says it was his intention to "revise and re-edit the sacred books."

These facts about what Pope St. Pius V really did in *Quo Primum* are not affected by asserting that in his revision he was substantially preserving the canon of the Mass which went all the way back to St. Gregory the Great. Paul VI's revision of the Roman Missal in 1969 also "substantially" preserved this same canon in the First Eucharistic Prayer.

Seeing how difficult it has been for some to accept the Roman Missal as revised by Pope Paul VI in our day, we can surely understand how concerned Pope St. Pius V was to see to it that his own prescriptions should be obeyed everywhere at a time when bishops, priests, and the faithful were not even accustomed to a uniform rite of Mass. That, precisely, was what Pope St. Pius V was trying to establish. And much of the strong language in *Quo Primum* was directed against those who might presume to go on celebrating their own, local, form of the Mass instead of accepting the revised Roman Missal which he was promulgating by this Apostolic Constitution.

If we read *Quo Primum* carefully we will see that, in its true context, Pope St. Pius' command that "no one whosoever is to be forced or coerced to alter this Missal," is intended to protect those priests wishing to follow the Pope against, say, a local bishop or religious superior desirous of continuing one of the local forms of the Mass which Pope St. Pius V was endeavoring to suppress by the very promulgation of *Quo Primum*. This language is quite clearly not directed against a subsequent Pope who might issue *his* Apostolic Constitution on the Mass by virtue of the same papal authority Pope St. Pius V was exercising in issuing *Quo Primum*.

Similarly, when the Pope in *Quo Primum* enumerates all the ecclesiastical dignitaries who are forbidden to alter the Missal he is establishing — "patriarch, administrator, and all other persons of whatever ecclesiastical dignity they may be, *even* cardinals of the Holy Roman Church" (emphasis added) —he most pointedly and significantly does not mention the future *Popes* whom some have imagined he intended to bind in this document; but, again, it is clear that he is not primarily addressing his successors, here or elsewhere in this disciplinary document; he is quite patently commanding and directing everybody over whom he himself was the supreme spiritual authority in 1570, including patriarchs and cardinals, to celebrate the Mass henceforth only as he, by virtue of his supreme authority as Pope over the liturgy and the sacraments, is now prescribing it in the revised Roman Missal he is promulgating.

That the primary intention of Pope St. Pius V in *Quo Primum* is to make his reform binding upon those who up to then have celebrated the Mass in diverse ways —rather than to restrict future Popes in their authority to regulate the liturgy and the administration of the sacraments —can also be seen from the following comment on the effects of St. Pius' reform, taken from the most authoritative present-day study of the history of the Mass of the Roman rite, Fr. Joseph A. Jungmann's *The Mass of the Roman Rite:*

> "Such a broad and sweeping unification could never have been completely accomplished before the day of the printing press. Even as things stood, there were bound to be many doubts and problems resulting from such widely diverse conditions and local customs, not to speak of the difficulties of making the change. To handle these doubts and problems, Pope Sixtus V, by the Constitution *"Immensa"* of January 22, 1588, founded the Congregation of Rites. Its charge was to see to it that everywhere in the Latin Church the prescribed manner of celebrating Mass and performing the other functions of the liturgy were carefully followed. It had to settle doubts, to give out dispensations and privileges, and since there was always a chance of introducing new feasts, it had to provide the proper formularies for them."[1]

Pope St. Pius V thus never intended by *Quo Primum* that no further revision of the Roman Missal could ever be made, or that no other form of the Roman Mass could henceforth ever be said. This can be further seen by the fact that the saintly Pope allowed for and indeed *provided* for the celebration of other forms of the Mass in *Quo Primum* itself: rites which had been followed for more than

200 years were specifically exempted from the provisions of *Quo Primum* and from the use of the St. Pius V Roman Missal. "In this way the older orders like the Carthusians and the Dominicans were enabled to retain their ancient liturgical usages," the old *Catholic Encyclopedia* article on the subject remarks, "but the new book was accepted throughout the greater part of Europe."[2]

If this canonized Pope was really attempting to bind his successors and all Catholics forever after to a single, fixed form of the Roman rite, it is remarkable that his successors did not seem aware that they had been so bound. Long before the revision of Pope Paul VI resulting in the present New Order of the Mass, there were a number of other revisions of the Roman Missal carried out down through the years. Fr. Jungmann has said apropos of this:

"Some real changes since the sixteenth century in the rubrics and in the text of the Missal of Pius V have resulted in certain instances from papal orders. For instance, in the new edition of the missal under Clement VIII (1604), the biblical chant pieces, which in some printings had been arbitrarily changed in favor of the new Vulgate, were restored to their original state, and new regulations were made regarding the final blessing. In another new edition of the Mass book under Urban VIII (1634), the wording of the rubrics was greatly improved and the revision of the hymns already accomplished in the breviary was carried out also in the few hymns of the missal. No new edition with any notable changes came out till that of 1920 which contained the revisions based on the reform of Pope Pius X. For the rest, excepting the increase in saints' feasts, very little was done to affect the arrangement of the Mass. Pope Clement XIII prescribed the Preface of the Holy Trinity for Sundays, and Pope Leo XIII ordered the prayers said after low Mass."[3]

The fact that few changes were made in the Missal did not mean, however, that the Popes were prohibited from making any by *Quo Primum*. A striking example of the fact that, even in the years immediately following the reign of Pope St. Pius V, his successors did not understand *Quo Primum* to mean that they could never make any changes in the Missal, comes from a history of the Jesuit missionaries in China in the early seventeenth century. The Jesuits had requested the right to allow the Mass to be translated and celebrated in Chinese by Chinese priests. Although this reform, in fact, never

went into effect for reasons too complicated to go into here, the
fact is that the reform was *approved* by Pope Paul V in 1615.

The story is recounted in *Generation of Giants* by George H.
Dunne, S.J.:

> ". . . in what must almost be a record for an institution
> noted for its prejudice against precipitate action, the Holy
> Office, in a meeting held on January 15, 1615, in the presence
> of Paul V in the Quirinal, granted the concessions asked for,
> namely, permission for priests to wear a headpiece while cele-
> brating Mass, permission to translate the Bible into literary
> Chinese; permission for Chinese priests to celebrate Mass and
> recite the canonical hours in literary Chinese.
>
> "Evidently some uncertainty remained as to the exact terms
> of the concessions, for the same subject was taken up again
> in another meeting of the Holy Office, held on March 26, also
> in the presence of the Holy Father. This time Bellarmine was
> chairman of the board of six cardinals. A new text was drafted
> and approved. It was substantially the same as the earlier de-
> cree, but with some important qualifications added. It was
> made clear that the permission to adopt the head-piece was
> granted to all missionaries in China. As for the liturgy it speci-
> fied that while Chinese could be used as the liturgical language,
> the Roman rite was still to be followed; nor was the permission
> to prejudice episcopal jurisdiction if and when bishops were
> constituted in China. To give the highest possible authority to
> this decree of March 26, 1615, Pope Paul V promulgated it by
> the Brief *Romanae Ecclesiae Antistes,* issued on June 17, 1615."[4]

The Popes, in short, did not understand *Quo Primum* to mean that
they could never change the Roman Missal or allow the Mass to be
celebrated in any other fashion than that prescribed by Pope St.
Pius V.

An interesting parallel to the case of the revised Missal of Pope
St. Pius V can be seen in that of the revised Roman Breviary promulgated by the same Pontiff. In 1568, in his Apostolic Constitution
Quod a Vobis, the Pope established the new Roman Breviary with
language fully as strong as the language he used in *Quo Primum.* In
fact, *Quod a Vobis* contains exactly the *same* concluding paragraph
as *Quo Primum,* warning anyone against making any change in what
had been enacted.

Yet, in spite of that, Pope St. Pius X, in 1911, did not hesitate to revise the Roman Breviary by means of his own Apostolic Constitution *Divino Afflatu*[5] —just as Pope Paul VI would later revise the Roman Missal by means of his Apostolic Constitution *Missale Romanum*. The fact that another canonized saint and a great foe of modernism did not see his saintly predecessor's prohibitions of any change as applying to *him* abundantly proves our point. Far from the same language in *Quo Primum* being a special caveat by which Pius V was permanently establishing his text of the Roman Missal beyond the possibility of future change, the identical paragraph to be found in both sixteenth-century documents was actually a conventional legal formula automatically attached to many documents issued by the Popes. It is worth reproducing the paragraph in question, as it is found at the end of both *Quo Primum* and *Quod a Vobis*:

> "Therefore, no one whosoever is permitted to alter this letter or heedlessly to venture to go contrary to this notice of Our permission, statute, ordinance, command, precept, grant, indult, declaration, will, decree, and prohibition. Should anyone, however, presume to commit such an act, he should know that he will incur the wrath of Almighty God and of the Blessed Apostles Peter and Paul" (See Appendix III).

Now so much was this paragraph a conventional legal formula in the papal documents of the day that the authors, checking the Latin text of *Quo Primum* in the course of their research upon this question, found that this paragraph was not even reproduced in full at the end of *Quo Primum* in the collection of papal bulls which we consulted![6] The Latin of this paragraph begins "*Nulli ergo omnino hominum liceat hanc paginam*," etc., but in the collection of papal bulls there is printed simply "*Nulli ergo, etc.*"—so much was this paragraph considered a mere conventional formula!

Certainly Pope St. Pius X considered it so when he revised the Roman Breviary in 1911 in spite of the identical caveat contained in St. Pius V's *Quod a Vobis*. He specifically says that he is ordering a "new arrangement" of the Roman Breviary "issued by St. Pius V and revised by Clement VIII, Urban VIII and Leo XIII." In doing so, this canonized Pope too concluded his Apostolic Constitution *Divino Afflatu* with an ecclesiastical caveat against anyone daring to change his decision which was the established legal form to be attached to papal decree in *his* time; it is remarkably similar to the caveat in *Quo Primum*.

"This we publish, declare, sanction, decreeing that these our letters always are and shall be valid and effective, notwithstanding apostolic ordinances, general and special, and everything else whatsoever to the contrary. Wherefore, let nobody infringe or temerariously oppose this page of our abolition, revocation, permission, ordinance, statute, indult, mandate and will. But if anyone shall presume to attempt this let him know that he will incur the indignation of almighty God and of his apostles the blessed Peter and Paul."[5]

By now it should be clear that such ecclesiastical formulas do *not* mean that a *Pope* cannot change the disciplinary decrees of a previous Pope. Pope St. Pius X did just that in *Divino Afflatu*.

Changes in the Roman Missal before Vatican II in this century have included the changes made by Pope Pius XII when, by a simple decree of a Roman Congregation, he completely revised the liturgy of Holy Week in 1955.[7] By means of his Apostolic *Rubricarum Instructum* of July 25, 1960, Pope John XXIII changed the rubrics of both the Roman Missal and the Roman Breviary.[8] And, of course, in a widely publicized move, it was also Pope John who introduced the name of St. Joseph into the prayers of the canon.[9] Even prior to Vatican II the Popes clearly did not see themselves bound by *Quo Primum* never to revise the Roman Missal.

Still further interim changes in the unrevised traditional Roman Missal were made by Pope Paul VI in 1965 and 1967 before he promulgated the revised Roman Missal by the issuance of his Apostolic Constitution *Missale Romanum* on April 3, 1969.[10]

What one Pope decrees in the way of liturgical or sacramental discipline, another Pope can modify or revoke. It is an axiom of law that what a given authority enacts the same authority can repeal; a subsequent Congress can repeal a law passed by an earlier Congress; one President can rescind or modify an executive order issued by an earlier President. These are illustrations taken from the civil realm but their logic applies equally to ecclesiastical law. We saw in the answer to Question #1 how the Council of Trent modified solemn decrees of earlier councils. Paul VI, possessing the same papal authority as his predecessor Pope St. Pius V, similarly repealed the Apostolic Constitution, *Quo Primum* by the fact of issuing a subsequent Apostolic Constitution, *Missale Romanum*, covering exactly the same subject matter, namely, the Roman Missal.

The fact of the repeal would, as we have said, be axiomatic in law, but, in any case, the principle is explicitly recognized by the current Code of Canon Law. Canon 22 states that "if the later law is equally general or equally particular with the former one"—and both *Quo Primum and Missale Romanum* are equally Apostolic Constitutions dealing with exactly the same subject matter, namely, the Roman Missal—"then the later law repeals the former law . . . if it deals with the entire subject matter of the former law."[11] This is, precisely, the case. (Technically, Pope Paul VI did not *abrogate* the older Roman Missal; he replaced it by the new revised Roman Missal and *derogated* the use of the older Missal to the case of aged or infirm priests allowed by their bishops to say the Tridentine Mass, but only without a congregation!)

Again, according to Canon Law, a later law also repeals the former one, "if it contains an explicit statement to that effect, a repealing clause."[12] And, here again, Pope Paul VI's Apostolic Constitution *Missale Romanum* both mentions (in the beginning) his predecessor's *Quo Primum* and says (at the end) that what he is promulgating is promulgated "notwithstanding, as far as is necessary, Apostolic Constitutions and Ordinances issued by Our Predecessors and other prescriptions even those worthy of special mention and derogation." *Quo Primum* is among the "prescriptions . . . worthy of special mention and derogation," as, indeed, is John XXIII's *Rubricarum Instructum* mentioned above.

Hence it becomes impossible for us to hold that Pope St. Pius V established the Tridentine Mass for all time or that Pope Paul VI did not validly promulgate the New Order of the Mass and make it obligatory and universal in the Roman rite through the issuance of his new Roman Missal in 1969.

But what about the explicit language in *Quo Primum* that says it is to apply "henceforth, now, and forever" and that "this present document cannot be revoked or modified"?

Two points have to be understood here. First, terms such as "forever" and "in perpetuity" in ecclesiastical documents refer to enactments that are to last *indefinitely,* that is, no specific date or time is set in advance (such as the death of the Pope) when they will automatically lapse; they thus remain in force until subsequently modified or repealed by legitimate authority. For example, when Clement XIV, in his brief *Dominus ac Redemptor,* dated July 21, 1773, suppressed the Society of Jesus, he declared that this measure should be *"perpetuo validas"*; but this in no way prevented his successor Pius VII from re-establishing the Society of Jesus anyway, in his

Sollicitudo Omnium of August 7, 1814.[13] The mere use of the term "perpetual" did not mean that a subsequent Pope no longer had the authority to revive the religious order which the previous Pope had dissolved. "Perpetual" merely *means* here until some further legitimate enactment is carried out by a sovereign Pontiff. It is worthy of note that Paul VI himself begins his Apostolic Constitution *Missale Romanum* with the formula *"Ad perpetuam rei memoriam"*; "For a perpetual record" (See Appendix I). This salutation is common on papal documents. In his document, Pope St. Pius V merely forbade his Constitution from being "revoked or modified" by any lower authority (than that of a Pope) not competent to modify or revoke it, even "cardinals of the Holy Roman Church," until a subsequent Pope might review or modify his decision.

Moreover, in his very use of the language that *Quo Primum* is to "remain always valid and retain its full force," the Pope specified: "notwithstanding any *previous* constitutions and decrees of the Holy See" (emphasis added). The Pope quite properly did not go on to specify that his Apostolic Constitution could never be modified by any subsequent constitutions or by a future Pope because, quite patently, any future Pope would enjoy exactly the same authority in the matter that he himself enjoyed.

The real intention and force of *Quo Primum* as a disciplinary document issued by the supreme authority in the Church, as we have been explaining it here, was, in fact, simply *assumed* by another subsequent Pope, Gregory XVI, in 1842. In a reference to *Quo Primum* this Pope described the document as meaning exactly what we have interpreted it above as meaning. We have argued that one of the principal intentions of Pope St. Pius V expressed in *Quo Primum* is to see that his revised Roman Missal is put into use everywhere that the Roman rite is celebrated. Pope Gregory XVI seemed to assume this primary meaning when he wrote in 1842 ". . . nothing would be more desirable than to see observed by all those under your care and in every place the constitutions of St. Pius V, our Predecessor of immortal memory, who wished that *no one should be dispensed from the obligation of adopting the Breviary and the Missal* published, according to the mind of the Council of Trent for the use of the Roman rite, except those who for over two centuries had used a different Breviary or Missal" (emphasis added).[14]

We should understand the language of *Quo Primum* as Pope Gregory XVI understood it, namely, as firmly establishing a geographically uniform Roman Missal wherever the Roman rite was celebrated, not as attempting to fix one particular version of the Roman Missal for all time. The article on the Mass in the old *Catholic Encyclopedia,* published during the reign of Pope St. Pius X, similarly describes the effect of *Quo Primum* as the establishment of "uniformity in the Roman rite and the abolition of nearly all the medieval variants."[15] There was no thought in this article that *Quo Primum* might have been intended to foreclose any future changes in the rite of the Mass, especially since the article documents in some detail the many, many changes made in the manner of celebrating the rite since Christ instituted it at the Last Supper—changes which can be verified by any reader by referring to such standard modern works as Fr. Jungmann's *The Mass of the Roman Rite* quoted above.[16]

Question # 5

EVEN IF WE ADMIT THAT POPE PAUL VI HAD THE AUTHORITY TO REVISE THE ROMAN MISSAL TO REPLACE THE TRIDENTINE MASS BY THE NEW ORDER OF THE MASS, ISN'T IT NEVERTHELESS TRUE THAT THE POPE DID NOT FOLLOW PROPER CANONICAL FORM IN MAKING THIS CHANGE? ISN'T IT THEREFORE STILL LICIT TO SAY THE TRIDENTINE MASS?

The answer to the previous question (#4) really made quite clear that Pope Paul VI licitly established the revised Roman Missal in his Apostolic Constitution *Missale Romanum*, thereby replacing the older Roman Missal containing the Tridentine Mass. In answer to the above questions, however, we will go on to deal with some of the specific objections which have often been raised to question whether the Pope in fact acted properly and canonically in replacing the Tridentine Mass by the New Order of the Mass.

An objection frequently leveled against Pope Paul's Apostolic Constitution *Missale Romanum*, promulgating the new revised Roman Missal (see Appendix I for the full text), is that this document nowhere expressly states that the Tridentine Mass is abrogated. It is worth noting in this connection that nowhere in *Quo Primum*, either, was it expressly stated that the various local Missals that were to be replaced by Pope St. Pius V's new Roman Missal were to be abrogated; St. Pius, in promulgating the Missal that he did wish to be used, seems to have assumed that it was evident that he did not wish the rites he was replacing to be allowed to continue if he was taking such pains to establish the Mass that he did want to be uniform in the Roman rite. Perhaps Pope Paul VI could be pardoned for doing exactly what his saintly predecessor did in this matter.

However, with regard to the claim that the Tridentine Mass is not expressly mentioned and abrogated, it is necessary to describe exactly what Pope Paul was doing in issuing this Apostolic Constitution and why the term "Tridentine Mass" did not have to be expressly mentioned. "Tridentine Mass" is not a legal, or a technical, or an official title for the Mass formerly celebrated throughout the Roman rite; it is simply a popular term for the rite of Mass formerly contained in the Roman Missal established by Pope St. Pius V, who similarly made no mention of any "Tridentine Mass." This Roman Missal was changed and modified to some extent, as we have seen (Question #4), by some Popes subsequent to St. Pius V.

In his 1969 Apostolic Constitution *Missale Romanum*, however, Pope Paul was addressing himself to the question of the revision of this Roman Missal; he did not say that a former liturgy, the "Tridentine Mass," was being abolished and replaced by a new and different liturgy; rather the whole thrust of his words was that the Mass of the Roman rite, popularly called the Tridentine Mass, was being modified and changed in some of its external features by means of certain additions, subtractions, and alterations in the Roman Missal; and that this revised version of the Mass of the Roman rite, now known as the "New Order of the Mass," was henceforth to *be* the official Mass of the Roman rite. It was not really necessary for Pope Paul VI to mention the "Tridentine Mass" and then abrogate it; he was not really "abrogating" anything; he was revising the Roman Missal, and establishing this revision as henceforth the normative Mass for Catholics of the Roman rite.

The older, unrevised Roman Missal (the "Tridentine Mass") was published in its last edition on January 27, 1965, with still further variations introduced on May 18, 1967, prior to the general revision which would result in the "New Order of the Mass."[1] When Pope Paul issued his Apostolic Constitution *Missale Romanum* promulgating this general revision, the further use of the older un-revised version of the Missal (the "Tridentine Mass") was *derogated*, not abrogated, that is, its use was henceforth to be limited to aged and infirm priests celebrating without a congregation, as allowed by their bishops.[2] And Pope Paul *did* thus derogate *Quo Primum*; and with express language:

> "We will that these our statutes and prescriptions be now and in the future firm and efficacious notwithstanding, as far as is necessary, Apostolic Constitutions and Ordinances issued by Our Predecessors and other prescriptions even those worthy of special mention and derogation." (See Appendix I for full text.)

These "other prescriptions. . .worthy of special mention and derogation" included, precisely, *Quo Primum; Quo Primum* is mentioned by name, both in the text and the notes of Paul VI's *Missale Romanum*; hence it is clearly included in what is derogated at the end.

Thus, to speak of the Tridentine Mass not having been expressly abrogated, is to get off the track of what is even involved here; the assertion is not a solid objection to the procedure followed by Pope Paul VI; it misses the point.

Similarly, the idea that Paul VI was merely establishing some kind of parallel rite alongside of which the "Tridentine Mass" could continue to be said is inexact; the "Tridentine Mass" and the "New Order of Mass" constitute different versions of the *same* Roman Missal, the latter version of which is now normative for Catholics of the Roman rite, while the use of the former version is lawfully limited to the cases of aged and infirm priests celebrating alone (and evidently, also to the case of the papal indult granted to the bishops of England and Wales to allow them to permit Masses to be celebrated from the older, unrevised Roman Missal under certain circumstances).

A further common objection denying that Pope Paul VI acted lawfully and according to proper canonical form in revising the Missal has been raised with the phrase quoted above from *Missale Romanum*: "We will that these our statutes and prescriptions be now and in the future firm and efficacious. . . ." The expression, "we will" (Latin: *"Volumus"*), translated also "we wish," or "it is our will," has been said by some to indicate only a wish or desire of the Pope, but not a firm command from the Chair of Peter binding upon all the faithful. We might wonder why a Pope would go to the trouble to issue an Apostolic Constitution only to express a wish or desire, but, in fact, that is not what Paul VI did.

Canonists agree that the public expression of the will of the legislator does make an enactment into a law binding upon those subject to it. In fact, the expression *"volumus,"* "we will" or "we wish," is precisely the language used in other recent Apostolic Constitutions issued by the Holy See, for example, the Apostolic Constitution on the Revision of Indulgences *Indulgentiarum Doctrina* of January 1, 1967, and the Apostolic Constitution on the Election of the Roman Pontiff *Romano Pontifici Eligendo* of October 13, 1975.[3] To continue to doubt that the Pope means what he says when he issues such documents, merely because he chooses a particular word, the meaning of which is nevertheless clear, or that, while possessing full authority to legislate on the matters in question, which nobody denies, he somehow inexplicably and by a mere form of words does not bring his full authority into play, is a singular way of understanding the exercise of authority.

Pope St. Pius X, stressing the fact that in any stable order the acts of authority must be received by those subject to it—otherwise everything can be called into question all the time, something that can scarcely be desired by any calling or considering themselves "conservatives" or "traditionalists"—Pope St. Pius X decreed that acts from the Holy See would be considered legitimately promulgated when they appeared in the *Acta Apostolicae Sedis*, the official "journal" of the Holy See:

> "We will it that Pontifical Constitutions, laws, decrees and other notifications emanating from the Supreme Pontiffs as well as Sacred Congregations and Offices be inserted and published in the *Acta Apostolicae Sedis* and for this precise reason, that they be considered legitimately promulgated each time a promulgation is made or the matter has not been otherwise disposed by the Holy See."[4]

Surely it is sufficient for Pope Paul VI to have promulgated his Apostolic Constitutions in this manner for Catholics to be confident that they have been validly promulgated.

Further, to the question of whether the will (or "wish") of the superior is binding regardless of whether it is promulgated in a specific form, we may cite St. Thomas Aquinas as another authority. Aquinas tells us that the specific object of obedience "is a command tacit or express; because the superior's will, *however it becomes known*, is a tacit precept" (emphasis added).[5] In other words, provided he makes known what he wants in a fashion that is unmistakable, the superior's command does bind those subject to his authority; the superior is *not* obliged to follow any particular form or to use any particular words in issuing his orders.

Thus regardless of whether or not Pope Paul VI followed proper canonical form in his *Missale Romanum*, as some traditionalists have questioned that he did, we *do* know his will in the matter of the New Order of the Mass for the simple reason that he has more than once made it clear. Surely the Pope himself was the best judge of what he meant by the words he used. "It is the law," he said of his reform of the Missal in his General Audience of November 19, 1969 (see full text in Appendix II).

In his Address to the Consistory of Cardinals on May 24, 1976, Pope Paul VI further made clear what his intention had been in issuing his Apostolic Constitution *Missale Romanum*: and, again, regardless of the form in which it was issued, the Pope quite clearly said: "The new *Ordo* was promulgated to take the place of the old, after mature deliberation, following upon the requests of the Second Vatican Council. In no different way did our holy predecessor Pius V make obligatory the Missal reformed under his authority, following the Council of Trent."[6]

The will of the Supreme Pontiff who revised the Roman Missal is thus clear beyond any shadow of a doubt; *since* it is clear, his will constitutes for Catholics a "tacit precept," as St. Thomas Aquinas says. Barring a new enactment by a successor of his, then, the New Order of the Mass remains the official Mass for Catholics of the Roman rite. It is, therefore, *not* still licit to celebrate the Tridentine rite without an indult from the Holy Father.

The Holy See, in fact, issued a further Note on the Obligation to Use the Roman Missal on October 28, 1974, which, while it no doubt by itself did not repeal the previous law in force regarding the Roman Missal, at any rate certainly again made clear the intentions of the Pope when he promulgated his new, revised Missal in his Apostolic Constitution *Missale Romanum*.

Upon his election as Pope, Pope John Paul II further declared in his *urbi et orbi* address that the New Order of the Mass was lawfully established when he said: "Fidelity. . .implies the observance of the liturgical norms laid down by ecclesiastical authority and therefore has nothing to do with the practice either of introducing innovations of one's own accord and without approval or of obstinately refusing to carry out what has been *lawfully* laid down and introduced into the sacred rites" (To the Cardinals and to the World, October 17, 1978; emphasis added).

Although our case is established, then, we may make mention here of still one other objection to Pope Paul's having lawfully replaced the Tridentine Mass by the New Order of the Mass; it comes from those who consider the celebration of the Tridentine Mass an "immemorial custom"; and who therefore invoke Canon 30 of the Code of Canon Law. Canon 30 states that "a law, general or particular, does not revoke customs which are centenary or immemorial, without express mention."[7] Some traditionalist priests have argued from this that they have a right to continue celebrating the Tridentine Mass.

However, the Tridentine Mass was never an "immemorial custom"; it was established by positive Church law promulgating the Roman Missal which contained it—precisely by Pope St. Pius V's *Quo Primum*. And Pope Paul's Apostolic Constitution does expressly mention *Quo Primum,* as Canon 22 required, and as we have already noted previously, and hence the objection here again falls to the ground.

From everything that has been said, we cannot conclude other than that the revised Roman Missal with the New Order of the Mass *has* been lawfully established and that the celebration of the Tridentine Mass is forbidden except where ecclesiastical law specifically allows it (aged or infirm priests celebrating *sine populo,* or under special circumstances where a papal indult applies, as in England and Wales under certain special circumstances).

Question # 6

BUT DOESN'T THE REPLACEMENT OF THE TRI-
DENTINE MASS INVOLVE THE WATERING DOWN
OR ABANDONMENT OF CATHOLIC TRADITION?
CAN CATHOLICS REALLY BE FAULTED FOR
FOLLOWING THE INJUNCTIONS OF ST. PAUL,
"STAND FIRM AND HOLD TO THE TRADITIONS
WHICH YOU WERE TAUGHT (II *Thess.*) 2:15)?

When we speak of "Catholic Tradition," we have to distinguish
what we mean by the term; for there is the unchangeable apostolic
Tradition, and there are changeable, ecclesiastical traditions, customs or discipline. We have to keep clear in our minds what we are
talking about. With regard to unchangeable, apostolic Tradition,
above all, we have to bear in mind: who decides what is, and what
is not, an unchangeable "Catholic Tradition"?

Tradition, understood as the sum of revealed Catholic doctrine, is,
along with Scripture, one of the twin pillars which make up the
sacred deposit of revelation, on which, in turn, our whole faith is
based. Obviously, Catholics—and the whole Church—must "stand
firm" and "hold to" sacred Tradition understood in this sense.

Against the Protestant Reformers whose slogan was *sola Scriptura,*
the great Council of Trent reaffirmed the importance of Tradition
when it taught that:

> "[The] Gospel was promised of old through the prophets in
> the Sacred Scriptures; Our Lord Jesus Christ, Son of God, first
> promulgated it from His own lips; He in turn ordered that it
> be preached through the apostles to all creatures as the source
> of all saving truth and rule of conduct. The Council clearly per-
> ceives that this truth and rule are contained in the written
> books and unwritten traditions which have come down to us,
> having been received by the apostles from the mouth of Christ

Himself, or from the apostles by the dictation of the Holy Spirit, and have been transmitted as it were from hand to hand. Following, then, the example of the orthodox Fathers, it receives and venerates with the same sense of loyalty and reverence all the books of the Old and New Testaments, for God alone is the author of both—together with all the traditions concerning faith and morals, as coming from the mouth of Christ or being inspired by the Holy Spirit and preserved in continuous succession in the Catholic Church."[1]

However, it is clear from what the Council of Trent says here that Catholic Tradition is something guarded and preserved *in the Church;* Catholic Tradition, in the true sense, is not merely what we think it is or ought to be; certainly it is not just what we may have been accustomed or used to; it is, finally, what the Church decides that it is; the Church herself, not private persons, is the judge of what belongs to the unchangeable Catholic Tradition, and what does not.

"God has given to His Church a living Teaching Authority," Pope Pius XII taught, "to elucidate and explain what is contained in the deposit of faith only obscurely and implicitly. This deposit of faith our Divine Redeemer has given for authentic interpretation not to each of the faithful, not even to theologians, but only to the Teaching Authority of the Church."[2]

Speaking of those who would presume to decide for themselves what Catholic Tradition is, and what it is not, Pope Pius IX wrote, in the language characteristic of the Pontiff who convoked, and presided over, the First Vatican Council in 1870, as follows:

"Like all the fomenters of heresy and schism, they make false boast of having kept the ancient Catholic faith while they are overturning the principal foundation of the faith and of Catholic doctrine. They certainly recognize in Scripture and Tradition the source of Divine Revelation, but they refuse to listen to the ever-living magisterium of the Church, although this clearly springs from Scripture and Tradition, and was instituted by God as the perpetual guardian of the infallible exposition and explanation of the dogmas transmitted by these two sources. Consequently, with their false and limited knowledge, independently and even in opposition to the authority of this divinely instituted magisterium they set themselves up as judges of the dogmas contained in these sources of Revelation."[3]

We should carefully note the fact that Pope Pius IX makes the Magisterium of the Church responsible for the "exposition and explanation" of sacred Tradition—just as the Magisterium has the same responsibility as regards sacred Scripture. Thus individuals, no matter how learned or devout, are not the interpreters of Tradition.

If the Church through her sacred Magisterium is the judge of Tradition, then, it follows, *a fortiori,* that the ultimate judge is—the Pope, the Holy See, since the Pope has the primacy over the whole Church, as defined by the First Vatican Council (See Question #3). This does not mean that the Pope is above Tradition; he is rather the servant of it; but from his office he is necessarily the ultimate judge and interpreter of it.

Moreover, the Pope's authority extends not merely to the dogmas handed down by Tradition in the Church (infallibility) but also to everything that pertains to the government of the Church committed by Christ to Peter and handed down to each of Peter's successors in turn. Even before Vatican I, Pope Gregory XVI had made it clear that the Pope's primacy over the Church extended not only to revealed Tradition concerning faith and morals but also to Church discipline. Pope Gregory wrote:

> "Can private individuals lay claim to power which is proper to the Roman Pontiffs alone? Even if it were question of points of discipline which are in vigor in the universal Church but are susceptible of change because they are of ecclesiastical institution, it nevertheless belongs to the Roman Pontiff alone, because Christ has put him at the head of his whole Church, to weigh the necessity of a change brought about by a new state of affairs."[4]

The voice of the Church speaks so consistently on this subject that we surely cannot doubt that the Popes are the ultimate guardians both of revealed Catholic Tradition pertaining to faith and morals as well as of Church discipline, customs and changeable "traditions" with a small "t." But does all this apply to the "changes in the Mass"? Do not Catholics, in fidelity to Tradition, have to stand firm and resist any effort to tamper with the Mass?

The confusion which surrounds this issue is very great. Some hold that the New Order of the Mass may be opposed by Catholics because "faith and morals"—and hence the Pope's infallibility—are *not* involved. Others seem to hold, precisely, that the supposed defects or omissions in the New Order of the Mass do involve the doctrine of the faith, and hence the revised Missal has to be opposed for that very reason! We have dealt already with similar confusions with regard to the assent and obedience owed by Catholics to the decisions of a general council (Question #2) and to those of a Supreme Pontiff (Question #3); we will be dealing in subsequent Questions with further difficulties which some have had in reconciling the New Order of the Mass with what they consider to be the Catholic Tradition and the doctrine of the faith.

Here we only make the point that, as we have already shown (Question #3), the Pope has full and supreme power of jurisdiction over the whole Church, not only in matters pertaining to faith and morals, but also in matters pertaining to the discipline and government of the Church throughout the whole world. As Catholics, we have to accept the decisions of the Pope and the Holy See not only with regard to the Tradition of the doctrine of the faith, but also with regard to what we have called changeable "traditions"—practices of worship and devotion which are related to our faith insofar as through them we express our faith in and love towards the Divine Majesty. But they are really "customs" or "practices," not part of Tradition which cannot be changed. Only the authentic revelation of *faith*, which came from Christ can be considered Tradition which cannot be changed, but only understood better.

Some of those who have objected, in the name of Catholic Tradition, to the changes in the Church since Vatican II are really objecting, not about matters of faith or to any heresy supposedly being fostered by the Church herself, but rather to new practices and modes of worship replacing older typical "customs" or "practices." However, these new practices and modes of worship they consider incompatible with Catholic Tradition. But—we are now obliged to point out here, based on what has been said and documented above— to the extent that they are protesting or rebelling against official liturgical enactments of the Holy See (and not against unauthorized *abuses* of actual, official Church regulations) they are, precisely, going contrary to Catholic Tradition by making themselves, rather than the Church, the judges of what the Catholic Tradition is.

As we have seen, the hierarchical Church is the only authentic interpreter of Catholic Tradition, whether in faith and morals, or in discipline and Catholic practice. If the Church officially approved of a particular practice—say, restricting Communion to one kind, *or* approving it under both kinds—it follows that what the Church approves is, by definition, compatible with Catholic Tradition; for the Church, especially the Holy See, is, again, the arbiter and judge of Tradition.

And it has always been an integral part of this Catholic Tradition that it is not the function of the Catholic faithful, even of individual priests, theologians, or bishops, to set themselves up as judges of what Catholic Tradition requires with regard to, say, liturgical practice, on the grounds that this only concerns discipline and not faith and morals; it is the function, rather, of the Church alone to decide such things. Way back in the eighteenth century, Pope Pius VI condemned as "false, temerarious, scandalous, pernicious, offensive to pious ears, [and] injurious to the Church and to the Spirit of God who guides her" the proposition of the false Synod of Pistoia (1786) that "we must distinguish. . .what concerns faith and the essence of religion from what is proper to discipline." Pius VI strongly stigmatized the idea that Catholics might "subject to scrutiny the discipline established and approved by the Church."[5]

Pope Gregory XVI was already asking even more pointedly back in 1833:

> "Is it possible that the Church, which is the pillar and ground of truth and which is continually receiving from the Holy Spirit the teaching of all truth, could this Church ordain, grant, permit what would turn to the detriment of the soul's salvation, to the contempt and harm of a sacrament instituted by Christ?"[6]

What seems clear from Catholic Tradition is that we Catholics must indeed "stand firm and hold to the traditions" which we were taught; but, as St. Paul himself adds, "by us" (II *Thess.* 2:15)—in other words, by the hierarchical Church. If the Church has officially decided that certain changes in her practices and worship are desirable, and has gone on to institute them, we must, as Catholics, accept and try to understand them. If we honestly feel that these changes officially instituted by the Church could be harmful to the faithful we certainly have the right to present our carefully reasoned and documented views privately to those in authority. This must be done responsibly, respectfully, and always with a readiness to obey the decision of the Holy See. Even if we do not agree with this decision, we must trust that Christ is ultimately in charge of His Church—

through His Vicar, who cannot lead the Church into perdition through any official mandate of his govening power.

The hypothesis that *all* the official changes were ill-advised, and that the Church must only suffer now because of them, is certainly not justified. We may indeed have to suffer, but then, as Catholics, we have always known that we had to suffer in this life because of our sins— to be purified of them. If our own suffering were to come about *because* of the Church we would surely be in no worse state than our divine Savior Who "loved the Church and gave Himself up for her" (*Eph.* 5 :25); "a servant is not greater than his Master" (*Jn.* 13:16).

As Catholics we know that suffering can be redemptive; as members of the Mystical Body our sufferings can, in God's Providence, contribute to the healing of the Church's own wounds. The Church possesses mysterious powers of regeneration and God is able to bring good even out of the errors and abuses which have proliferated during the period when the Church has been attempting to implement the changes which the Second Vatican Council called for.

But not all the changes have been errors or abuses; far from it! Some changes were legitimately called for, and to these necessary changes we may apply a saying of Pope Benedict XV: "*Non nova, sed noviter,*" he said, "Not new things, but in a new way." Moreover, as this Pope of World War I remarked, Tradition as interpreted by the Church must "serve as the norm for those matters which are subject to change."[7]

We must honestly concede that the changes decided by Vatican II and officially promulgated by the Holy See, especially the revised Roman Missal requested by Vatican II and promulgated by Pope Paul VI, do *not* represent the abandonment or watering down of Catholic Tradition, but are the *realization* of a *part* of that Tradition. It should be recalled that the authorized reforms, especially those in the liturgical sphere, were the product of a liturgical movement extending back over 100 years. Pius XII's encyclicals *Mystici Corporis* (1943) and *Mediator Dei* (1947), like Vatican II's Constitution on the Sacred Liturgy *Sacrosanctum Concilium* (1963), would have been impossible had it not been for the remarkable efforts of such liturgical scholars as Dom Gueranger, Dom Cabrol, Dom Cagin, Cardinal Pitra, Dom Leclercq, and Dom Beauduin (to mention just a few) to obtain a deeper knowledge of the history of the liturgy and a more profound understanding of the Mass as both sacrifice and sacrament. There are standard books in which can be found some of the fruits of this liturgical scholarship going back a century and more. It was inevitable that some of the discoveries in this sphere would eventually have found their way into the Church's official liturgy even if there had never been any Second Vatican Council.[8]

The great Pope St. Pius X, in his *Divino Afflatu* (1911) and in his *Abhinc Duos Annos* (1913), was concerned with the reform of the Psalter and the Roman Breviary.[9] Both of these papal documents were concerned with the restoration of the true spirit animating the liturgy, and indeed both were prophetic about the changes that would come. Pope St. Pius prepared the way for the recent attempts to develop a solid Christian spirituality through encouragement of a more intense and more active participation of all Catholics in the liturgy; in a 1903 *Motu Proprio* he urged more "active participation in the most sacred mysteries and in the public and solemn prayer of the Church."[10]

Thus the canonized Pope most identified with opposition to the heresy of modernism was *in favor of* orderly liturgical change, as required by the times, and carefully introduced by the Church in response to the liturgical movement. Opposition to modernism certainly *cannot,* therefore, be equated with opposition to liturgical change, nor can liturgical change be dismissed as purely a "liberal" thing. St. Pius X was for it, after all.

Thus, the growth of a vigorous liturgical movement seeking to unfold to the entire Church the immense liturgical treasures contained in the various Western rites (Gallican, Mozarabic, Celtic and Ambrosian) and Eastern rites (Byzantine, Coptic, Armenian, Syriac, etc.), as well as the liturgical insights of the great Fathers of the Church, represented an effort to tap the fullness of Catholic practices and traditions to meet the spiritual needs of our own time — to penetrate further the profundities of the Paschal Mystery of Christ. As we have noted, the *Novus Ordo* of Pope Paul VI is the result of studies conducted by patristic and liturgical scholars and historians going back at least a hundred years. The Second Vatican Council merely accelerated the process which was begun in the days of Pope Pius IX and which was continued by successive Popes.

In his Motu Proprio of July 25, 1960, *Rubricarum Instructum,* a document further reforming the rubrics of both the Roman Breviary and the Roman Missal, Pope John XXIII noted:

". . .in 1956, while the prepatory studies for the general reform of the liturgy advanced, our predecessor, Pope Pius XII, wished to hear for himself the opinion of the bishops concerning a future liturgical reform of the Roman Breviary. . . . And after having examined the matter well, We came to the decision to place before the Fathers of the future Council the fundamental principles concerning the liturgical reform and not to delay any longer the reform of the Roman Missal."[11]

Thus it was Pope Pius XII himself who commissioned the preparatory work ultimately placed before the Second Vatican Council—from which issued the reforms of the Council. In one of the last acts of his life, Pope Pius XII issued an instruction on sacred music in which he explicitly recognized and encouraged the fundamental principle underlying most of the reforms recommended by the Council, namely, greater participation by the faithful in the celebration of the Mass by the priest. "Of its nature the Mass *demands* that all those who are present should participate, each in his own proper way," Pius XII said.[12] He specifically encouraged responses, prayers, and singing by the faithful at Mass. Thus he anticipated and confirmed trends which would be acted upon by the Council and in the implementation of the post-conciliar liturgical changes. The typical conciliar liturgical reforms were already present in the thinking of Pius XII before the Council was ever convened.

The *Novus Ordo* and the other post-conciliar liturgical reforms were thus hardly novel and unheard of when they came about. They represented the product of a liturgico-biblical movement seeking to use untapped riches of the Catholic Tradition; they represented the fruit of studies pursued and encouraged under seven successive pontificates. The further work of the conciliar Liturgical Commission and its sub-commissions dealing with the Mass during the proceedings of the Second Vatican Council (1962-1965) was in no way the result of hasty improvisations or lack of critical study. During the Council itself, there were 22 meetings of the Commission on the Liturgy, with 630 interventions made by the conciliar Fathers. At the conclusion of their deliberations, 2147 Council Fathers voted in favor of the definitive text of the Constitution on the Sacred Liturgy mandating a revision of the Roman Missal, while only four voted against.[13] On December 4, 1963, the Pope used his apostolic authority as Successor of Peter to confirm this decree on the Sacred Liturgy *Sacrosanctum Concilium.*

Incidentally, Archbishop Marcel Lefebvre did not take the floor
during the discussion of the draft that became the Constitution on
the Sacred Liturgy at the first session of the Council; he was content
to present his written text in which he spoke of ambiguities in the
principles of liturgical adaptation being discussed and also ventured
his opinion that authority over the liturgy should not be shared with
bishops' conferences, but should remain entirely in the hands of the
Pope.[14]

Like the Council of Trent, the Second Vatican Council was an
ecumenical council of the Church, and was thus guided by the Holy
Spirit in its decrees and declarations touching upon doctrinal matters
(see Question #2). It is inconceivable, on Catholic principles, that
such an ecumenical council of the Church, convoked and confirmed
by a Pope, could or would sanction liturgical innovations which
would contradict any truth of the Catholic Tradition, compromise the validity of the Eucharistic Sacrifice which our Divine Lord
left to us as the perpetuation in time of His sacrifice on the cross,
or otherwise go contrary to Catholic doctrine, practice, or Tradition.

Vatican II, an ecumenical council possessing the *same* authority
possessed by the Council of Trent, determined, as we have already
seen in the answer to Question #3, that "The rite of the Mass is to be
revised in such a way that the intrinsic nature and purpose of its
several parts, as well as the connection between them, may be more
clearly manifested, and that devout and active participation by
by the faithful may be more easily achieved. . . . For this purpose
the rites are to be simplified, due care being taken to preserve their
substance." (Vatican II, Constitution on the Sacred Liturgy *Sacrosanctum Concilium,* #50) The revision of the Roman Missal which
resulted in the *Novus Ordo* was thus carried out in response to the
specific request of the council that the rite of the Mass be "simplified."

Far from this decision of the Council being contrary to the Catholic Tradition, especially the Tradition of the Roman rite, we should
remember that the Roman or Latin rite has always tended towards
brevity and simplicity. Writing in the old *Catholic Encyclopedia*
published during the reign of Pope St. Pius X, Fr. Adrian Fortescue,
in the article on the Mass, speaks of "the characteristic Roman tendency," evident throughout the history of the development of the rite
of the Mass, "to shorten the service and leave out what had become
superfluous." This liturgical writer believed that the replacement
by Latin of the Greek in which even the Roman Mass was originally
said was a factor which contributed to making habitual in the sub-

sequent history of the Roman Rite a concern that "the rites are to be simplified"—the very words of Vatican II!

"No doubt the use of Latin was a factor in the Roman tendency to shorten the prayers, leave out whatever seemed redundant in formulas, and abridge the whole service," Fr. Fortescue writes in the article on the Mass just quoted. "Latin is naturally terse, compared with the rhetorical abundance of Greek. This difference is one of the most obvious distinctions between the Roman and the Eastern rites."[15]

Thus, far from being "untraditional," the revisions in the Roman Missal which Vatican II called for, and which Pope Paul VI carried out in promulgating the revised Roman Missal containing the New Order of the Mass, were actually characteristic of a long history going back to the very earliest times in the Roman rite.

In any case, the fact that a general council of the Catholic Church called for certain changes in the rite of the Mass (just as the Council of Trent had called for the reforms that Pope St. Pius V instituted in 1570) *meant* that the changes being called for were not contrary to Catholic Tradition; this is so because, as we have seen, it is for the Church herself, not private persons, to decide what accords with Catholic Tradition and what does not.

We have already quoted Pope Leo XIII to the effect that it is up to the authority of the Church to decide what accords with Catholic Tradition (Question #1). We have quoted further Pontiffs to the same or similar effect in this section. We may now, therefore, conclude this section by recalling that it was further clearly and precisely stated by the Holy Office under Pope Pius XII, in 1949, that "the Savior did not leave it to private judgment to explain what is contained in the deposit of faith, but to the doctrinal authority of the Church."[16] The Church is the arbiter and judge of Catholic Tradition; thus we "stand firm and hold to the traditions" which we were taught when we follow the hierarchical Church and accept her legitimate decisions.

Question # 7

BUT ISN'T THERE ABUNDANT PROOF THAT THE NEW ORDER OF THE MASS WAS REALLY DESIGNED TO PLEASE PROTESTANTS — TO BE A MERE "MEMORIAL" OF THE LORD'S SUPPER RATHER THAN THE HOLY SACRIFICE THE CHURCH HAS ALWAYS OFFERED IN THE MASS?

With respect to the charge that the Mass has been reduced to a mere "memorial" as with the "Lord's Supper" of the Protestants, it must be recalled that the Church has *always* regarded the Eucharistic Sacrifice as, among other things, a "memorial." The Council of Trent itself described the Mass as a "memorial," since Our Lord Himself told His Apostles: "Do this as a memorial of Me" (*Lk.* 22:-19).[1] The word "memorial" must, however, be understood in the Church's understanding of the term—one that harkens back to its authentic biblical sense. This means that the Mass is not solely a commemoration of the *past* events of Christ's life, and especially His Passion, Death, Resurrection and Ascension, but a memorial (*"anamnesis"* in the Greek) whereby a priest uttering the words of consecration, *brings about or represents* the same mystery which Christ brought about at the Last Supper on "the night before He suffered." The one sacrifice of the Cross is thus rendered present, though in an unbloody manner, and the divine Victim of the Cross is *both* offerer and offered in the Church's liturgical rite.

This Catholic doctrine is worlds apart from the Protestant concept of "the Lord's Supper." Protestants generally do not believe Christ can be made present; hence, for them there can be no sacrifice. Believing only in the "priesthood of all believers," they reject the Catholic belief that the ordained priest offers the sacrifice for all the people in the person of Christ. Certainly the Protestant idea of what Jesus commanded His disciples to do as a memorial of Himself is very different from the action which the Church has always carried out in the Holy Mass. And the idea that some Protestant observers, at working sessions of the Commission established in 1963 to carry out the liturgical reforms called for by the Second Vatican Council, might have influenced the revision of the Roman Missal in a Protestant direction is without foundation. We can see this by examining the doctrine on the Mass actually to be found in the revised Roman Missal—just as we can see from the documents of Vatican II itself on the Mass that no Protestant influence crept in as a result of Protestant observers at the Council. Both the revised Roman Missal and the documents of Vatican II are sound and verifiably contain only Catholic doctrine.

In any case, on July 4, 1976, the Sacred Congregation for Divine Worship unequivocally declared: "The Protestant observers did not participate in the composition of the texts of the new Missal."[2] Discussions and consultations with Protestant observers on liturgical matters no more resulted in a consequent abandonment of the Mass as a sacrifice than other ecumenical dialogues during the Council with observers from Protestant, Eastern Orthodox and other Eastern churches led to a rejection by the Second Vatican Council of the other specific Catholic doctrines denied by these "separated brethren."

Let us take, for example, the following definition of the Mass contained in a document issued by the Holy See subsequent to Vatican II and in connection with the reforms desired by that Council; it should demonstrate that the traditional Catholic understanding of what the Mass is has in no way been changed by the Church since Vatican II, although some additional terminology has also been included (the "Lord's Supper") in order, possibly, to attract those Protestants who, understanding better what the Mass is, might come to accept it. Here, then, is the Church's latest "definition" of the Mass, the *official* definition, in fact, of the post-Vatican II Church:

> "Hence the Mass, the Lord's Supper, is at the same time and inseparably:
>
> 1) a sacrifice in which the sacrifice of the cross is perpetuated;
>
> 2) a memorial of the death and resurrection of the Lord, who said "do this in memory of me" (*Lk.* 22:19);
>
> 3) a sacred banquet in which, through the communion of the Body and Blood of the Lord, the People of God share the benefits of the Paschal Sacrifice, renew the New Covenant which God has made with man once for all through the Blood of Christ, and in faith and hope foreshadow and anticipate the

eschatalogical banquet in the kingdom of the Father, proclaiming the Lord's death "till his coming" (Instruction on the Worship of the Eucharistic Mystery *Eucharisticum Mysterium,* #C1).[3]

In the Foreword to the General Instruction on the Roman Missal— the revised Roman Missal containing the text of the New Order of the Mass—it is also clearly stated:

> "The sacrificial character of the Mass was solemnly defined by the Council of Trent in accordance with the universal tradition of the Church (Session 22, September 17, 1562). The Second Vatican Council has enunciated this same teaching once again, and made this highly significant comment: 'At the Last Supper our Saviour instituted the Eucharistic Sacrifice of his Body and Blood. He did this in order to perpetuate the sacrifice of the cross until he should come again; and he wished to entrust to his beloved spouse, the Church, a memorial of his death and resurrection'" (Constitution on the Sacred Liturgy, #47).[4]

Speaking of how the Council's teaching on this point finds an enduring expression in the texts of the Mass, the Foreword to the General Instruction on the Roman Missal goes on to describe how the priest, during the *anamnesis* (memorial or prayer of remembrance), "addresses himself to God in the name of all the people; he gives thanks to God and offers to Him in a holy and living sacrifice, the Church's offering, the Victim whose death has reconciled man with God; he prays that the Body and Blood of Christ may be the acceptable sacrifice which brings salvation to the whole world."

In other words, the Foreword to the General Instruction describes the New Order of the Mass as a sacrifice of praise, thanksgiving, propitiation and satisfaction, thus affirming doctrines which Protestants specifically deny, namely, that the Mass is a sacrifice of propitiation and of satisfaction for our sins. The *Novus Ordo* is that; it was not designed to "please Protestants" by compromising the integrity of any Catholic doctrine whatever. We should note here that the priest offering the sacrifice exactly functions as the Church has always taught, while Protestants reject the very idea of a priest functioning in this way.

In short, the holy Mass remains the Eucharistic Sacrifice that it has always been since the time the obligation to offer it perpetually was committed by Christ to the Church—just as it continues to be all the other things it has always been! And, as we can see from the Foreword to the General Instruction on the Roman Missal quoted above, the Second Vatican Council itself explicitly taught the essential Catholic doctrine about the Eucharistic Sacrifice, or the Mass. This may come as a surprise to those who may have thought that the presence of a few non-Catholic "observers" at the Council could really have outweighed the promised influence of the Holy Spirit at any general council of the Catholic Church; or that such "observers" on a post-conciliar Commission could introduce Protestant ideas into the revised Missal which the Pope could then uncritically approve.

That both the conciliar and the post-conciliar teaching on the Mass is completely in accord with Catholic Tradition, and, in particular, with the Council of Trent, ought to constitute the *proof* that Protestant and other observers at or after the Council certainly did not lead the Catholic bishops of the world or the Pope astray. Whatever may have happened at the Council itself, or whatever non-Catholic observers, Council *periti,* or even some "progressive" bishops may have wanted is all irrelevant to the final, official acts of the Council enshrined in its documents and ratified by the Pope; these are the only things about the Council that really count; and, as we have demonstrated (Question #2) these conciliar acts are both protected by the Holy Spirit from error and are binding upon the faithful, just as the decisions of the Council of Trent were protected by the Holy Spirit from error and became binding upon the faithful as soon as ratified by the Popes of the time.

Just as it is not the function of the faithful, or even of the theologians, to subject to critical questioning the teachings and rulings of the Popes (see Questions #3 and #6), so it is for official authority in the Church to provide the official interpretation of what the acts of a general council are and mean and how they have to be implemented. It has occasionally been repeated by some traditionalists that, owing to the confusion which has followed the Council, the only course now open to Catholics is to examine the Council's directives and relevant points of doctrinal teaching to discover whether or not they accord with the Church's traditional teaching.

But the idea that it is incumbent upon "Catholics" to do this, rather than upon the Church herself to decide upon the meaning and significance of the various documents of one of her Councils, is a most *un*traditional idea; as we have already thoroughly documented, it is for the official Magisterium of the Church alone to do this.

It is, indeed, a *Protestant* idea that individuals should judge the official acts of the Church. The essence of Protestantism lies primarily in the individual believer's claim to "private judgment"; historically, the Protestant exercised this claim principally in the interpretation of sacred Scripture, but to assert that the Church's sacred Tradition is equally subject to the private interpretation of individuals would also seem to involve nothing else than old-fashioned "Protestant" private judgment.

The word "Protestant" originally came from those "protesting" against the decrees of the Diet of Speyer (1529); later the word came to apply generally to all those "protesting" against what they regarded as the errors of the Catholic Church. If *we* suddenly find ourselves "protesting" about the official decrees and decisions of the same Catholic Church, perhaps it becomes incumbent upon us to re-examine just how "Catholic" or "traditional" our action really is. We do not, after all, have any ground to stand on in complaining about the unauthorized abuses of the Church's liturgical prescriptions if we do not ourselves accept these prescriptions.

If the Church at and following Vatican II did adopt some new practices which at one time seemed to be more characteristic of Protestant worship —hymn-singing, vernacular liturgy, greater emphasis on the Scriptures, etc.—we should remember that none of these things really affects the substance of Catholic doctrine or of the Mass; that these kinds of things in our worship can be changed (Questions #1, #6) if the Church so decides; that in the past the Church adopted and adapted many pagan customs, thereby ennobling them; that the early Church specifically had some of these same things —hymn-singing, vernacular liturgy, greater emphasis on the Scriptures — and that, finally, the fact that the Church has adopted these particular things today *means* that they are really compatible with Catholic worship.

Certainly the Church authorities had a duty to impose the changes deemed necessary with tact and understanding and—unfortunately this was not always done;—nevertheless the substance of the question is not affected by the widespread failure of the authority to understand how upsetting rapid, widespread and continuing change can be.

Moreover, we should remember that Catholic reluctance to accept changes in the Church can itself be a matter of custom and habit. Established custom is always a deterrent to change. By grace built on faith, however, it should be easier for us Catholics to change than for non-Catholics to do so whenever there is an authoritative mandate to do so. If we wish to bring non-Catholics into full communion with the Church, thereby obeying the mandate given to us by Our Lord Jesus Christ Himself, we ought to be willing to modify such non-essentials in our worship as might make our Holy Sacrifice more understandable and attractive and accessible to those who do not enjoy the inestimable privilege of having been born into the Catholic Church.

Thus the first Council of Jerusalem was willing to accommodate the worship of the Church to *both* the Jewish and the gentile converts (Cf. *Acts* 21:17-26); and thus the Second Vatican Council too wished to make the Church more accessible to those outside her fold. If this dream of the Council has hardly yet been realized, we must never forget that that failure partly devolves upon our shoulders: what have we been doing to try to share the treasures of the "Catholic faith that comes to us from the apostles" with those outside the Church?

The existence of a false ecumenism among some Catholics, like the existence of false renewal generally, should not cause Catholics to disparage genuine efforts to find common ground in doctrinal matters with other Christians. Rather it is of the essence of Christian charity to take advantage of whatever opportunities present themselves for open and irenic dialogue with those seeking explanations of Catholic faith and practice.

Blessed Peter Favre, one of the original small band which gathered around St. Ignatius Loyola—later to become the mighty Society of Jesus which following the sixteenth century not only reconverted a good part of Europe but helped to evangelize several other continents as well—had a philosophy for dealing with those not of the Catholic faith which the Jesuits frequently used to great advantage. We could perhaps do worse than adopt it today. "In the first place," Blessed Peter wrote to one of the other original Jesuits, Fr. Diego Laynez, later one of the important *"periti"* at the Council of Trent, "it is necessary that anyone who desires to be serviceable to heretics of the present age should hold them in great affection and love them very truly, putting out of his heart all thoughts and feelings that tend to their discredit. The next thing he must do is to win their good-will and love by friendly intercourse and converse on matters about which there is no difference between us, taking care to avoid all controversial subjects that lead to bickering and mutual recrimin-

ation. The things that unite us ought to be the first ground of our
approach, not the things that keep us apart."[5]

The Church said no more than this at Vatican II. And Pope John
Paul II decisively seconded the judgment of the Council when, in
his encyclical *Redemptor Hominis,* he declared that a sincere ecumenical effort is one of the imperatives for the Church in the de-
Christianized world of today. "It is . . . certain," Pope John Paul
said in this encyclical, "that in the present historical situation of
Christianity and the world, the only possibility we see of fulfilling
the Church's universal mission, with regard to ecumenical questions,
is that of seeking sincerely, perseveringly, humbly and also courageously the ways of drawing closer and of union."

It is not that John Paul II does not see the problems and difficulties involved or that he is unaware of the ignorance and prejudice
that commonnly exist where the Church and authentic Catholic doctrine are concerned. It is just that he sees no alternative; he has been
called. *We* have been called: "I must preach the good news of the
Kingdom of God" (*Lk.* 4:43).

Hence Pope John Paul went on to say in *Redemptor Hominis*
(#6):

> "There are people who in the face of difficulties or because
> they consider that the first ecumenical endeavors have brought
> negative results would have liked to turn back. Some even
> express the opinion that these efforts are harmful to the cause
> of the Gospel, are leading to a further rupture in the Church,
> are causing confusion of ideas in questions of faith and morals
> and are ending up with a specific indifferentism. It is perhaps
> a good thing that the spokesmen for these opinions should ex-
> press their fears. However, in this respect also, correct limits
> must be maintained. It is obvious that this new stage in the
> Church's life demands of us a faith that is practically aware,
> profound and responsible. True ecumenical activity means
> openness, drawing closer, availability for dialogue, and a shared
> investigation of the truth in the full evangelical and Christian
> sense; but in no way does it or can it mean giving up or in any
> way diminishing the treasures of divine truth that the Church
> has constantly confessed and taught. To all who, for whatever
> motive, would wish to dissuade the Church from seeking the
> universal unity of Christians the question must once again be
> put: Have we the right not to do it? Can we fail to have trust—

in spite of all human weakness and all the faults of past centuries — in our Lord's grace as revealed recently through what the Holy Spirit said and we heard during the Council?"

So much for true ecumenism. Can we doubt the Vicar of Christ? It is unfortunate that some of today's ecumenical efforts have been so little in the true spirit of what John Paul II is really calling for — and what Vatican II really called for, which was the same thing. This is a continuing problem which we must continue to be conscious of.

But the belief that the Church's genuine efforts at ecumenism since the Council have somehow resulted in a "Protestantized" Mass fails to take into account the fact that no Protestant Church or group has *accepted* the New Order of the Mass. No conscientious Protestant could really be pleased with the *Novus Ordo Missae* since it reflects traditional Catholic doctrine concerning the Eucharistic Sacrifice as a propitiatory work offered for the living and the dead; concerning the Transubstantiation of the bread and wine into the body, blood, soul and divinity of Our Lord Jesus Christ; concerning the intercession of the Blessed Virgin Mary and the saints; concerning prayer for the dead; concerning the necessity for a validly ordained priest to celebrate Mass — all points on which Protestants continue to disagree with the Catholic Church but all of which are explicitly present in the *Novus Ordo*.

If there be found Protestants who favor those elements contained in the *Novus Ordo,* it would be those who have benefited from the remarkable biblical, patristic, liturgical and theological renaissance of the past century and who now agree that such Catholic doctrines are essential (or at least permissible) elements of Christian faith and practice.

Brother Max Thurian, a Calvinist monk at the Monastery of Taizé in France, whose various comments have been invoked by a number of authors to "prove" that the Mass has now been "Protestantized," replied as follows when directly questioned on the matter: "I have no difficulty in affirming that in the new Order of Mass, nothing has been changed with respect to traditional Catholic doctrine concerning the Eucharistic Sacrifice."[6]

Subsequently, Brother Max Thurian wrote the following:

"Recently a Protestant liturgical commission was given the task of revising the prayers of the Last Supper. It was proposed that they adopt the second Catholic Eucharistic Prayer (inspired by St. Hippolytus). That proposition was rejected, because the commission considered that the doctrine implied in that prayer did not correspond to the actual common faith of Protestants. . .the invocation of the Spirit on the bread and wine presupposed Transubstantiation."[7]

Thus a Protestant, Brother Max Thurian, on the subject of the supposedly "Protestantized" New Order of the Mass! If *he* thinks that the form of our Second Eucharistic Prayer necessarily implies the Catholic doctrine of Transubstantiation, perhaps we Catholics can reaffirm our faith in the matter, since we *know* on supernatural faith that the substance of the bread and wine is changed into the substance of the Body and Blood of Christ in this holy sacrament of the Eucharist. The Council of Trent defined this and Our Lord, in any case, promised that "the bread which I shall give for the life of the world is my flesh" (*Jn.* 6:51). All this still remains true in the case of the New Order of the Mass.

The idea that mere contacts or discussions with Protestants or others could result in compromising the decisions of a general council of the Church in any way is an idea that Pope Pius IX firmly excluded more than a century ago in a similar situation where certain decisions of the First Vatican Council were called into question Of those who questioned some of the acts of that Council, Pius IX wrote:

> "If they believed firmly with other Catholics that the Ecumenical Council is governed by the Holy Spirit, that it is solely by the impulse of this Divine Spirit that the Council defines and proposes what must be believed, it would never have occurred to them that matters which have not been revealed or which could be harmful to the Church could be defined in its sessions and imposed upon their faith; and they would never have imagined that human maneuvers could arrest the power of the Holy Spirit and impede the definition of revealed truths or truths helpful to the Church."[8]

No more at Vatican II did "human maneuvers" result in a "Protestantized" Mass; the Mass is the same as always.

Nevertheless, the regularity with which the charge continues to be repeated that the Roman Missal was revised with the help of Protestants suggests that we should conclude this section by listing the names of the persons—all Catholics, not a single non-Catholic—who did participate in the work of the post-conciliar Commission (or *"consilium"*) headed by Cardinal Lercaro of Bologna which, under official ecclesiastical authority, was responsible for the actual preparation of the revised Roman Missal. More than 30 diocesan bishops from all over the world were represented on this commission; Pope Paul VI actually submitted the text prepared by the Commission to the Fathers of the first Synod of Bishops, and accepted suggestions made by them, before finally promulgating his revised Roman Missal in 1969 (See Questions #3, #4, and #5 and Appendix I).

The liturgical experts on this Commission who actually worked on the preparation of the revised Roman Missal were as follows, according to one of them, French priest Pierre Jounel; some of them are renowned scholars in the liturgy; none of them can be questioned on the grounds of orthodoxy or loyalty to the Catholic Church, as far as the authors have been able to determine. These are the names:

J. Wagner, Director of the Liturgical Institute of Trier;

A. Haenaggi, University of Fribourg, Switzerland (later replaced by A. Franquesa, a monk from Monserrat, Spain);

Joseph A. Jungmann, S.J., Innsbruck, Austria (his authoritative books on the Mass have been several times quoted in these pages, and he, in turn, quotes a number of the other names in this list in his scholarly pages);

C. Vagaggini, Professor at Sant' Anselmo, Rome;

T. Schnitzler, parish priest from Cologne, Germany;

P. M. Gy and Pierre Jounel of the Institute of the Liturgy, Paris, France;

L. Agustoni, a parish priest from Switzerland;

L. Bouyer and L. Gelineau, French religious order priests.[9]

Question # 8

IS THE NEW ORDER OF THE MASS THUS OBLIGATORY FOR CATHOLICS OF THE ROMAN RITE? AND DOES THIS MEAN I MAY NOT ATTEND A TRIDENTINE MASS CELEBRATED BY A VALIDLY ORDAINED PRIEST?

In previous sections (Questions #2, #3, #5 and #6) we have established that the Second Vatican Council possessed the authority to require disciplinary changes in the celebration of the liturgy and the administration of the sacraments; and that Pope Paul VI both possessed the authority to implement the changes required by the Council and did, in fact, lawfully implement them. We have also established that the decisions of the Council and the Pope on these matters are binding upon the Catholic faithful; "binding" means that the Catholic faithful are obliged to accept them with trusting obedience.

In 1974, the Sacred Congregation for Divine Worship in Rome issued a Note on the Obligation to Use the New Roman Missal which we have already had the occasion to quote (Questions #4 and #5). This Note, entitled *Conferentiarum Episcopalium*, makes clear that, with the exception of aged priests celebrating Mass without a congregation (and of a special papal indult granted to the English hierarchy) ordinaries are *not* permitted to authorize the celebration of a Tridentine Mass; here is what the Note actually says:

> ". . .Mass may not be celebrated, whether in Latin or in the vernacular, save according to the rite of the Roman Missal promulgated by the authority of Paul VI on 7 April, 1969.
>
> "With regard to the regulations issued by this sacred congregation in favor of priests who, on account of advanced years or infirm health, find it difficult to use the new Order of the Roman Missal or the Mass Lectionary: it is clear that an ordinary may grant permission to use, in whole or in part, the 1962

edition of the Roman Missal, with the changes introduced by the Decrees of 1965 and 1967. But this permission can only be granted for Masses celebrated without a congregation. Ordinaries may not grant it for Masses celebrated with a congregation. Ordinaries, both religious and local, should rather endeavor to secure the acceptance of the Order of the Mass of the new Roman Missal by priests and laity. They should see to it that priests and laity, by dint of greater effort and with greater reverence comprehend the treasures of divine wisdom and of liturgical and pastoral teaching which it contains. What has been said does not apply to officially recognized non-Roman rites, but it does hold against any pretext of even an immemorial custom."[1]

The only condition attached to the above directive from the Holy See was that the episcopal conference must have approved its own vernacular version of the new Roman Missal. As far as the United States is concerned, this condition was fulfilled when the National Conference of Catholic Bishops approved the translations of the New Order of the Mass at their meeting in November, 1969.[2] As many will remember, it was decreed at that time that the New Order of the Mass could be used beginning on Palm Sunday, 1970, and that it had to be used from the First Sunday in Advent in 1971.

Confirmation of this episcopal action by the Holy See was reported in the Bishops' Committee on the Liturgy Newsletter for February-March, 1970.[3]

The question of the language, Latin or English, was always separate from the New Order of the Mass itself, incidentally; the U.S. bishops had resolved to request permission to celebrate Mass in the vernacular at a meeting back in November, 1966; the Holy See granted this permission on May, 1967.[4] Thus "Tridentine Masses"—but in English—were legally celebrated in this country from October 22, 1967. Pope Paul's revised Roman Missal was then still nearly two years in the future, and more than four years would pass before the *Novus Ordo* would become obligatory. But the vernacular had already been generally substituted for the Latin well before that; and this situation came about with the express approval of the Holy See at every step of the way.

The question of Latin should therefore *not* be linked with the question of the *Novus Ordo*; public Latin Masses according to the revised Roman Missal are, in fact, still celebrated in many dioceses;

the authors have both been privileged to attend some singularly beautiful and reverent *Novus Ordo* Masses in Latin and devoutly wish that some who have called the new rite "inherently sacrilegious" or such similar things could have been present along with them to see how reverently the New Order of the Mass *can* be celebrated. But the point is: the Tridentine Mass is not the same thing as the Latin Mass.

The approval of the translation of the new Roman Missal having been received by the U.S. bishops, however, they were no longer permitted by the Holy See to allow the celebration of any regular Tridentine Masses with a congregation, whether in English or in Latin; and Masses which the bishops are not even permitted to allow, the faithful would surely not be allowed to attend in order to fulfill their Sunday Mass obligation. The unbroken Tradition of the Catholic Church in such matters is surely that the pastors of the Church establish the discipline and the faithful follow it.

Pope Pius XII perfectly expressed this Catholic tradition when he wrote that "clerics and laity may not exempt themselves from this discipline [of the Church]; rather all should be concerned to obey it, so that by the loyal observance of the Church's discipline the action of the shepherd may be easier and more efficacious, and the union between him and his flock stronger."[5] On another occasion the same Pope Pius XII taught that "private individuals... even though they be clerics, may not be left to decide for themselves in these holy and venerable matters, involving as they do the religious life of Christian society along with the exercise of the priesthood of Jesus Christ and worship of God."[6]

His predecessor, the great Pope Pius XI, spoke in a similar vein about the obligation of the faithful to accept the discipline established by the Church:

"Whoever desires to fight under Christ's standard must hold this principle as certain, that in rejecting the yoke of discipline they will reap not the palm of victory, but ignoble defeat. For it has been divinely ordained that youth cannot progress either in intellectual or moral culture, or in the general formation of life according to Christian principles, unless it submits to the direction of another. Now if the other disciplines require a great docility, still more is this the case when the soul is being formed to the work and duty of the apostolate: this duty, since it is attached to the function of the Church received from Christ, cannot be carried out in a holy or useful fashion except in sub-ordination to those whom the Holy Spirit 'hath placed, bishops, to rule the Church of God'" (*Acts* 20:28).[7]

In his first speech to the Church and the world on October 17, 1978, Pope John Paul II quoted exactly the same spiritual passage from the Acts of the Apostles to make exactly the same point, namely, that one form of the witness of the faithful to the truths *is* "by obedience to their sacred pastors."

From all this the Tradition of the Church is clear: the faithful must fulfill their Sunday Mass obligation in the manner prescribed by the hierarchical Church. At present the Mass prescribed by the authority of the hierarchical Church is the New Order of the Mass.

But it is said by many attending Tridentine Masses that they cannot in *conscience* hear Mass according to the New Order of the Mass, since they regard it as invalid, sacrilegious or as having been unlawfully imposed. Now conscience is a serious matter, and the Church has traditionally recognized that consciences must be obeyed; however, the Church has also taught that there is a serious, unavoidable moral obligation to form one's conscience in accordance with the truth.[8]

And for Catholics, the truth means—the teaching of the Church. "The Divine Redeemer has consigned His revelation, *of which moral obligations are an essential part*," Pope Pius XII declared, "not to any mere men, but to His Church, to which He has given the mission of bringing men to embrace this sacred deposit with faith" (emphasis added).[9]

Included among the teachings of the Church—as we have shown in the quotations above from Popes Pius XI, Pius XII and John Paul II—and also in the answers to Questions #2, #3 and #6—is the firm teaching that the faithful must accept the decisions of competent Church authorities in liturgical and disciplinary matters. The very existence of such a traditional Church teaching about the necessity of forming one's conscience in accordance with the Church should immediately alert us whenever we might be tempted to think that the Church herself might have erred in what she has established or imposed, or might have established "a useless discipline," in the words of Pope Pius VI,[10] "or one which would be too onerous for Christian liberty to bear": it should remind us that, as we have just quoted Pope Pius XII as saying, it is not left to us, private individuals, to decide what is appropriate and fitting in the liturgy and ad-

ministration of the sacraments. In his encyclical *Mirari Vos* Pope
Gregory XVI said: "It would beyond any doubt be blameworthy and
entirely contrary to the respect with which the laws of the Church
should be received. . .to find fault with the discipline which she has
established. . . ."[11]

If the Church decides through her competent authorities to institute officially that which we might otherwise be tempted to question, we nevertheless can be entirely at peace in our consciences
because we know that the Holy Spirit would not allow the duly constituted authorities of the Church, in officially promulgated acts guaranteed by the Holy See, to lead us astray on anything which might
jeopardize our own eternal salvation.

This would be true if the discipline decided upon proved not to
be of the wisest or best or for the general welfare of the Church;
that would be a responsibility for which the authorities of the
Church, not individuals, would have to answer; it would not be
a matter of conscience for us. When we go before our maker and
Judge, we will not be asked about what the Pope or the bishops did,
but about what *we* did; and dispositions about the Mass to be celebrated in the Roman rite were simply not placed in our hands. God
will *not* condemn us for obeying the authorities whom He placed
over us, acting within their proper sphere.

It is, of course, a truism of moral theology that we may never
commit a sin even if the Pope or a bishop should command us to do
so; but here enters a vast question indeed; for it has not been shown
(indeed cannot be shown) that attendance at a *Novus Ordo* Mass *is*
a sin. . . .

On the contrary, we have already shown in the answers to previous
questions that the New Order of the Mass is both lawful and lawfully
imposed; in subsequent questions we intend to deal with further
specific objections which some have tried to use to show that the
New Order of the Mass is invalid, sacrilegious, and the like. Here we
can summarize by noting the teaching of St. Thomas Aquinas on
obedience to authority. St. Thomas Aquinas in the *Summa Theologica* tells us that there are two reasons for which a subject may not
be bound to obey his superior: first on account of the command of
a higher power; secondly in a matter wherein he is not subject to
his superior.[12]

It is clear that in liturgical matters, all of the faithful are subject
to the Pope, and bishops in communion with him. Even St. Pius V's
Quo Primum, for example, makes that manifestly clear. On the other

hand the objection has been raised that we must obey God rather than men, even if the men are the Pope and bishops. However, it is the traditional doctrine of the Catholic Church that the will of God is made known to men here and now through the teachings of reigning Popes and bishops in communion with them; the Church is a living Church, and although her teaching and discipline are grounded firmly in Scripture and Tradition, it is the reigning Pope and the bishops in communion with him who interpret Scripture and Tradition as they apply to us today; it is to these living shepherds then that our obedience is owed.

We therefore cannot appeal to any higher authority than that of the Pope and the Catholic bishops in the matter of which Mass we are obliged to attend. And there can be no real doubt, according to this criterion, that attendance at a Mass celebrated according to the revised Roman Missal is now obligatory for Catholics of the Roman rite. Those who would claim exemption on the grounds of conscience should ponder what Pope St. Pius X said about the votaries of another school of thought who claimed the right to remove themselves from the direction of the hierarchy of the Church on grounds of "conscience." This is what this holy, canonized Pope said about them:

> "What is imputed to them as a fault they regard as a sacred duty. They understand the needs of conscience better than anyone else, since they come into closer touch with them than does the ecclesiastical authority. Nay, they embody them, so to speak, in themselves. Hence, for them to speak and to write publicly is a bounden duty. Let authority rebuke them if it pleases — they have their own conscience on their side and an intimate experience which tells them with certainty that what they deserve is not blame but praise. Then they reflect that, after all, there is no progress without a battle and no battle without its victims; and victims they are willing to be, like the prophets and Christ Himself."

Pope St. Pius X was writing here, of course, about the modernists, and these words come from his famous encyclical *Pascendi Dominici Gregis*.[13] We should beware of invoking the same false principle of "conscience" which the modernists found so convenient.

EXCURSUS: A FURTHER NOTE ON LATIN
AND VERNACULAR MASSES

Because of the persistent confusion of the Latin Mass with the Tridentine Mass—in the press and media the whole problem of "traditionalism" is often reduced to the question of the "Latin Mass"—it seems advisable to add here a further word on this subject. The Latin Mass and the Tridentine Mass are not identical. As was made clear in the reply to Question #8, the Tridentine Mass was actually celebrated in English in the United States for a period before the publication of the revised Roman Missal, while the New Order of the Mass can be and is sometimes celebrated in Latin, which is, of course, the official, normative text of the revised Roman Missal.

In the popular mind these distinctions are lost sight of. What is recalled is that the Mass used to be celebrated in Latin but that, since the Council, it has been widely celebrated in the vernacular. This is especially surprising—and even painful—to some when it is recalled that Vatican Council II, in its Constitution on the Sacred Liturgy *Sacrosanctum Concilium* (#36) decreed that "the use of the Latin language, with due respect to particular law, is to be preserved in the Latin rites." In the same document, the Council said (#54) that care must be taken to ensure that the faithful may. . .be able to say or sing together in Latin those parts of the Ordinary of the Mass which pertain to them." How has it happened, many have wondered, that the actual post-conciliar practice virtually everywhere is so different from what the Council decreed?

Basically this happened because in the immediate post-conciliar years hierarchies from all over the world steadily petitioned the Holy See to allow a wider and wider use of the vernacular. Vatican II's Constitution on the Sacred Liturgy *Sacrosanctum Concilium* had itself allowed a wider use of the vernacular along with Latin. "Since the use of the vernacular, whether in the Mass, the administration of the sacraments, or in other parts of the liturgy, may frequently be of great advantage to the people," this Council document said (#36), "a wider use may be made of it. . . ." The same document also provided (#40) that national hierarchies could petition the Holy See for further adaptations of the liturgy to suit conditions in their countries and cultures. In the event, that is what these national hierarchies did, virtually everywhere; the Holy See, in acceding to their requests, gradually lifted previous restrictions on the use of the vernacular, thus heavily emphasizing Vatican II's call for a wider use of the vernacular over the Council's wish for the retention of Latin.[1] It must be stated that it was entirely within the authority of the Holy See to do this, although given the Council's position, it would certainly also be entirely within the rights of the faithful to petition for a restoration of a greater use of Latin in the Mass again.

On June 14, 1971, the Sacred Congregation for Divine Worship issued a "Note on the Roman Missal and the Liturgy of the Hours" in which the whole question of the vernacular in the Mass was, finally, simply committed into the hands of the various episcopal conferences: the bishops could decide when vernacular editions of the Roman Missal become obligatory, and they could decide on the use of the vernacular in all parts of the Mass, or on the advisability of continuing some Masses in Latin. According to this "Note," priests may use Latin or the vernacular in the celebration of private Masses; and the Liturgy of the Hours may also be celebrated in Latin or in the vernacular, in private or in common. This "Note" represents the instructions from the Holy See under which we are currently living; and it means, as a practical matter, that the bishops have the authority to decide whether we may also have Latin Masses and to what extent.

As far as the United States is concerned, while the celebration of the Mass in the vernacular is now the established norm in accordance with the permission accorded by the Holy See to the American bishops, there seems to have been no action by the bishops' conference to "restrict" or "ban" Latin Masses celebrated according to the new Roman Missal. Provided always that the local ordinary agrees, therefore, lovers of the Latin Mass and of traditional sacred music would seem to be perfectly free to work for a revival of them in this country. In 1974, intending to encourage such a revival, Pope Paul VI himself sent out to all the bishops of the world *Jubilate Deo*,[2] a collection of the simpler Gregorian chants which the faithful should learn "according to the mind of the Second Vatican Council's Constitution on the Sacred Liturgy." Promotion of the use of *Jubilate Deo* is long overdue.

The retention both of Latin as a liturgical language and of Gregorian chant and other sacred music in Latin would seem to depend heavily upon the initiative of those interested in seeing them retained, and it is to be hoped that some constructive initiatives of this kind will be multiplied. James Hitchcock has persuasively argued in an excellent book, *The Recovery of the Sacred*,[3] that we can most profitably work back to greater reverence and a sense of the sacred by carefully building on the liturgy that the Church has adopted, not by expecting a simple return to the old Latin Mass.

Question # 9

BUT HOW CAN I HAVE CONFIDENCE IN THE *NOVUS ORDO* MASS IN MY OWN PARISH, CONSIDERING THAT THE LATIN WORDS *"PRO VOBIS ET PRO MULTIS"* IN THE FORMULA OF CONSECRATION ARE MISTRANSLATED AS "FOR YOU AND FOR ALL MEN"? THE LATIN DOES NOT SAY *"PRO OMNIBUS"! DOESN'T THIS IMPLY AN HERETICAL IDEA, NAMELY, THAT ALL MEN WILL NECESSARILY BE SAVED?*

The actual words of the consecration of the wine into the Precious Blood, in the English translation now familiar, are as follows:

"Take this, all of you, and drink from it: this is the cup of my blood, the blood of the new and everlasting covenant. It will be shed for you and for all men so that sins may be forgiven. Do this in memory of me."

Is any "heretical idea" being asserted by these words? Did not Christ, in fact, shed His blood for all men according to the traditional Catholic faith? There are a number of scriptural texts that plainly state that Our Lord died for all men, among which, for example, we find:

"He. . .did not spare his own son but gave him up for us all. . ." (*Rom.* 8:32);
"For as in Adam all die, so also in Christ shall all be made alive" (I *Cor.* 15:22);
"And He died for all, that those who live might live no longer for themselves but for Him who for their sake died and was raised" (II *Cor.* 15:15);
"He is the expiation for our sins, and not for ours only but also for the sins of the whole world" (I *Jn.* 2:2);
"And we have seen and testify that the Father has sent His Son as the Savior of the world" (I *Jn.* 4:14);

97

"For there is one God, and there is one mediator between God and men, the man Christ Jesus, who gave Himself as a ransom for all" (I *Tim.* 2:5-6).

Moreover, the contrary proposition, that Christ did *not* die or shed His blood for all men—a proposition which Cornelius Jansen held was "semi-Pelagian"—has been formally *condemned* by the authority of the Church, that is by Pope Innocent X in 1653, in a case involving the Jansenists.[1]

Thus, on the face of it, nothing heretical is being asserted by the use of the words "for all men" in the consecrating formula; Christ's blood *was* shed "for all men"; that is a simple statement of fact. Nevertheless, as the Council of Trent defined, "even though 'Christ died for all' (II *Cor.* 5:15), still not all receive the benefit of His death, but only those to whom the merit of His passion is imparted."[2]

Traditional Catholic theology has thus always distinguished between the "objective redemption" of all men by Christ and the "subjective redemption" whereby the grace merited by Christ on the Cross actually proves fruitful only in the case of those who cooperate with His grace and achieve salvation.

Ludwig Ott says in this connection:

"The universality of Christ's vicarious atonement is to be related to the objective redemption only. Christ rendered sufficient atonement for all men without exception. The subjective appropriation of the fruits of redemption is, however, dependent on the fulfilment of certain conditions, on faith (*Mk.* 16:-16), and on the observation of the commandments (*Hebr.* 5:9; 2 *Pet.* 1:10)."[3]

Most informed Catholics have thus been aware that the Church teaches that not all men are necessarily saved. But that Christ died not for the faithful only, but for all mankind without exception, is a logical conclusion from the scriptural passages quoted from Saints John and Paul above; Ludwig Ott, again, holds it to be a teaching "proximate to faith" *(sententia fidei proxima).*[4] It certainly expresses correctly Christ's intention to offer His Sacrifice on the Cross for the salvation of mankind. Why would it be wrong, therefore, for the Church to incorporate into the words of consecration of the Mass the revealed truth that Christ *did die* for all men (signifying of course, the "objective redemption")?

The inclusion of the words "for all men" in the consecratory formula no more implies the heresy that all men *will* necessarily be saved than the previous consecratory formula "for you and for many" (still found in the Latin text of the *Novus Ordo,* incidentally) necessarily implied the opposite heresy that Christ did *not* give Himself for the redemption of all. The consecratory formula of the Mass is not, in the nature of the case, the place where the Church's full doctrine is, or could possibly be, expressed.

This does not mean that otherwise we would not know what the Church teaches about this; we know, for example, from the teaching of the Council of Trent quoted above; and the Church's teaching remains what it is, guaranteed by her infallible Magisterium, regardless of the formula used in the Mass. The Church's full teaching on this (or any other matter) is not required to be recited in order to effect the Transubstantiation of the wine into the Precious Blood. It may be added that the use of "for many" in the words of consecration has never signified any defined belief of the Church that *many* (if that word *is* interpreted in its ordinary English sense) will be saved. We do not know, and the Church has not said. It is still possible (and there have been theologians who have defended this thesis) that in reality *few* will be saved, as, for instance, in the case of Our Lord's words, "For many are called, but few are chosen" (*Mt.* 22:14); or, "For the gate is narrow and the way is hard that leads to life, and those who find it are few" (*Mt.* 7:14).

With respect to the question of the form of the sacrament, the consensus of theologians of past centuries has been that only the words "This is My Body" and "This is My Blood" are absolutely necessary (we will take up this matter in detail in the answer to Question #10). The Church can vary other words in each consecratory formula to express whatever aspect of revealed truth she wishes.

It may be asked, however, why the translators of the Latin *Novus Ordo,* in which the Latin words *"pro vobis et pro multis"* are retained, exactly as in the old Missal, and this by the express stipulation of Pope Paul's Apostolic Constitution *Missale Romanum* (See Appendix I), have nevertheless preferred "for you and for all men" in the official approved English translation. (The same question can be asked of the translators of the approved vernacular version of the Novus Ordo in Italian, since they also seem to have preferred the same translation, "for you and for all men": *"Per voi e per tutti."* This is the version celebrated by the Pope himself when he says Mass in Italian, as one of the authors has verified with his own ears from not too many feet away from the high altar in St. Peter's Vatican Basilica!)

At first sight, the official Latin *"pro multis"* would seem to require "for many." Regarding the motive of the translators for introducing a different translation—into more than one vernacular translation!—the authors have no information and decline to speculate. We have already seen that the translation is not heretical. But in addition to the fact that the translation "for all men" is not heretical, there *is* perhaps a further rationale for it.

If we examine the Fifth Chapter of St. Paul's Letter to the Romans, for example, we find the following:

> "For if many died through one man's trespass, much more have the grace of God and the free gift in the grace of that one man Jesus Christ abounded for many" (*Rom.* 5:15).

It is necessary, however, to read the first half of this scriptural passage more carefully. St. Paul says that "many died through one man's trespass." Now, unless "many" here can actually be translated as "all men," this phrase from St. Paul would actually constitute a formal denial of the Church's dogma, defined *inter alia* by the Council of Trent, that the original sin of Adam and its consequences were in fact transmitted to all men rather than just to "many"!

But an inspired letter of St. Paul would be the last place where we would expect to find denials of defined Catholic dogma. Indeed the Council of Trent used a passage from the very same Fifth Chapter of the Letter to the Romans in its definition![5]

Thus the phrase "for many" *must* be susceptible of more than one interpretation. And, in fact, in the same Fifth Chapter of his Epistle to the Romans, in verses 12-13, St. Paul, introducing his discussion of the effects of Adam's sin, employs the phrase "all men" as a *synonym* for the phrase "many," already quoted, which he uses a few verses later on! Thus, if we are to make a capital case out of translating *pro multis* as "for all men" in the English New Order of the Mass, we are going to have to start with the inspired Apostle to the Gentiles himself, who apparently finds it possible to use the two phrases interchangeably.

This same interchangeability of meaning can also be found in the Old Testament. In Isaiah 53:14, for instance, we read that "He bore the sin of many and made intercession for the transgressors." Yet earlier in the same chapter of Isaiah, verse 6, we find the familiar words: "All we like sheep have gone astray; we have turned every one to his own way; and the Lord has laid on Him the iniquity of us all."

Actually, orthodox biblical scholars have explained the apparent discrepancy, by pointing out that Hebrew and Aramaic words for "many," familiar to the Apostles, had a common meaning of "the all who are many" or an "undefined multitude." In other words, the Bible on occasion used the words *many* and *all* interchangeably. That is to say, the expression "for many" has a semitic meaning that is equivalent in some cases to "for all men." The original Hebrew or Aramaic words came into the Greek New Testament simply as *polloi,* which in turn was perhaps somewhat simplistically translated into the Latin Vulgate as *"multis"* rather than *"omnibus."* In our day, there has been a greater awareness of the various meanings of all the words involved—and of the semitic nuances underlying them. The Church has accordingly found no contradiction in doctrine in approving "for all men" in English—or *"per tutti"* in Italian—as a valid translation of the Latin *"pro multis."* Some scripture scholars believe "for all men" might even be a more faithful translation of the original sense of the holy scriptures.

The great biblical scholar Pierre Benoit, O.P., writes as follows of the meaning of the word "many" in the scriptures:

> "The word which we translate as 'many' stresses the sense of a great number and does not exclude anyone. . .Jesus certainly makes this fullness of salvation his own and it is the whole of mankind to the end of space and time that he includes in this 'many' for whom he was going to give his life as a 'ransom'" (*Matthew* 20:28; *Mark* 10:45).[6]

Still another biblical study, by Edward J. Kilmartin, S.J., independently finds that "the semitic phrase 'for many' stands for a totality and not for a multitude in contrast to the whole. Hence it indicates the universality of Christ's redemptive work."[7]

It may be of further interest that St. Thomas Aquinas, who was well versed in the scriptures and frequently quoted them, remarks: "St. Augustine explains *'multi'* to mean 'all men'; and *this manner of speaking is frequently found in sacred scripture*" (emphasis added).[8]

Finally, a standard pre-Vatican II work, *The Canon of the Mass* by Jerome Gassner, O.S.B., simply finds *either* meaning acceptable in commenting on the consecration:

"'Many' can be taken for (a) all, with a special connotation
of the immense multitude of the children of Adam; or (b)
with reference to those who actually are saved: many, but not
all men, cooperate with the grace of Christ."[9]

Thus, we can see that there certainly is justification for the translation of "*pro multis*" as "for all men" found in vernacular translations of the Mass; and, from the point of view of Catholic doctrine,
the issue simply does not have the importance that has unfortunately
been attributed to it.

The doctrine of the Church remains what it is, and always has
been and always will be, regardless of the verbal variations in the
formula used for the consecration of the chalice at Mass: the sacrifice
of Christ *did* redeem "all men," though not all may actually profit
because the merits of Christ's sacrifice have to be applied to everybody in particular, and some, employing their free will, may reject
God's grace. But this doctrine remains what it is regardless of the
variations in the formulas of consecration found in the Church's
liturgies, both Eastern and Western. Our Catholic belief in the merits
of Christ's sacrifice remains the same whether the formula for consecration of the chalice includes "for all men," "for many," "for
you," or *none* of them!

We have instances in the history of the Church of valid consecrations where *none* of the above formulas have been included, in fact,
some of which we will cite in the reply to Question #10.

As we can see from the history of liturgical development, the
Church may add to or subtract from the consecration formulas in
perfect consciousness that she has left the *substance* of the sacramental rite intact, and not altered anything essential Our Lord has
laid down, for the liturgy and the sacraments have been committed
into her hands by Christ.

For example, the *Novus Ordo* has added the scriptural words
"which will be given up for you" to the previous consecratory
formula of the Tridentine Mass. Does this added scriptural phrase
taken from St. Luke (22:19) and from St. Paul (I *Cor.* 11:24),
bringing out more clearly, by the way, the sacrificial nature of the
Mass, alter the orthodoxy of the consecratory formula for the
bread? The words "for all men," which also express an important
scriptural truth (II *Cor.* 5:14; I *Tim.* 2:5-6; I *Jn.* 2:2), no more
render heretical the consecration formula for the chalice.

Those who have brought such charges should consider those wise words written back in 1963 by a theologian who was setting forth a common Catholic teaching:

> "Turning now to the 'form' [of the Eucharist], the words that signify the meaning of this Sacrament, their diversity makes it plain that *Christ had no intention of establishing a rigid formula*. What is essential is that the words, in different languages, should respect the meaning Christ gave the rite when He instituted it" (emphasis added).[10]

For those who nevertheless continue to have anxieties about the problem of translation of *"pro multis"* as "for all men" instead of "for many," however, we may conclude this section by noting the existence of an official Declaration on the Meaning of Translations of Sacramental Formulae which the Holy See issued in 1974 to cover questions of difficulties in translations which, as we can imagine, once the Holy See decided to approve vernacular liturgies, are occurring with regard to other questions besides *"pro multis"*—and with regard to other languages besides English!

This particular Declaration entitled *Instauratio Liturgica*, dated January 25, 1974, and issued by the Sacred Congregation for the Doctrine of the Faith (formerly "the Holy Office") requires that translations of the authoritative Latin texts of sacramental and liturgical documents be as faithful as possible; but then it goes on to specify that, whatever the translation of a formula, its *meaning* remains that of the original Latin text which is approved by the Church. The Declaration is short enough to be reproduced in its entirety below; it should put to rest once and for all the anxieties that have been expressed over the translation of *"pro multis"* as "for all men" in the New Order of the Mass (and over some of the other renderings in the vernacular version of the Mass):

> "The liturgical reform which has been carried out in accordance with the Constitution of the Second Vatican Council has made certain changes in the essential formulae of the sacramental rites. These new expressions, like the other ones, have had to be translated into modern languages in such a way that the original sense finds expression in the idiom proper to each language. This has given rise to certain difficulties, which have come to light now that the translations have been sent by episcopal conferences to the Holy See for approval. In these circum

stances, the Sacred Congregation for the Doctrine of the Faith again calls attention to the necessity that the essential formulae of the sacramental rites render faithfully the original sense of the Latin 'typical text.' With that in mind it declares:

"When a vernacular translation of a sacramental formula is submitted to the Holy See for approval, it examines it carefully. When it is satisfied that it expresses the meaning intended by the Church, it approves and confirms it, stipulating, however, that it must be understood in accordance with the mind of the Church as expressed in the original Latin text."[11]

BUT QUITE APART FROM THE TRANSLATION QUESTION,
ISN'T IT TRUE THAT THE FORMULA FOR CON-
SECRATION, FIXED FOR ALL TIME BY CHRIST,
INCLUDED "FOR MANY"? WOULDN'T ALL
CONSECRATIONS WITHOUT "FOR MANY,"
OR WITH SOME DIFFERENT FORMULA,
THEREFORE BE INVALID?

The principal sources for the idea that the Church's formula for consecration, "fixed for all time," included "for many" seem to be the *Catechism of the Council of Trent* and St. Thomas Aquinas. Both of these eminently respectable traditional sources held that the form to be used for the consecration of the wine must include not merely the words "This is the chalice of my blood" but the additional words which follow this in the unrevised, pre-1969 Roman Missal, so that the complete form which would always have to be used for the consecration of the wine would be (in English): "This is the chalice of My Blood, of the new and eternal Testament, the mystery of faith, which shall be shed for you and for many, unto the remission of sins."

Not only does the *Catechism of the Council of Trent* hold that "we are firmly to believe" that all of these words belong to the form of the sacrament; it goes on to specify that "with reason . . . were the words 'for all' not used."[1]

St. Thomas Aquinas similarly considers the form of the sacrament of the holy Eucharist in several articles of his *Summa Theologica*, and concludes—not, however, it must be said, with very great conviction—that "it seems incorrect" to hold that "the words 'This is the chalice of my blood' alone belong to the substance of this form but not those words which follow."

"Others say more accurately," the Angelic Doctor notes, "that all of the words which follow are of the substance of the form."[2]

Now, while both St. Thomas Aquinas and the *Catechism of the Council of Trent* are normally of very great authority, it nevertheless does not seem necessary to follow them in this case. However pre-eminent, St. Thomas Aquinas is still only a single theologian, not the official Church; and despite its name the *Catechism of the Council of Trent* was not itself a conciliar document. And as we shall see, the Church has recognized and recognizes liturgies in which the formula for the consecration of the wine neither included "for many" nor the other words above held by these two authorities (and by some traditionalists today) to belong to the substance of the formula; hence though we would normally assign the greatest weight to these authorities we may not follow them against decisions of the Church herself.

Certainly the question does not involve the form of the sacrament as fixed by Our Lord because, as we shall note further on about the four New Testament accounts of the institution of the Eucharist, two of them do not include "for many" or the other words above. The *Catechism of the Council of Trent* itself notes that the words "the new and eternal testament" have "been added," as have the words "the mystery of faith," just as, indeed, the words "for you and for many" are again not found in that form in the New Testament, but, according to the *Catechism,* have been "joined together by the Catholic Church under the guidance of the Spirit of God."[3] The *Catechism* itself thus recognizes that the Church is responsible for determining what the proper form of a sacrament must be; and if the Church recognizes a form different from that believed by the *Catechism* to be essential, the authority of the latter can scarcely be adduced against such an official decision of the Church since, as we have noted, it is not itself a dogmatic source but rather was published as a manual of instruction for priests; it was not issued *by* the Council of Trent but was only prepared afterwards at the request of the Council.

As for St. Thomas, in his reply to an objection that the words, "This is the chalice of my blood," do effect a perfect consecration of the blood, he does not really speak to the question of whether the words are *necessary* for a consecration; he merely points out how by the use of these other words mention is fittingly made of "the fruits of the passion in the consecration of the blood."[4] It could be that St. Thomas was purposefully vague here because he really was not sure; the Church of his day had not decided; and historical variations in the liturgy and the sacraments were perhaps not as well known or appreciated then as they are today. It may be of some interest, though, that the editors of the Latin edition of the *Summa Theologica* note apropos of the conclusion of St. Thomas which is neither forceful nor precise that, on the contrary, "it seems to us probable that only the words 'This is the chalice of my blood' or 'This is my blood' are the essential form of [the consecration of] the chalice," contrary to St. Thomas' own view; thus even his own editors do not consider his arguments as probative.[5]

Nor would it be amiss here to remark on another of St. Thomas' opinions, namely, that we should be bound by the decisions of the Church not by the opinions of any theologian whatever, even St. Thomas himself; he would no doubt have been the first to renounce his own opinion in favor of the judgment of the Vicar of Christ. He said: "We must abide rather by the Pope's judgment than by the opinion of any of the theologians, however well-versed he may be in divine Scripture."[6]

It seems, in short, that neither St. Thomas Aquinas nor the *Catechism of the Council of Trent* can really be invoked as demonstrating or proving that all of the words used for the consecration of the wine in the Tridentine Mass are necessary for a valid consecration. It seems that they were really justifying the use of the words that were in fact used by the Roman rite of their day; and making a case — which indeed they do make — of how fitting the additional words are if they are used.

The same thing seems to be true of the Decree for the Armenians issued by the Council of Florence in 1439. The Church was at that time endeavoring to achieve union with the Armenian Orthodox (Monophysite) Church, and the Council of Florence therefore set forth a statement of Latin sacramental practice which included the same form for the consecration of the Precious Blood as found in St. Thomas Aquinas and the *Catechism of the Council of Trent*. However, again, this conciliar Decree appears to be describing and justifying the Latin sacramental practice of the time.

It is of crucial importance, in this regard, that standard Church reference works published long before Vatican II and the revision of the Roman Missal have *not* necessarily followed St. Thomas and the *Catechism* in this matter. The 1961 edition of Donald Attwater's *A Catholic Dictionary*, for example, mentions only the words "This is the chalice of my blood" and only adds: "It is disputed among theologians as to how much of the usual form is necessary."[7] There was not, in other words, any definitive judgment of the Church that the form of the consecration had to include any more than those words; it was "disputed among theologians."

Wilmers' *Handbook of the Christian Religion* published in 1891 states that the form consists of "the words of Christ . . . 'this is my blood.'"[8] F. M. Capello's *Tractatus Canonico-Moralis de Sacramentis* states that the words *"Hic est enim calix sanguinis mei"* are "certainly essential."[9] The four-volume *Moral and Pastoral Theology* by Henry Davis, S. J., one of the commonest parish reference works in the 1940's and 1950's, says the same thing. Fr. Davis does add that "possibly the rest of the form is essential" and that "if any of the subsequent words are omitted, a grievous sin is committed" (because the Church's *discipline* required them).[10] Finally, the highly respected and authoritative Ludwig Ott, in his *Fundamentals of Catholic Dogma,* says that "the words of instruction demonstrate, at least with a high degree of probability, that at the Last Supper Jesus effected the transmutation with the words, 'This is my body, this is my blood.'"[11]

The overall testimony of opinions on this subject prior to the changes ushered in with Vatican II is thus far from establishing that the words of consecration were absolutely fixed and henceforth forever necessary according to the "Tridentine" form. In the post-Vatican II years, Fr. Joseph Jungmann, summarizing a long history, similarly declares, "the words 'this is my body,' 'this is my blood' are the minimum required and are sufficient for the sacrament to be actualized."[12]

It is for the Church, in any case, to decide the form of the consecration; and what she sanctions in the way of variant liturgical or sacramental practice shows that her approved forms can also vary. We should constantly remember that "the Church" is not limited to the Roman rite. Attwater's *Catholic Dictionary,* already quoted above, states in this connection with regard to the situation before the Council:

> "The Catholic Church recognizes nine rites, each one of which has its own right and proper way of doing things, from celebrating the Holy Eucharist downwards; they are: the Latin (including variants), Byzantine, Armenian, Chaldean, Coptic, Ethiopic, Malabar, Maronite and Syrian rites. All these except the Latin and the Maronite are also used by numbers of Christians who are no longer Catholics. It should be noted that all rites are local in origin; historical events have extended their use to whole churches."[13]

A certain flexibility and variation in the words of consecration in the Mass have thus always been present in the Church's liturgies, as a matter of fact, as we can see by examining the consecratory formulae of the Eastern liturgies in the Church. It is interesting to note that in the Byzantine Greek Liturgy, right after the priest says: "Drink of this, all of you, this is My Blood of the New Testament, which is shed for you and for many, for the remission of sins," the words of Our Lord, "Do this in memory of me" (*Lk.* 22:19; I *Cor.* 11:23), do not appear—still another variation in the formula for consecration which has been held to be "unchangeable." According to Dom Leclerq, in fact, there have been no fewer than eighty-nine variations in the formulas for consecration in the history of the Church![14] And among all these variations there are a number where not only the phrase "for many" but other words of the "Tridentine" form of the consecration are not to be found.

To cite examples, we may begin with one of the very earliest consecrations of which we have any record; we refer to one described by St. Paul the Apostle:

"For I received from the Lord what I also delivered to you, that the Lord Jesus on the night when he was betrayed took bread, and when he had given thanks, he broke it, and said, 'This is my body which is for you. Do this in remembrance of me.' In the same way also the cup, after supper, saying, 'This cup is the new covenant in my blood. Do this, as often as you drink it, in remembrance of me.' For as often as you eat this bread and drink the cup, you proclaim the Lord's death until he comes" (I *Cor.* 11:23-26).

We should note that St. Paul reports having received the formula of consecration he uses "from the Lord" Himself. And yet this formula does *not* include the phrase "for many." Could we say, therefore, that St. Paul's Masses were consequently invalid? Paul's disciple, St. Luke, similarly reports the institution of the Holy Eucharist by Christ (*Lk.* 22:14-20), and, again, the use of the phrase "for many" is nowhere to be found. Instead, as with St. Paul quoted above, only the phrase "for you" is used. Should we therefore argue from this that the merits of Christ's sacrifice could be applied only to those with whom Christ was talking at the moment, namely to the Apostles themselves? No, once again, our *faith* remains the same regardless of the form of consecration used.

It is true that the phrase "for many" does occur in the account of the institution of the Holy Eucharist which we find in both the

Gospels according to Sts. Matthew and Mark (*Mt.* 26:28; *Mk.* 14:24); but the fact that Sts. Paul and Luke do not include it clearly implies that it was never an *essential* part of the formula for consecration fixed by Our Lord Himself. Moreover, although the accounts in Matthew and Mark do include "for many" they do *not* include the word "chalice" which has equally been held to be part of the "fixed form."

Church history presents other clear examples of Masses where *none* of the phrases "for many," "for you" or "for all men" were used. What the standard historical work on the subject calls "the oldest known text of the Roman Mass," the Mass of St. Hippolytus, which dates from the early part of the third century — and which was, incidentally, in Greek! — has the following text, which includes the form of the consecration:

> "And when He was delivered up to voluntary suffering that He might abolish death and rend asunder the bonds of the devil and tread upon hell and enlighten the righteous and show forth the resurrection, [He] took bread and giving thanks to Thee, He said: *this is My Body which is broken for you.* And likewise taking the cup, He said, *this is My Blood which is shed for you.* When you do this, make memory of Me. Making memory therefore of His death and resurrection, we offer to Thee this bread and chalice giving thanks unto Thee for finding us worthy to stand before Thee and to minister unto Thee. And we beseech Thee to send Thy Holy Spirit upon the oblation of Thy Church, to gather into one [body] all Thy holy ones who partake of it that they may be filled with the Holy Spirit for the strengthening of their faith in truth, that we may praise and glorify Thee through Thy Child Jesus Christ, through Whom glory be to Thee and honour, to the Father and the Son, with the Holy Spirit in Thy holy Church now and forever. Amen."[15]

Moreover, the following Oriental Liturgies in use today do not include "for many" in the consecration of the chalice:

Catholic Ethiopian Rite

> "And likewise also the cup, giving thanks, he blessed it, and hallowed it, and gave it to his disciples, and said unto them, Take, drink, this is my blood (pointing and bowing profoundly), which is shed for you for the remission of sins."[16]

Liturgy of the Abyssinian Jacobites

"Take, drink this cup: my blood it is, which is shed for , ‿‿ for the remission of sin."[17]

Two of the most interesting liturgical finds of recent history have been manuscripts of ancient Egyptian liturgies. The first, the Sacramentary of Serapion, was written about 353-356 A.D. by Serapion, Bishop of Thmuis, a friend both of St. Athanasius and of St. Anthony, the father of monasticism. This ancient liturgical text has the following words for the consecration of the chalice:

"We have offered also the cup, the likeness of the blood, because the Lord Jesus Christ, taking a cup after supper, said to his disciples, 'Take ye, drink, this is the new covenant, which is my blood, which is being shed for you for remission of sins.'"

The second new find, the so-called Deir Balizeh manuscript, belongs to the seventh or eighth century, but its text is said to reach back to the third century. The words of the priest for the consecration of the chalice in this rite are:

"Likewise after supper he took the cup, and when he had blessed it and had drunk, he gave it to them saying, Take, drink all of it. This is my blood which is being shed for you unto remission of sins."[18]

Scholars studying the Eastern rites can point to many *anaphoras,* or eucharistic prayers, which do not include the "for many."[19] The "for many" *is* included in the contemporary liturgy of almost all of the Eastern rites or churches today (except the Ethiopian); *but the fact that it has not always and everywhere been included in rites whose validity the Catholic Church has never questioned or doubted, amply demonstrates that it is not essential for validity.* And whether it is essential has been precisely the question we are concerned with here.

To reinforce the point we may cite further ancient *anaphoras* (eucharistic prayers) of the ancient Ethiopian Church where *none* of the phrases "for many," "for you," or "for all men" is used, indicating that none of these phrases is *essential* for a valid consecration. The following examples are quite old, going back as far as the

seventh century, and are included in books published by the Holy
See for Ethiopian Catholics:

Anaphora of the Lord Jesus Christ

"And as often as ye do this, make memorial of Me. And likewise also the cup, putting wine into it, giving thanks, blessing
(three signings of the cross) and sanctifying, Thou gavest unto
them. Truly, This is Thy Blood which was shed for our sins."

Anaphora of the Evangelist John

"And, likewise, He gave praise over the cup (three signings
of the cross) and said: This (pointing) cup is My Blood of the
New Testament (some MSS. add: 'whoso drinketh of it shall
not die, and whoso partaketh of it shall not perish'): Take,
drink of it, all of you."[20]

We may conclude from all this that, just as the use in the consecratory formula for the Precious Blood in the New Order of the
Mass of the phrase "for all men" as the translation of the Latin *"pro
multis"* does not constitute heresy (Question #9), so the use of this
phrase in no way invalidates a Mass celebrated according to the
New Order.

If it is to be determined whether or not any rite of the Mass is
valid with respect to the form of consecration employed—and in
whatever language—it really only has to be determined whether the
words "This is my body, this is my blood" are present; if they are
present, then consecration according to that rite would undoubtedly
be valid, as the authority of the Church has determined over the
centuries.

The New Order of the Mass contains the essential forms for valid
consecration, whether in Latin or in the vernacular. Therefore,
arguments contesting its validity on that score should henceforth
be laid aside.

Question # 11

DOESN'T THE REMOVAL OF THE WORDS "*MYSTERIUM FIDEI*" FROM THE WORDS OF CONSECRATION AND THEIR USE INSTEAD FOR ACCLAMATIONS, THREE OUT OF FOUR OF WHICH CONCENTRATE ON CHRIST'S COMING AGAIN RATHER THAN ON HIS PRESENCE HERE AND NOW ON THE ALTAR — WASN'T THIS REARRANGEMENT DELIBERATELY INTENDED TO DOWNGRADE OR DENY THE CATHOLIC BELIEF IN THE REAL PRESENCE?

The words "mystery of faith" are evidently originally taken from St. Paul, who says about deacons that they "must be serious, not double-tongued, not addicted to much wine, not greedy for gain; they must hold the mystery of faith with a clear conscience" (I *Tim.* 3:8-9).

There may be some connection between the fact that this phrase is used by St. Paul about deacons and the fact that some scholars believe that the words were originally inserted into the Mass at this point to be proclaimed by the deacon to announce that the consecration had taken place (since the faithful could not see the priest at this point, as is still the case in the Byzantine Greek Church).

The foremost historian of the Mass of the Roman rite, Fr. Joseph Jungmann, S.J., is of the opinion, however, that the "explanation that the words were originally spoken by the deacon to reveal to the congregation what had been performed at the altar, which was screened from view by curtains, is poetry, not history. The phrase is found inserted in the earliest texts of the [Latin] sacramentaries, and mentioned even in the seventh century. It is missing only in some later sources. . . . How or why this insertion was made," Fr. Jungmann adds, "or what external event occasioned it, cannot be readily ascertained."[1]

What seems to be certain, however, is that the words are not those of Our Lord at the institution of the Eucharist; as we have seen in the reply to Question #10, none of the scriptural accounts of the institution records these words; they are not to be found in other formulas of consecration recognized as valid by the Church; and hence they are not required for a valid consecration.

It is because these words are not among those spoken by Our Lord that they have been rearranged in the revised Roman Missal containing the New Order of the Mass. "The words 'Mystery of Faith'. . . taken out of the context of the words of Our Lord and pronounced by the priest," Pope Paul VI explained in his 1969 Apostolic Constitution *Missale Romanum* (See Appendix I), "serve as it were as an introduction to the acclamation of the faithful."

Perhaps it should be recalled that the words of consecration involve an *action* as contrasted to a declaiming; and these words of consecration are, of course, substantially the actual words of Jesus Christ. Even though the additional words "mystery of faith" can fittingly recall the Real Presence of Christ in the Eucharist when placed within the words of consecration, and have done so for many centuries in the Roman rite, in another sense they really are more words of a declamatory nature, and thus not so strictly a part of the great Action or Deed of the consecration. They constitute more of "a being-outside-and-speaking-about" this great sacred Action, a sort of declaration of what the consecration has brought about. So it is also appropriate and fitting that these words be said after the words of consecration which actually effect the Transubstantiation of the bread and wine into the body, blood, soul and divinity of Jesus Christ.

After the consecration, the Latin text of the *Novus Ordo* has the priest declare: *"mysterium fidei,"* which signifies, as in the early days of the Church, that the awesome Transubstantiation of the elements has taken place. Then follows the acclamation of the people: *"Mortem tuam annuntiamus, Domine, et tuam resurrectionem confitemur, donec venias"*; "We proclaim your death, O Lord, and we confess your resurrection, until you come in glory." This acclamation (not rendered accurately in the present English vernacular) is an adaptation of the words of St. Paul used immediately following his formula of the words of consecration. *"Quotiescumque enim manducabitis panem hunc, et calicem bibetis, mortem Domini annuntiabitis, donec veniat"*; "for as often as you eat this bread and drink this cup, you proclaim the death of the Lord until He comes" (I *Cor.* 11:27). If St. Paul admitted such an acclamation, it is hard to see why it is inappropriate for the faithful today to use the words of the great Apostle to the gentiles, especially when the acclamation is approved by the Church.

It is, in fact, most appropriate that the People of God should realize that here present is the Crucified and Risen Christ. Here is Christ's Body as He died, as He rose, and as He is now glorious. Here is *"Jesus heri, hodie et in saecula"*; "Jesus yesterday, today and forever"—the whole Christ. Here He is in the "mystery of faith" with His glorified five wounds. Now we see our Redeemer in a veiled way, but soon we shall see Him with our bodily eyes as our Judge and Redeemer: "The Son of Man coming in clouds with great power and glory" (*Mk.* 13:24). There is in all this *no* disparagement or denial of the Real Presence; rather there is a new welcome emphasis on the Second Coming of Jesus Christ Who will transform the suffering and persecuted Church Militant into the Church Triumphant!

We should recall that the Pope who authorized the rearrangement of these words "mystery of faith" in the Mass in no way wished to deny or downgrade the Catholic belief in the Real Presence. In fact, in 1965, the same Pope wrote an encyclical with the express intention of reaffirming the Catholic belief in Transubstantiation and the Real Presence; and he entitled it, precisely, *Mysterium Fidei*!

In this encyclical in which the Pontiff vigorously upheld the Catholic beliefs in Transubstantiation and the Real Presence —using the very language of the Council of Trent—he taught at the outset that "the Catholic Church has always devoutly guarded as a most precious treasure the Mystery of Faith, that is, the ineffable gift of the Eucharist which she received from Christ her Spouse as a pledge of His immense love. . . ."

Paul VI explained further in the encyclical that he was writing it precisely because of errors that had arisen, because of a tendency to downgrade or deny the Catholic belief in Transubstantiation and the Real Presence. "The awareness of our apostolic duty does not allow us to be silent in the face of these problems," he wrote. "Indeed, we are aware of the fact that among those who deal with this Most Holy Mystery, there are some who. . .spread abroad opinions which disturb the faithful and fill their minds with confusion about matters of faith. It is as if everyone were permitted to consign to oblivion doctrine already defined by the Church, or else to interpret it in such a way as to weaken the genuine meaning of the words or the recognized force of the concepts involved."

But it is *not* allowable to set aside doctrine already defined by the Church, according to Pope Paul VI. In particular, he stigmatizes in the encyclical *Mysterium Fidei* three modern errors, as follows:

1) ". . .it is not allowable. . .to exaggerate the element of

sacramental sign as if the symbolism. . .expresses fully and exhausts completely the mode of Christ's presence in this sacrament."

2) "Nor is it allowable to discuss the mystery of Transubstantiation without mentioning what the Council of Trent stated about the marvelous conversion of the whole substance of the bread into the Body and the whole substance of the wine into the Blood of Christ. . . ."

3) ". . .or, finally, [it is not allowable] to propose and act upon the opinion according to which, in the Consecrated Hosts which remain after the celebration of the sacrifice of the Mass, Christ Our Lord is no longer present" (Encyclical *Mysterium Fidei*).

Thus Pope Paul VI on the "mystery of faith"! The very Pope who is accused of having wished to downgrade or deny the Catholic belief in the Real Presence proves to be the one who is reaffirming and upholding the dogma before the whole world against those who would deny it today. Those who would like to know what Pope Paul VI taught about the Real Presence (and other Catholic dogmas) should consult the great teaching documents of his pontificate, in which all traditional Catholic belief is uniformly upheld, and not look to the rearrangement of words in the revised Roman Missal as evidence of his having fallen away.

The Mass, after all, involves primarily the worship of the Divine Majesty; it expresses orthodox Catholic belief (the *Novus Ordo* still does so!); but it is not primarily the vehicle for the Church's teaching in its fullness; for that we have the sacred Magisterium of the Church. And it will be found that the sacred Magisterium of the Church continued to uphold all traditional Catholic doctrine during the pontificate of Pope Paul VI. Indeed, for what is possibly the most complete statement of the Catholic belief in the Real Presence to date in the history of the Church, one could not do better than to consult Paul VI's encyclical *Mysterium Fidei*.

With respect to the consecration let us be thankful that the Church possesses the tremendous power to bring about this great *mysterium fidei* for the benefit of our sanctification and salvation, but let us be content with the faith of St. Cyril of Alexandria as to the words required to bring it about—the very words which we have already shown to be alone essential in the reply to Question #10. St. Cyril wrote about these words as follows:

"Christ said indicating the bread and wine: 'This is My Body,' and 'This is My Blood,' in order that you might not judge what you see to be a mere figure. The offerings, by the hidden power of God Almighty, are changed into Christ's Body and Blood, and by receiving these we come to share in the life-giving and sanctifying efficacy of Christ."[2]

QUESTION # 12

BUT HOW CAN THE *NOVUS ORDO* BE HELD TO OFFER A TRUE SACRIFICE WHEN THE *TE IGITUR,* THE *MEMENTO DOMINE,* THE *HANC IGITUR* AND OTHER ELEMENTS WHICH AFFIRMED THE CATHOLIC DOCTRINE OF TRANSUBSTAN— TIATION HAVE BEEN ELIMINATED?

Before proceeding to reply to this question, we should add that those who commonly ask it usually go on to say: "It is not enough to reply that the word sacrifice is found in the vernacular translations of the New Order of the Mass, because the word 'sacrifice' can always be understood as Protestants understand it, namely, as a 'sacrifice of thanks and praise,' not as the sacrifice of Christ's own Body and Blood for the living and the dead."

It may be well to give our readers the passages of the above prayers whose "elimination" the question refers to. Below will be placed in adjoining columns: 1) a translation of these prayers as they appear in an older Missal for the laity published in 1957, and 2) as they presently appear in the present approved vernacular version in use in our churches:

"Therefore, most merciful Father, we humbly beg and entreat you through Jesus Christ your Son, our Lord, to accept these gifts, these offerings, these holy and spotless sacrifices which we offer you first for your holy Catholic Church, that you may grant her peace and protection, unity and direction throughout the world, together with your servant, N., our Holy Father, and N., our Bishop, and all faithful guardians of the Catholic and Apostolic faith." (*Te Igitur* — Maryknoll Missal, 1957)

"We come to you, Father, with praise and thanksgiving, through Jesus Christ your Son. Through him we ask you to accept and bless these gifts we offer you in sacrifice. We offer them for your holy catholic Church, watch over it, Lord, and guide it; grant it peace and unity throughout the world. We offer them for N., our Pope, for N., our Bishop, and for all who hold and teach the catholic faith that comes to us from the apostles." (*Te Igitur* — Vernacular English Text Approved for Use in the United States, 1970)

"Remember, O Lord, your servants N. and N., and all here present, whose faith and devotion are known to you. For whom we offer, or who themselves offer, to you this sacrifice of praise, in their own behalf and in behalf of all who are theirs, for the redemption of their souls, for the hope of their salvation and protection from harm, and who now offer their promises to you, the eternal living, and true God." (*Memento, Domine* – Maryknoll Missal, 1957)

"Remember, Lord, your people, especially those for whom we now pray, N. and N. Remember all of us gathered here before you. You know how firmly we believe in you and dedicate ourselves to you. We offer you this sacrifice of praise for ourselves and those who are dear to us. We pray to you, our living and true God, for our well-being and redemption." (*Memento Domine* – Approved English Version, 1970)

"We therefore beg you to accept, O Lord, this offering of our worship and that of your whole household. Regulate the days of our lives so that they may be spent in your peace; spare us from eternal damnation and help us to be numbered in the fold of your chosen. Through Christ our Lord. Amen." (*Hanc Igitur* – Maryknoll Missal, 1957)

"Father, accept this offering from your whole family. Grant us your peace in this life, save us from final damnation, and count us among those you have chosen. (Through Christ our Lord, Amen)." (*Hanc Igitur* – Approved English Version, 1970)

Though the present English translation of the Latin text of the *Novus Ordo* sometimes leaves something to be desired, it is quite false to say that these prayers of the celebrant have been *eliminated* in the vernacular New Order of Mass. Rather, they *remain* part of the traditional Roman Canon (Eucharistic Prayer I) which is still supposed to retain the place of preeminence among the four chief Eucharistic Prayers approved in the revised Roman Missal.

It is true that some of these elements are lacking in the other Eucharistic Prayers, but, in this connection, the following needs to be remarked:

1. These elements are the result of later insertions into the primitive Eucharistic Prayer (or Canon, or *anaphora*) of the Roman Church, and did not exist in their present form before the Fourth Century.[1]

2. Such intercessions also generally appear in the Eastern liturgies *after* the Consecration, not before, as in the present Roman Canon. Thus, simply because such passages do not appear in Eucharistic Prayers (or Canons) II, III, and IV, the conclusion cannot be justified (anymore than in the case of the Eastern liturgies in the Church) that the Church has sought to downgrade the offering of the Mass as

a sacrifice or downgrade the Church's own doctrine of Transubstantiation. We have already seen in the reply to Question #11 that the same Pope who promulgated the *Novus Ordo* specifically re-affirmed the Church's doctrine of Transubstantiation as defined by the Council of Trent in his encyclical *Mysterium Fidei*.

3. Actually, in its new Eucharistic Prayers as well as in the revised offertory of the New Rite, the Church has taken pains to avoid the misleading impression of a sacrifice of bread and wine during the offertory, for there is only the one sacrifice of the Body and Blood of Christ accomplished during the consecration of the elements. In the offertory of the Tridentine Mass such expressions as "Receive, O Holy Father. . .this immaculate host which I. . .offer Thee. . .," and "We offer unto Thee, O Lord, the Chalice of salvation. . ." caused many erroneous theories to crop up concerning a "natural" sacrifice which many thought preceded the real sacrifice. Many generations of liturgists as well as many of the faithful were troubled by this. In the days of St. Pius V, eminent liturgists had discussed a reform of the Roman Canon to eliminate all misunderstanding of the meaning of sacrifice. For the offering of bread and wine in the offertory does *not* constitute the sacrifice of Christ. There is no other salvific sacrifice than that of Christ on Calvary, and the sacrifice of Christ is perpetually renewed on the altar *at the moment of consecration* by a validly-ordained priest, and not before, as the Council of Trent clearly teaches.[2]

4. The clearest concept of sacrifice is found in the *Novus Ordo* where, theologically, it ought to be: in the *anamnesis,* that is to say, in the prayer which follows the words of consecration and which "makes memory" of the death and resurrection of the Lord by priest and people offering His Body and Blood (made present by Transubstantiation) to the Father. Thus, the Second Eucharistic Prayer of the New Order of the Mass (substantially that of St. Hippolytus going back to the year 215 A.D.)[3] declares:

"Memores igitur mortis et resurrectionis ejus, tibi, Domine, panem vitae et calicem salutis OFFERIMUS . . ." (Latin text)

"In memory of his death and resurrection, we offer you, Father, this life-giving bread, this saving cup." (Approved English Version)

Eucharistic Prayer III:

". . .OFFERIMUS *tibi, gratias referentes, hoc* SACRIFICIUM *vivum et sanctum. Respice, quaesumus, in oblationem Ecclesiae tuae et, agnoscens* HOSTIAM, *cujus volusti immolatione placari . . .*" (Latin text)

". . . *we offer* you in thanksgiving *this holy and living sacrifice.* Look with favor on your Church's offering, and see *the Victim* whose death has reconciled us to yourself." (Approved English Version)

We also find that the Fourth Eucharistic Prayer in the New Order of the Mass makes abundantly clear that the Mass is a sacrifice:

"OFFERIMUS *tibi* EJUS CORPUS ET SANGUINEM, SACRIFICIUM *tibi acceptabile, et toti mundo salutare. . .*" (Latin text)

"We offer you his body and blood, the acceptable *sacrifice* which brings salvation to the whole world . . ." (Approved English Text)

These expressions (together with yet other expressions that we could readily cite from the text of the Mass referring to reception of the actual Body and Blood of Christ in Holy Communion) can leave no doubt that the *Novus Ordo* manifests a complete Catholic orthodoxy—because it is a sacrifice of the Body and Blood of Jesus Christ who is both Priest and Victim, and who offers Himself as a Victim in propitiation for the living and dead.

The words of a Lutheran scholar, Jean Pleyber, are worthy of consideration on this subject, because the allegation that the New Order of Mass is no longer "Catholic" is rejected, first of all, by Protestants who have at all examined the issue. Jean Pleyber says:

"I believe that an essential point of Catholic doctrine is that the Pope is the beneficiary of a particular assistance of the Holy Spirit who has conferred upon him infallibility in matters of faith and morals. There cannot be Catholic archbishops and bishops outside of their total communion with the Pope. On this score, then, the position of Archbishop Lefebvre seems to me indefensible. Without doubt, he says, the question is only 'pastoral,' that is to say, disciplinary, and not 'doctrinal,' i.e., dogmatic. But he directly adds that the new canon of the Mass excludes the 'sacrificial' character of the Eucharistic celebration, reducing it to a mere 'memorial' of the Passion of the Savior and to a bare community meal. This matter clearly no longer involves the pastoral, but dogma. The position of Archbishop Lefebvre seems to me illogical. For if it is a question of dogma, the Pope is infallible and he ought then to be obeyed without hesitation or murmur.

"As to the matter in question, I have often assisted at Masses celebrated according to the new canon, and each Sunday I have viewed a televised Mass. I have never seen evidence that such Masses deny the sacrificial character of the Eucharist. And when I hear said and when I read that 'they have fabricated a Protestant Mass,' I know only too well that this is not true and that such persons are wide of the mark. I have even asked the priest in my village to forward the new liturgical texts to me, and I am convinced upon reading them that nothing has changed in Catholic Eucharistic doctrine. I believe it is useful to say that the Catholics who speak of a 'Protestantized Mass' are quite ignorant of Protestantism and perhaps of a great deal of Catholicism. . . ."[4]

We may conclude this particular discussion by saying that there is abundant evidence in the text of the *Novus Ordo* itself—notably in the three additional Canons or Eucharistic Prayers—that the Catholic doctrine of Transubstantiation is affirmed in this revised form of the Mass and that this Mass remains the true sacrifice of the Cross.

Pope John Paul II confirms all this when he speaks of the Mass — he is talking about the *Novus Ordo*—in his encyclical *Redemptor Hominis* (#20), in the following language which no one can argue is anything but "traditional":

"By Christ's will there is in this sacrament a continual renewing of the mystery of the sacrifice of Himself that Christ offered to the Father on the altar of the cross, a sacrifice that the Father accepted, giving, in return for this total self-giving by His Son, who 'became obedient unto death' (*Phil.* 2:8), His own paternal gift, that is to say the grant of new immortal life in the resurrection, since the Father is the first source and the giver of life from the beginning. That new life, which involves the bodily glorification of the crucified Christ, became an efficacious sign of the new gift granted to humanity, the gift that is the Holy Spirit, through whom the divine life that the Father has in Himself and gives to His Son is communicated to all men who are united with Christ."

REGARDLESS OF PARTICULAR WORDS, FORMULAS OR
PARTS IN THE TEXT OF THE MASS ITSELF, WASN'T
THE DEFINITION OF THE MASS PUBLISHED IN THE
GENERAL INSTRUCTION ON THE NEW ROMAN
MISSAL PROOF ENOUGH THAT WITH THE
NOVUS ORDO WE ARE SURELY CONFRONTED
WITH A PROTESTANTIZED VERSION
OF THE MASS?

The "definition of the Mass" referred to in this question, still widely diffused in some traditionalist literature, is as follows:

"The Lord's Supper (or the Mass) is the assembly or congregation of the People of God, with a priest presiding, to celebrate the memorial of the Lord."

Before discussing this "definition of the Mass," we should point out that it appeared in the original General Instruction on the Roman Missal and because of criticism leveled at it was revised. The following is the revision actually to be found in the definitive General Instruction on the Roman Missal approved and promulgated by the Pope and currently in effect; there is nothing "Protestant" about this paragraph:

"In the Mass or Lord's Supper the People of God are called together into one place where the priest presides over them and acts in the person of Christ. They assemble to celebrate the Memorial of the Lord, which is the sacrifice of the Eucharist. Hence the promise of Christ: 'Wherever two or three are gathered together in my name, there am I in the midst of them' (*Mt.* 18:20) applies in a special way to this gathering of the local church. For in the celebration of the Mass whereby the sacrifice of the Cross is perpetuated Christ is really present in the very community which has gathered in his name, in the person of his minister, and also substantially and continuously under the eucharistic species." (General Instruction on the Roman Missal, Chapter II, # 7)[1]

It is misleading to continue to circulate the first version above as if it represented an official post-Vatican II Church "definition" or proved anything at all about the nature of the New Order of the Mass. To those who might reply that the General Instruction was revised only after the incompleteness of the first formulation was pointed out, we could further rejoin in our turn that this simply proves that those, if any, whose intention it might have been to see the first, controversial "definition of the Mass" quoted above, published in an official Roman document, were finally not able to succeed in doing so! This should give added confidence in the ultimate judgment of the Holy See in such matters, not create doubts. The Church, on her human side, has never been free of confusion; throughout her history some men have tried to use her for their own ends. A remarkable fact about her history, however, is that she keeps landing on her feet in spite of efforts to trip her. We should never underestimate this ability of the Church to continue to land on her feet.

Having noted this, we may go on to add that even the first, incomplete version quoted above was never intended as a *full definition* of the Holy Mass, but only as a *brief description,* quite traditional and orthodox in itself as one description among others, which, moreover, was to be understood in the context of the many other paragraphs (341 in all) of the *"Institutio Generalis"* or General Instruction on the Roman Missal. This particular description, moreover, comes in a chapter of the Instruction entitled, "Structure, Component Elements and Parts of the Mass," and in a section entitled, "The Structure of the Mass as a Whole." A description of the "structure" of something surely does not imply or require a strict *definition* of it.

Pope Paul VI himself, in his Apostolic Constitution *Missale Romanum,* explained that the General Instruction was meant only to be a description of the new rubrics; the Pope specified (See Appendix I):

"It explains the functions and duties of each participant and describes the material things and special arrangements."

It was, in other words, not meant to be a full-fledged treatise on the theology of the Eucharist; for that, as we have noted earlier

(Question #11), we would urge those interested to consult Pope Paul's 1965 encyclical *Mysterium Fidei* in which the full faith of the Church on the central mystery of our faith is admirably set forth.

Even though the General Instruction on the Roman Missal is primarily devoted to the rubrics and to the way the Mass is to be celebrated, it nevertheless does contain further references to the sacrificial character of the Mass. In Chapter I, #2, we are told, for example, that the Eucharist "is the sacrifice of His Body and Blood."[2] In Chapter II, #48, the whole Last Supper narrative is repeated, and it is again re-affirmed that in the Mass "the sacrifice of the Cross is continually made present in the Church whenever the priest, who represents Christ Our Lord, does what Christ Himself did and commanded his disciples to do in memory of Himself."[3] #259 of Chapter V, referring to the altar, states clearly that on it "the Sacrifice of the Cross is made present under sacramental signs."[4] Going back to the Foreword of the General Instruction, we find, as we have already noted in the reply to Question #7, that the document quite explicitly recognizes the Council of Trent's definition of the Mass.[5]

We could go on but the point is made; all who are interested should read the General Instruction on the Roman Missal to satisfy themselves that the Mass described in it is truly the sacrifice which the Church has always offered.

But even in the original version quoted above, brief and inadequate a "definition" of the Mass as it no doubt was, there was, as we have already noted, nothing particularly "Protestant." The words "assembly," or "congregation of the People of God," have been objected to. But the original Latin is *"sacra synaxis seu congregatio."* The expression *"sacra synaxis"* is a term used in the early Church to refer to the Mass. It has mystical overtones pointing to a sacred body of people brought together—the Mystical Body of Christ. In fact, the word "Mass" only certainly came into use with St. Ambrose in the late fourth century, coming from the words, *"Ite, Missa est,"* as the old *Catholic Encyclopedia*, in an article by Fr. Adrian Fortescue, made clear many years ago.[6]

The words *"congregatio"* and *"convocatio"* were often used in tradition to refer to the Church.[7] These words, as well as "memorial of the Lord" are rich in sacrificial resonances, and are in no way "Protestant."

The words—"with a priest presiding," or, as some have translated them, "under the presidency of the priest"—do represent a rather unfortunate translation of what is, however, a very traditional expression, *"sacerdote praeside."*

"To preside" comes from the word *"praesidere,"* "to preside, to have the care or management of"—this word in the Latin does not have the "democratic" connotation which attaches to "president" in English but simply refers to the power the priest has to officiate at the sacrifice. As Pope Pius XII says, the priest represents Christ "Who is head of all his members and offers Himself in their stead . . . [the priest is] superior to the people." (Pope Pius XII, Encyclical *Mediator Dei*, #84)

The word *"praeside"* is therefore rich in theological overtones of the history of the Latin West and does not bear the objectionable "democratic" or Protestantizing flavor that some have chosen to misread into it.

It is, however, important to note that there is a new emphasis in the Church on the perennial doctrine of the participation of the faithful in the priesthood of Christ (Cf. I *Pet.* 2:9), though, of course, the laity does not possess the power of the ministerial priesthood. But there is a greater awareness that, because the priest bears the person of Christ and offers in the person of Christ, he acts for the people, *who* in one sense thus all offer the oblation together with him. This has always been true in the Catholic Church. The oldest description which we possess of the celebration of a Holy Mass in post-apostolic times, the account of St. Justin Martyr in his *First Apology* which dates from around 150 A.D., includes the following:

> ". . .After finishing the prayers we greet each other with a kiss. Then bread and a cup with water and wine mixed are brought to the one *presiding* over the brethren. He takes it, gives praise and glory to the Father of all in the name of the Son and of the Holy Ghost, and gives thanks at length for the gifts that we were worthy to receive from him. When he has finished the prayers and thanksgiving, the whole crowd standing by cries out in agreement: Amen. Amen is a Hebrew word and means: So may it be. . . ." (Emphasis added)[8]

If priests were understood as "presiding" over the faithful at Mass in the Catholic Church of the second century, as this passage from St. Justin Martyr indicates, surely neither the word nor the idea can be ascribed to the Protestant Reformation of the sixteenth century.

With regard to the supposed approval of a "Protestantized" Mass in the General Instruction on the Roman Missal because of the use of this word, then, we may surely accept the testimony of St. Justin Martyr to the contrary; and we may, in any case, surely lay aside any doubts we might have had if we will only take the trouble to read through the General Instruction as definitively promulgated by the Pope and now found in our altar missals: in it we will find many references to the sacrificial nature of the Mass such as those quoted above.

Question # 14

DIDN'T CARDINAL OTTAVIANI, FORMER HEAD OF THE "HOLY OFFICE," INTERVENE TO CRITICIZE SEVERELY THE MANNER IN WHICH THE *NOVUS ORDO* DOWNPLAYED THE IDEA OF SACRIFICE?

When a small group of French and Italian theologians wrote in 1969 a 29-page "Critical Study of the *Novus Ordo Missae*," the late Alfredo Cardinal Ottaviani was joined by his colleague Antonio Cardinal Bacci in writing a letter to Pope Paul VI enunciating their opinion that:

> ". . .the *Novus Ordo Missae* — considering the new elements, susceptible of widely differing evaluations, which appear to be implied or taken for granted — represents, as a whole and in detail, a striking departure from the Catholic theology of the Holy Mass as it was formulated in Session XXII of the Council of Trent. . . . Therefore, we most earnestly beseech your Holiness not to deprive us — at a time of such painful divisions and ever-increasing perils for the purity of the Faith and the unity of the Church — of the possibility of continuing to have recourse to the fruitful integrity of that *Missale Romanum* of St. Pius V, so highly praised by your Holiness and so deeply venerated and loved by the whole Catholic Church."[1]

This was the principal substantive point of the so-called "Ottaviani intervention." However, it is also true that a letter dated February 17, 1970, was subsequently published in which the same Cardinal Ottaviani declared to the author of a work dealing with the *Novus Ordo*:

> "I have rejoiced profoundly to read the Discourse by the Holy Father on the question of the new *Ordo Missae*, and especially the doctrinal precisions contained in his Discourses

at the public Audiences of November 19 and 26 [see texts of both in Appendix II], after which, I believe, no one can any longer be genuinely scandalized. As for the rest, a prudent and intelligent catechesis must be undertaken to solve some legitimate perplexities which the text is capable of arousing. In this sense I wish your 'Doctrinal Note' [on the *Novus Ordo*] and the activity of the *Militia Sanctae Mariae* wide diffusion and success."[2]

This second letter, although it has been a matter of public record since 1970, has not been publicized to the extent that the original "Ottaviani intervention" was publicized; many Catholics are unaware of the existence of this letter in which the respected Cardinal declared that "no one can any longer be genuinely scandalized." Though a few writers, aware of the second letter, have alleged that the blind Cardinal was the victim of a fraud in obtaining his signature to it,* Cardinal Ottaviani never in any way repudiated the sentiments expressed in this letter; never did he go on record to disavow it although he could have easily done so.

In fact, later on, Cardinal Ottaviani published still another statement in which he said:

> "The beauty of the Church is equally resplendent in the variety of the liturgical rites which enrich her divine cult—when they are legitimate and conform to the faith. *Precisely the legitimacy of their origin protects and guards them against the infiltration of errors. . . .* The purity and unity of the faith is in this manner also upheld by the supreme Magisterium of the Pope through the liturgical laws" (emphasis added).[3]

Here Cardinal Ottaviani gives the most powerful and conclusive argument that the New Order of the Mass cannot really contain, or tend towards heresy, namely, that its doctrine is guaranteed by the divinely assisted Magisterium of the Catholic Church. Those who attempt to justify their rejection of the *Novus Ordo* on the basis of Cardinal Ottaviani's opinion of it delivered before its definitive version was even available, conveniently ignore these other wise words of this same humble servant of the Holy See—words delivered in October, 1963, at the Second Session of the Second Vatican Council. Cardinal Ottaviani said on that occasion:

*A highly respected and reliable Catholic publisher revealed to Catholics United for the Faith that Cardinal Ottaviani expressed to him his distress and anger that these allegations had been circulated by the French publisher Jean Madiran of *Itineraires*.

"The words of Christ 'feed My sheep' are words which have
been addressed only to His Vicar, and it follows that whoever
would wish to be counted among the Flock of Christ must submit to the Universal Pastor appointed by Christ. No one can be
an exception to this rule, not even Bishops."[4]

Though the promulgation of the new Roman Missal (containing
the New Order of the Mass) by Pope Paul VI was not a dogmatic
definition—in the nature of the case the promulgation of Paul VI's
new Missal was a disciplinary act, as was the promulgation of St.
Pius V's Missal in 1570, not an exercise of the Pope's teaching authority—the virtually universal acceptance of the new Missal by the
bishops of the entire Catholic world is further proof of the fact
that there is nothing heretical or contrary to Catholic tradition which
would prevent its acceptance by the Roman rite of the Church—unless virtually the whole Church is now irremediably in error, something Christ promised would never happen.

Since Cardinal Ottaviani said the Tridentine Mass over a lifetime of
outstanding service to the Church, it is easy to understand his *feeling*
that the Church should not be "deprived" of the Mass which had
become so familiar. This was the feeling of many priests and bishops.
However, this Prince of the Church also accepted and, as quoted
above, indeed "rejoiced" in the explanations offered by the Supreme
Authority in the Church in response to his earlier doubts and ques-
tionings. In this, as in his entire priestly life, Cardinal Ottaviani
could well serve as a model for all of us.

If the testimonies of other eminent servants of the Church can be
added, it may not be amiss here to add that of the late Charles
Cardinal Journet, one of the most erudite Thomistic theologians of
our time, and the author of what is perhaps the greatest work on the
Church published in this century. Cardinal Journet delivered these
touching remarks about his feelings on the day before he ceased to
celebrate the Tridentine Mass which he so loved (November 29,
1969):

"The Holy Father has very pointedly asked for obedience
when the new *Ordo Missae* begins to be celebrated in the different dioceses [of Switzerland] . . . . Tomorrow morning, for the
first time, I will say the new *Ordo Missae* with profound obedience, pleased to have something to give to God. It will not be a
little thing! For many years I have celebrated the old *Ordo*,

which I know almost by heart; each time that I celebrate it, I discover new things. It is as dear to me as my own flesh and blood. I must now leave it. I am pleased to give something to God.

"Let me take care to say, there is no renouncing of anything essential—I will return to this point in a moment. One renounces nothing essential pertaining to what is of divine law; the substance of the Mass remains absolutely the same: there is the Offertory, the Consecration. . . . And the Sovereign Pontiff has recalled expressly what was not expressed sufficiently in the rubrics of the new *Ordo*: that the Mass is a *sacrifice*.* He has recalled that there is a change of bread and wine into the Body and Blood of Christ. All these things, which are not Protestant, are truly Catholic—and also orthodox. Thus there is the reaffirmation of the classic Catholic doctrine on the Eucharistic sacrifice.

". . .Certainly in all this there is our acute sense of uprootedness. Must one accept it or not? Ah, yes! When one tears something dear away from us, and when this is demanded of us in the name of obedience—for a future which is hidden from us—one must say *yes*, one must be content in saying *yes*, one must be content even to feel suffering. . . . But it is with happiness that one suffers, for he has something to give to God. . . . Thus, let us not get into a frenzy. There is no necessity for any uproar concerning the Mass."[5]

In a letter dated January 13, 1975, the distinguished Cardinal also spoke his mind concerning Archbishop Marcel Lefebvre's seminary at Ecône; this letter was addressed to a religious sister who had inquired about his views:

"I have your letter. I have been very moved by what you write me. In the face of one drift towards the modernist heresy, there has been created another drift towards an *"intégriste"* (traditionalist) schism."

---

*See the text of the Pope's remarks which Cardinal Journet is referring to in Appendix II.

It is interesting that Cardinal Journet distinguishes the modernist *heresy* from the traditionalist *schism*. It is surely true that the traditionalists began by denying no Catholic doctrine; indeed they began by attempting to defend doctrines which they saw endangered. Soon, however, to defend their own position, they had to deny, at least as a practical matter, the *doctrine* that the Pope is the operating head of the Church on earth, in disciplinary matters as well as in his teaching office. The evolution of the traditionalist position fits the pattern that St. Augustine once described, namely, that a heresy is a schism grown old. One may start with schism, and, in defending it, fall into heresy. Cardinal Journet describes the process in the rest of the letter he sent to the religious sister who had inquired about his views:

> "There is a new Port-Royal which is lacerating France, and not only France, but the Church. And it is a much more grave threat than the first, since in order to defend itself from being schismatic, it is obliged to see heresies in the decisions of the Pope and of an Ecumenical Council.
>
> "It is necessary to convince your fellow sisters that they are engaged on a path which will separate them more and more from the Church. For the Church of all time *(l'Église de toujours)* is the Church which has a Pope. . . ."[6]

This last is a point on which Cardinal Journet, Cardinal Ottaviani—and all Catholics—ought to be able to agree: the Catholic Church "is the Church which has a Pope."

Question # 15

IF, AS THE CHURCH HAS ALWAYS BELIEVED, *LEX ORANDI, LEX CREDENDI,* THE RULE OF PRAYER DETERMINES THE RULE OF FAITH, CAN WE NOT ATTRIBUTE THE DRASTIC DECLINE IN CATHOLIC FAITH AND PRACTICE IN THE PAST FEW YEARS TO THE ILL-ADVISED LITURGICAL REFORMS DECIDED UPON BY THE SECOND VATICAN COUNCIL AND IMPLEMENTED BY THE POPE?

First of all, we must quote the great Pope Pius XII who, in his encyclical *Mediator Dei* said that the familiar maxim "*Lex orandi, lex credendi*" was not strictly true in matters of the liturgy. "This is not what the Church teaches and enjoins" (#46). "The sacred liturgy does not decide and determine independently and of itself what is of Catholic faith" (#48).

Indeed, Pius XII was quite severe in speaking of "the error and fallacious reasoning of those who have claimed that the sacred liturgy is a kind of proving ground for the truths to be held of faith" (#46). The thing the Pope of the 'forties and 'fifties stigmatized here would seem to be precisely the same thing being done by those who point not to the teaching documents of Pope Paul VI, such as his 1968 Credo of the People of God or his 1965 Encyclical *Mysterium Fidei,* for evidence of the faith he professed about the Mass, but rather to his revisions in the Roman Missal which supposedly prove that this Post-Vatican II Pope abandoned orthodoxy. Actually, as Pope Pius XII pointed out, it is the liturgy which is "subject. . .to the Supreme Teaching Authority of the Church," as expressed in such documents as encyclicals and Pope Paul's VI's Credo. It is to these magisterial documents that we must look first, as far as the faith is concerned, and not exclusively and in a spirit of suspicion at the Mass.

Another point that is well worth making about the phrase *lex orandi, lex credendi* is that its use in recent times was actually popularized by the modernists, and thus the weight assigned to it by some traditionalists is surprising to say the least. In the 1961 edition of Pius XII's *Mediator Dei* published by the America Press, Fr. Gerald Ellard commented on the paragraphs 46-48 of the encyclical which we have just quoted above in a way which makes unmistakably clear the role the modernists have had in distorting the meaning of this maxim; his comments are worth quoting at some length in view of the importance that has been attached to this maxim in a traditionalist context. Fr. Ellard noted that Pius XII made mention of the phrase primarily "to reaffirm the meaning. . .twisted out of its original significance by modernist heretics" who held that in any dispute on points of faith one might appeal to liturgical prayers; these prayers would be found to reflect the correct underlying faith:

> "In the hands of the modernists this appeal to liturgical practice was by way of asserting 'that the sacred liturgy is a kind of proving ground for the truths to be held by faith; meaning by this that the Church is obliged to declare such a doctrine sound when it is found to have produced fruits of piety and sanctity through the sacred rites of liturgy, and to reject it otherwise.'
>
> "The most conspicuous of the English modernists published a volume under the title, *Lex Orandi,* the whole theme of which is well summarized in one sentence: 'Beliefs that have been found by a continuous and invariable *experience* to foster and promote the spiritual life of the soul must so far be in accord with the nature and the laws of that will-world with which it is the aim of religion to bring us into harmony; their practical value results from, and is founded in, their representative value. . . .'
>
> "But the correct use of the appeal to the Church's prayer-forms, as a theological source, requires that a distinction be kept constantly in mind. The ancient liturgies are not the norm of the primitive faith, as though they had determined and formulated the beliefs. Rather it is the doctrinal belief of the Church that is always prior, and that gives form and expression to that faith expressed in prayer."[1]

This is a truth that constantly has to be borne in mind today. Considering the use to which the modernists wished to put an expression such as *lex orandi, lex credendi,* we should be wary of invoking it uncritically, and, indeed, should not depend upon such phrases, or slogans, at all when dealing with Church affairs, but should look exclusively to the living Magisterium of the Church.

Having made these fundamental points about the maxim *lex orandi, lex credendi,* we may now proceed to respond to the question asking whether the liturgical changes since Vatican II have not caused the decline of Catholic faith and practice so evident in the past few years. This "explanation" may appear plausible to some, but it is convincing only to those who have not reflected upon the inroads a virulent secularism and revived modernism had made in the Church long before the Second Vatican Council. We have only to read the vigorous encyclical *Humani Generis* published by Pope Pius XII in 1950 to see the proportions of the doctrinal crisis already threatening the Church's life and vitality then. This document, which highlighted the main deviations of the "new theology" and the "new morality," truly reads as if it were written for our own day when a veritable "epidemic of errors" still remains a principal concern of the Chief Shepherd of the flock.

From the beginning of his pontificate Pope John Paul II has certainly been aware of these problems of the Church, of what he called in his encyclical *Redemptor Hominis* "the various internal weaknesses that affected her in the post-conciliar period" (#4). These same problems have been a steady concern of the Pontiffs. In his historic pilgrimage to Fatima, Pope Paul VI delivered a sermon, on May 13, 1967, in which he took occasion to say:

"You know Our special intentions which characterize this pilgrimage. Now We recall them, so that they give voice to Our prayer and enlightenment to those who hear them. The first intention is for the Church —the Church, one, holy, Catholic and apostolic. We want to pray, as We have said, for her internal peace. The ecumenical Council has reawakened many energies in the heart of the Church, has opened wider vistas in the field of her doctrine, has called all her children to a greater awareness, to a more intimate collaboration, to a more fervent apostolate. We desire that these be preserved and extended.

"What terrible damage could be provoked in this reawakening, by arbitrary interpretations, not authorized by the teaching of the Church, disrupting the traditional and constitutional structures, replacing the theology of the true and great teachers of the Church with new and peculiar ideologies, interpretations intent upon no longer holding as matters of faith positions which modern thought, often lacking rational judgment, does not understand and does not care for. Such interpretations would change the apostolic concern of redeeming love into acquiescence to the negative forms of secular mentality and a mere human ethic. What a delusion our efforts to arrive at universal unity would suffer, if we failed to offer to our Christian brethren, at this moment divided from us, and to the rest of humanity which lacks our faith in its clearcut authenticity and in its original beauty, the patrimony of truth and charity—of which the Church is the guardian and the dispenser.

"We want to ask of Mary a living Church, a true Church, a united Church, a holy Church."

In innumerable other discourses, Pope Paul VI further attempted to deal with the "ferments of infidelity here and there in the Church unfortunately attempting to undermine her from within" (*Apostolic Exhortation,* December 8, 1974).

But the persistence of modernist errors despite the crushing Syllabus *Lamentabili Sane* of St. Pius X, July 3, 1907, through the pontificate of Pius XII with his encyclical, *Humani Generis,* August 12, 1950, and into our own days, simply witnesses to the depth of the *crisis of faith* affecting all too many Christians in modern society. What must be emphasized is that this increasingly serious doctrinal crisis was able to develop during the time of the Tridentine Mass. The "Mass of St. Pius V," with all its admirable features which even Paul VI remarked on, was no barrier to the doctrinal deviations that have been the true cause of the decline of Catholic faith and practice in the Church in the twentieth century. The root causes for the present "crisis of faith" and "crisis of authority," crises which affect both Church and society, lie far deeper than which Mass is being celebrated and it would be a profound mistake to think otherwise.

Conversely, it can be noted that in countries such as Poland where the *Novus Ordo* and all the legitimate liturgical reforms *have* been correctly introduced and where modernism has made hardly any inroads up to very recent times, the faith is very strong and there are many vocations to the priesthood, belying the assertion that the *Novus Ordo* in itself necessarily has the adverse results for the faith which some claim it has. All this was dramatically brought to the attention of the world at the time of the election of the Polish Pope John Paul II, and, subsequently, during his visit to Poland as Pope in June, 1979.

A clear distinction must be made between the authorized and correctly implemented liturgical reforms, on the one hand, and, on the other hand, the abuses, aberrations and even sacrileges which have cropped up at the same time like cockle next to the wheat, making the two almost indistinguishable in the eyes of many of the faithful. The resulting confusion has contributed to the further spread of modernism since so many of the attempts to "fight" modernism have not been properly grounded first in humble and obedient loyalty to the Pope and the Church and then in acceptance of the official changes.

The false doctrine which has been and is being disseminated within the Church, and which drew such new strength from widespread misinterpretations of the *aggiornamento* of the Second Vatican Council, was identified by Pope Paul in his General Audience of January 19, 1972, when he said: "Modernism was the characteristic expression of these errors, and it still exists today under other names."

A few months later, he stated even more precisely:

"It was believed that after the Council there would be a day of sunshine in the history of the Church. There came instead a day of clouds, storm and darkness, of search and uncertainty. By means of some fissure the smoke of Satan has entered the Temple of God" (General Audience, June 29, 1972).

Pope John Paul II, characteristically, said the same thing more bluntly in his address to the Latin American bishops in Mexico in early 1979: "Some people fall into forms of interpretation at variance with the Church's faith."

The intellectual and spiritual disorientation underlying this modernism is clearly linked to the work of the devil. "An enemy has done this," Our Lord noted for all future generations of the faithful in one of His striking parables (*Mt.* 13:28), and He went on to identify the enemy in question who sowed the bad seeds: "The enemy who sowed them is the devil" (*Mt.* 13:39). The devil in his own way is quite astute: he knows how to take advantage of the spiritual dizziness infecting souls in order to try to ruin the work of the Second Vatican Council. It is assuredly this larger perspective with which concerned Catholics should view the present decline in Catholic faith and practice whose roots reach back into the philosophical errors of the nineteenth century and earlier. It is highly misleading to blame either the work of an ecumenical council of the Church or the Popes for the deviations which have caused such havoc. Neither a Pope nor a Council can avail if no one will obey them. The lack of obedience, which can be noted on all sides, is thus one of the principal elements in the present crisis.

As we noted, a similar disobedience to the dictates of Pius XII's *Humani Generis* was rife in France and Germany years before the Council and thus perforce even before the introduction of the *Novus Ordo*. The Mass is not the issue; unbelief and disobedience are the issue. The Council became the occasion or the pretext for some in the Church to place the mantle of the Council over their errors, twisting what the Council actually said; there are those who are still trying to do that; but it is also clear that the official acts of the Council, ratified by the Pope, are guaranteed by the Holy Spirit (See Question #2). No heretical affirmations have been or can be found in the Council's decrees and declarations; and those who assert or repeat the contrary can scarcely claim to be representing, of all things, the Catholic Tradition.

It needs to be repeated without any equivocation: It is *not* the fault of the Council or of the Popes that clergy and laity afflicted with modernism and its variants, with worldliness, with simple ignorance, or whatever, are not following the plain teaching of that Council and those Popes. The distinction we make between the machinations of Council *periti* and the final decrees of the Council (See Question #13) are not merely facile distinctions; there *is* a difference between what a theologian or even a bishop may assert and what the Church officially enacts. This was so at Vatican I and at all the previous Church councils. Considering the history of these previous councils, Cardinal Newman remarked, "we may well feel indignant at the intrigue, trickery, and imperiousness which is the human side of [their] history." But even in the light of the knowledge of this human side of the Church Newman did not hesitate to affirm: "Of course what a general council speaks is the word of God."[2]

There is no evidence to show that Vatican II was different from other Church councils in this regard. It had its human side too, of course; even then what happened at this twentieth-century Council was mild and restrained compared to the intrigue and the strife and the tumult that characterized some of the earlier general councils of the Church. At the Council of Ephesus, the main protagonists actually brought their own bodyguards: Nestorius, gladiators from the circus, St. Cyril of Alexandria, sailors from Alexandria. "Disputes were frequent, [and] fights and riots with the Nestorian minority. . . ."[3] The Council formally ended with groups of bishops deadlocked and mutually excommunicating and anathematizing each other—yet this was the same council that defined the dogma, which has of course stood ever since, that Our Lady was *Theotokos,* the Mother of God.

So it was with Vatican II: the Council's final documents are what count; and they were in no way nullified by the intrigues or "politics" that may have gone on at or after the Council. Supposing that "the Rhine flowed into the Tiber" during the years of the Council, the Tiber still remained the Tiber—and remains the Tiber today.

We must not be scandalized at the evidence that the Church has her "human side." "The divine mission of the Church that works among men and must work through men may be lamentably obscured by human failings," Pope Pius XI wrote in his encyclical *Mit Brennender Sorge*—failings which "again and again sprout up as tares amid the wheat of God's kingdom." Still we must not forget amid all this that the Church is in the world primarily to sanctify and save souls and that this work continues to go on in the midst of and in spite of the tares which may sprout up. We must not forget, Pius XI insisted, that there always remains in the Church an "immense sum of sincere pursuit of virtue, of the spirit of sacrifice, of brotherly love, or heroic striving after holiness"; we must not, taught the Pope who condemned Communism as intrinsically evil, "make a career, and in many instances, a low profession, of busying [ourselves] with the human failings in the Church" (*Ibid.*). Rather we should again be grateful to God that He redeems and elevates sinful humanity anyway through that same Church with her "human side."

The Second Vatican Council has clearly been the *occasion* for increased disorders in the Church rather than the *cause*. Pope Paul VI, in season and out of season and until his death interpreted the Council properly for those willing to listen; he also struggled mightily with the immense task of trying to discipline those not always noted for caring to listen. Similarly, Pope John Paul II announced at the outset of his pontificate his intention of insisting on "purity of doctrine and sound discipline" (Address to Bishops of the Seventh Pastoral Region of the United States, November 9, 1978), and we may be confident that the Successor of Peter will continue to feed the sheep and confirm his brethren.

The actions of the Holy See in late 1979 in the cases of Fr. Hans Küng and Fr. Edward Schillebeeckx certainly underline that the Pope meant what he said when he said that his pontificate would emphasize doctrine and discipline.

We may also be sure, however, that none of his efforts has been or will be easy in view of the obstinate "ferments of infidelity" which exist today and especially in view of the nature of today's communications media. Leaders of the Church in past ages didn't have to worry about the mass media hanging on their every act and trumpeting their own superficial "media" impression of it to the four corners of the world, reaching even the Catholic faithful with this "media" interpretation ahead of the leaders of the Church with the real message. Today Church leaders do have to cope with this situation, and they have to be circumspect for the sake of the Church.

It is not a question of cowardice, of "worrying about what the media might think" if strong disciplinary measures were to be imposed; it is a question of recognizing and taking into account the simple fact of the real *power* of the media today, a power that can harm the Church. For the media *are* a power, as even Presidents of the United States have learned to their grief. One thinks also of the cartoon of Fidel Castro saying, "I got my job through the *New York Times*." And just as the Church once had to reckon with the power of princes and feudal barons, so today she does have to reckon with the power of the media. Whatever disciplinary measures may have to be taken have to be taken in the full glare of the lights of these hostile media.

Nevertheless Pope Paul VI did not fail to "speak out" anyway, and more than once; let us be fair to him about that; we cite only one example:

"Deviations in the faith or in the sacramental practice are certainly very grave, wherever they occur. For a long period of time they have been the object of our full doctrinal and pastoral attention. Certainly one must not forget the positive signs of spiritual renewal or of increased responsibility in a good number of Catholics, or the complexity of the cause of the crisis: the immense change in today's world affects believers at the depth of their being, and renders ever more necessary apostolic concern for those 'who are far away.'

"But it remains true that some priests and members of the faithful mask with the name 'conciliar' those personal inter-

pretations and erroneous practices that are injurious, even
scandalous, and at times sacrilegious. But these abuses cannot
be attributed either to the Council itself or to the reforms that
have legitimately issued therefrom, but rather to a lack of authentic fidelity in their regard" (See Appendix IV).

The testimony of such a great champion of orthodoxy as Alfredo
Cardinal Ottaviani is another testimony that can be brought against
the thesis that all the troubles in the post-conciliar Church were not
caused either by this Council or by the actions of the Holy See in
implementing this Council's decrees. In the issue of *L'Osservatore
Romano* of February 16, 1956 — six years before the opening of the
Second Vatican Council — Cardinal Ottaviani wrote about some of
the theologians of the day; he could have been writing today, about
the same phenomenon which we have experienced more virulently
since the Council; but he was writing of something already long before the Council:

> "Today certain individuals make a pretense of putting a
> theology together as one might make up a crossword puzzle.
> They are composing the 'new theology,' the 'theology of labor,'
> the 'theology of sport,' and the rest. The theologies and the
> teachers 'with itching ears' are increasing in number, and the
> authoritative teaching of the competent organs of the ecclesi-
> astical Magisterium is being ignored. People have never been so
> indulgent towards error as they are today. And they have never
> been as severe, as disobedient, and as insolent towards the
> Church as they are today. Today the ecclesiatical Magisterium
> has nothing more to say as far as some little men are concerned.
> These are the supermen of culture, who believe they can act
> on their own even in the field of theology. Certain intellectuals,
> who are watered-down Christians and also fanatical in their
> stand, hardly ever open their mouths except to say something
> bad about our history, our household, our brethren, and our-
> selves. But is this not a vile procedure? Is it not primarily a
> surrender to the enemy? These people seek delight, not as Mary
> did, at the feet of Jesus, but as Eve did, listening to the ser-
> pent."

Thus the respected Cardinal Ottaviani. Should we blame Vatican
II for the state of affairs he describes? Should we blame Pope John

XXIII or Pope Paul VI? The true answer of the authentic Catholic Tradition would have to be that the supreme authorities in the Church ought to be the last to be blamed for errors and abuses committed in the first place *against* their very authority. Rather than carp and blame, even where undeniable abuses exist, we ought to try to reaffirm legitimate Church authority by the generous spirit in which *we*, at least, hasten to obey legitimate authority, regardless of what others may be doing.

Nearly a century ago, St. John Bosco surely spoke for the authentic Catholic Tradition when he wrote about the disposition which the faithful ought to cultivate towards the supreme living Teacher whom God has placed in the world to help us get to heaven:

"Always have the highest esteem and deepest respect for the Roman Pontiff, hating the errors that are spread concerning his quality as head of the Church; speak of him with the highest regard, scolding severely those who abuse him in your presence; refute as ably as you can, the errors and calumnies that might be hurled against him; always reject writing that attack his authority and jurisdiction. This you can do by destroying them or refuting them or opposing them by spreading good literature even at the cost of much expense. Pray every day for the Church and for the Roman Pontiff, reciting one Our Father, Hail Mary and Glory be. . .with the words *Credo Sanctam Catholicam Ecclesiam* (I believe in the holy Catholic Church), in order to make an act of faith in the divinity of the Church of which the Pope is the visible head on earth."[4]

Question # 16

HASN'T IT BEEN DEMONSTRATED THAT SOME OF THE VATICAN OFFICIALS RESPONSIBLE FOR THE NEW ORDER OF THE MASS WERE, IN FACT, MASONS HOPING TO SUBVERT THE FAITH?

No, it has not been so demonstrated. There has certainly been no *proof* given for such allegations, although they have been widely disseminated in pamphlets and brochures attacking the *Novus Ordo*. Mere publication of calumnies does not constitute proof. In the October 10, 1976, issue of *L'Osservatore Romano*, it was officially denied that the high ranking prelates named in various Italian newspapers and magazines (and uncritically repeated by certain British and American publications) had anything to do with the Masons: "Not one prelate of the Vatican ever had anything to do with Freemasonry."

Archbishop Annibale Bugnini, in particular, denied that he ever had the slightest connection with Freemasonry or with any other secret organization."[1] The Vatican Secretary of state, the late Jean Cardinal Villot, also accused of being a Mason, declared forcefully that he had never had the slightest connection with Freemasonry or any other secret organization.

Naturally such denials on the part of the very persons accused did not carry much weight with those who were accusing them; but, the whole question of the alleged Masons (or Communists, or Protestants) in the Vatican raises in acute form the question of the power that the media—in this case, the medium of print—has come to exert over the thinking even of those Catholics who profess to be more concerned about the Church. The power we refer to is this: all that needs to be done, apparently, to get some Catholics today to doubt immediately of the dispositions made by the shepherds of the Church is to have printed in some journal or newspaper some accusation or other casting doubt upon this or that of their actions. Catholics of nearly all tendencies today seem ready, even strangely eager, to believe whatever might be alleged against the Pope or the bishops. There has come about what Pope Leo XIII sadly described as "a loosening of that bond of love and submission which ought to bind all the faithful to their pastors, and the faithful and the pastors to the Supreme Pastor, the bond in which is principally to be found security and common salvation."[3]

Often it doesn't matter how outlandish the accusation is; the new "authority of print" immediately outweighs the authority which the shepherds of the Church possess from God. Often it doesn't even matter where the slander is printed. Some points in an article in the scarcely pro-Catholic *New York Times* awhile back about an unpopular Church official, for example, were very quickly picked up and repeated thenceforth as absolute gospel truth by various Catholic publications of a conservative or traditionalist bent.

In the case of the stories about the Masons (or Communists or Protestants) in the Vatican, the original printed sources were scarcely credible, yet they were immediately believed and very widely disseminated by papers calling themselves Catholic. Why are those who profess to be so proud of being Catholic, or orthodox, so often ready to believe, without real proof, the worst about the motives or actions of the shepherds of the Church or the officials of the Holy See? In 1957 Pope Pius XII warned against what he called that "'free examination' more fitting to the heterodox mentality than to the pride of the Christian and according to which no one hesitates to summon before the tribunal of his own judgment even those things which have their origin in the Apostolic See."[4]

Earlier in the same letter already quoted above, Pope Leo XIII had also warned that "if it should happen that those who have no right to do so should attribute authority to themselves, if they presume to become judges and teachers, if inferiors in the government of the universal Church attempt to try or exert an influence different from that of the supreme authority, there follows a reversal of the true order, many minds are thrown into confusion, and souls leave the right path."[3]

The main result of some of the fantasy and gossip about the Church officials that has reached print has in fact been to deflect some souls from the right path. In addition to the stories of the Masons in the Vatican, there have been even more inplausible ones which many Catholics have nevertheless rushed to believe. Thus there were the incredible rumors and stories about Pope Paul VI in his last years being the virtual prisoner of Freemason Cardinals, or the drugged victim of Communist agents operating in the Vatican, or a heretic who had proceeded with devious cunning to "Protestantize the Mass." In apparitions allegedly stemming from the Mother of God, it was even claimed that the Pope seen by millions of people was an imposter who had been cleverly substituted in the real Pope's place. The imposter could be identified by the size and markings of one of his ears! No absurdity was too foolish for some to believe.

In evaluating such stories—where real "proof" of any kind is in the nature of the case excluded—we should ask ourselves to whose benefit it is that the Catholic faithful should be persuaded to doubt of their own Church leaders? *Cui bono?* As the old Latin adage has it, "to whose advantage?" Could it be that some of these rumors were launched or planted *by* the Masons, the Communists or other enemies of the Church in order to sow confusion among the faithful? Who, after all, does profit most if the confidence of Catholics is shaken in their divinely-established Church, in fact beset by many enemies both from within and without? *Cui bono?* Catholics should ask themselves this question before simply proceeding to believe whatever scandal or rumor against the Church, her leaders or her personnel manages to reach print.

We should remember that the tactic of starting false rumors has always been a well-known tactic of the enemies of the Church. It was a tactic which St. Peter Canisius, for example, often faced in Reformation times in the sixteenth century; rumors were regularly spread about various people, including even the Holy Roman Emperor, as having gone over to the Lutherans or as having at least dropped their opposition to Lutheranism. Soon the common people—understandably, in some cases—began to believe and say, *"der Glaube ist frei,"* a man may believe what he likes.[5] Thus can mere rumors without any foundation in fact undermine people's beliefs, including belief in the Church and the integrity of her leaders.

Moreover, we should also remember that to the extent that enemies of the Church might even manage to infiltrate the Vatican, they still would not be able to harm the Church by such measures as, say, imposing an "invalid" Mass on her and depriving the faithful of the very sacraments which Christ instituted for their spiritual benefit.

The validity of the New Order of the Mass is guaranteed by the supreme teaching and ruling authority of the Church, the Vicar of Christ, who is always safeguarded by the Holy Spirit in feeding the flock of Christ with sound doctrine and sacraments. Catholics need not fear that any plots or maneuverings by possible Freemasons, or Communists, or any other "enemies" whatever in the labyrinthine corridors of the Vatican will prevail against the solemn assurance of the Son of God that His Vicar will always confirm his brethren in the truth and in those liturgical practices conformable to the Gospel of our salvation. It has never happened, no matter what tribulations the Church ever had to pass through; and it will not happen "in the one communion which the apostolic See proclaims, in which the whole truth and perfect security of the Christian religion resides," as the First Vatican Council expressed it in one of its dogmatic constitutions, adopting language first formulated by Pope St. Hormisdas in 515 A.D.[6] Catholics can therefore *believe* it; they must believe it; it is *de fide*. But they should rather fear being taken in by the modern demon of the media that would cause them to *doubt* of the Church Christ founded upon a Rock. . . .

"It is *safer*," Newman wrote, "to acquiesce with, than without, an authority; safer with the belief that the Church is the pillar and ground of truth, than with the belief that in so great a matter she is likely to err" (emphasis added).[7]

The Rock-man Peter is not at the mercy of conspirators of whatever persuasion. When Peter acts and speaks as the supreme authority in the Church to enjoin upon the faithful a form of worship, it is traditional Catholic doctrine that the faithful should obey, and not spend time reading sensationalist exposés of conspiracies casting doubt upon the authority of the Church. Our Lord Jesus Christ asked his disciples for *faith,* and of those He appointed to teach, rule and sanctify in the Church, He said: "He who hears you, hears Me" (*Mt.* 10:16). Our faith is not, in other words, in "the authority of print" which the modern world finds so persuasive. The notion that we should spend our time seeking to find conspiratorial reasons to *doubt* the supreme Shepherd of the Church in the exercise of his legitimate authority in liturgical matters, violates reason as well as the basic dictum that our obedience is due the successor of Peter in his authoritative decrees. Our Catholic faith must needs be that of a little child trusting his spiritual father in the faith.

Moreover we should not make the excuse that we are loyal to the Pope, but not to his underlings. The Popes have necessarily depended for many centuries on a vast amount of "staff work" performed by others in their onerous and unique task of teaching, ruling and sanctifying in the Church; entire *palazzi* in Rome house the offices of the Roman Curia. But when the Pope confirms with his own authority the work of his own subordinates, it thereby *becomes* his work; this is the basic principle of management whether in industry, in government, in the armed forces—or in the Church. Canon law forbids the transaction of important business or the issuing of documents without the approval of the Pope (Canons 243, 244). We should, therefore, not waste our time trying to identify possible heroes or villains in the Pope's entourage, as, again, the media love to do; in the media the Church is considered nothing else but just another "political entity"—though we know she is the Ark of Salvation.

In connection with all this, there comes to mind a remarkable allocution of Pope St. Pius X delivered in 1912, in which the saintly Pontiff taught that the faithful ought to learn, literally, to *love* the Pope, and his acts, and his decrees, including those carried out for him by his subordinates; we might profitably heed these words of St. Pius X today:

> ". . .when we love the Pope, we do not dispute whether he commands or requires a thing, or seek to know where the strict obligation of obedience lies, or in what matter we must obey; when we love the Pope we do not say that he has not yet spoken clearly—as if he were required to speak his will in every man's ear, and to utter it not only by word of mouth but in letters and other public documents as well. Nor do we cast doubt on his orders, alleging the pretext which comes easily to the man who does not want to obey, that it is not the Pope who is commanding, but some one in his entourage. We do not limit the field in which he can and ought to exercise his authority; we do not oppose to the Pope's authority that of other persons—no matter how learned—who differ from the Pope. For whatever may be their learning, they are not holy, for where there is holiness there cannot be disagreement with the Pope."[8]

Thus, Pope St. Pius X, the foe of modernism, on the spirit in which Catholics ought to receive and accept the decisions and dispositions of the Vicar of Christ on earth.

Question # 17

QUITE APART FROM THE MOTIVES OF THOSE WHO
PRODUCED THE *NOVUS ORDO,* OR OF THE
PARTICULAR ELEMENTS, WORDS OR PHRASES
IN THE NEW RITE, HASN'T IT CAUSED AN
UNPRECEDENTED DESACRALIZATION OF THE
CHURCH? SHOULDN'T WE JUDGE IT AS A MIS-
TAKE BY ITS ALREADY EVIDENT "FRUITS"?

The word "desacralization" is practically a description of our
present age: having ceased to believe in God, our age no longer believes in, or even understands, the sacred. The prevailing philosophy
of the age is called, precisely, secular humanism, "secular" being
opposed to "sacred," and "human" to "divine." It is therefore not
surprising that "desacralization" is rather general.

One knowledgeable observer even speaks of "a frenzied determination to desacralize, to fight against whatever is 'sacred,' against
every *'sacrum'* at every level of human life, particularly in social and
public life. The firm intention is to force man to live totally apart
from any *'sacrum'* whatsoever, so as to make him 'man' and nothing
more—that is to say 'desacralized.'" The identity of this particular
observer is of special interest: Karol Wojtyla, Cardinal Archbishop of
Cracow, soon to be elected Pope John Paul II.[1] And he testifies
here to what should be in any case obvious, that we live in a radically
desacralized era. The Church is swimming against the tide in attempting to maintain any sense of the sacred at all among the people of
today.

Some or even much of what we sometimes encounter in Catholic
worship today which may strike us as irreverent or desacralized,
therefore, is scarcely to be ascribed to the New Order of the Mass. It
is rather a reflection of what people today happen to think is appropriate for worship or the liturgy—and, of course, most people today
have been radically secularized by the desacralized world around
them, often without even realizing it.

Thus, we now have the many familiar abuses in the liturgy, which can be conveniently subsumed under the phrase "do your own thing," and thus, too, we have such in-between things as "rock Masses" and an all too common casual, breezy irreverence which, while not actually abuses of concrete existing regulations of the Holy See, certainly do not lend themselves very easily to anything that we could properly call "sacred."

Then there is the fact of change itself in today's "future shock" society; change steadily undermines the liturgy which of its nature makes use of fixed, repeated hieratic words and actions; the Mass is the *reenactment* of the sacrifice of Christ. It is, necessarily, carried out over and over again in the same way. To change this habitual action without good reason is to risk undermining belief in it, is to risk reinforcing the impression that what *appears* to be different *is* different. What St. Thomas Aquinas says about changing laws applies also to changing the liturgy: ". . .to a certain extent," the Angelic Doctor teaches, "the mere change of law is of itself prejudicial to the common good because custom avails much for the observance of laws, seeing that what is done contrary to general custom, even in slight matters, is looked upon as grave."[2] In other words, custom equally "avails much" for the proper celebration of the Mass—and, especially, for repeatedly reinforcing the belief of the faithful in its efficacy. Newman aptly notes on this subject:

"To the devotional mind what is new and strange is as repulsive, often as dangerous, as falsehood is to the scientific. Novelty is often error to those who are unprepared for it, from the refraction with which it enters into their conceptions. . . .

"The history of the Latin versions of the Scriptures furnishes a familiar illustration of [the] conflict between popular and educated faith. The Gallican version of the Psalter, St. Jerome's earlier work, got such possession of the West, that to this day we use it instead of his later and more correct version from the Hebrew. Devotional use prevailed over scholastic accuracy in a matter of secondary concern. 'Jerome,' says Dr. Westcott, 'was accused of disturbing the repose of the Church, and shaking the foundations of faith.'"[3]

To regard change as something good in itself as far as liturgy is concerned, therefore, is to misunderstand the nature both of liturgy and of the sacred.

This is not to say that change is never necessary. St. Thomas Aquinas, again, teaches that "on the part of man whose acts are regulated by the law, the law can rightly be changed on account of the *changed condition of man*, to whom different things are expedient according to the difference of his condition" (emphasis added).[4] It was the changed condition of man in the modern world which Pope John XXIII adduced in his "Opening speech to the Council" as the principal reason for convoking Vatican II (See Question #1); and the Council recommended changes intended to respond to the changed condition of man in the modern world.

So it is not true to say that changes, even in the Church's manner of celebrating Mass, are never necessary. The Mass has very often been changed in its externals. A classic like Fr. Joseph Jungmann's *The Mass of the Roman Rite,* or even the same author's shorter, more readable *The Mass,* demonstrates exhaustively the fact of these changes down through the centuries.[5] It is correct to say, however, that when change is required it should be carefully prepared for and explained and carried out with a minimum of disruption—and with an understanding that people can be deeply affected when cherished habits of any kind, but especially habits of worship, are upset.

On the evidence, too few people have understood this as far as the Vatican II changes were concerned. The occasion of the liturgical changes officially instituted by the Church during and following the Council provided all too many such people the opportunity to demonstrate to all and sundry just how little they did understand about liturgy and the sacred all along. Included among such people are not only priests who celebrate in an irreverant or offhand manner, of course, but all the members of the congregations who go along with and favor the new matter-of-fact secularized liturgical atmosphere and the sometimes curious innovations that we have witnessed over the past few years.

Of course we must not exaggerate either. Correctly and reverently celebrated, the New Order of the Mass has been a truly sacred experience for millions of Catholics in many countries; the New Order does constitute a fitting mode of worship of the divine majesty, and this is true even when it is celebrated in the vernacular. Also, many Catholics in countless parishes have been spared some of the more common abuses. The New Order of the Mass in itself is in no way desacralized, as we have shown in some previous sections (e.g., Question #12), though it did suffer the misfortune of being born in a desacralized age. Fair-minded Catholics must admit this even though both the existence of desacralization today and its seriousness must also be admitted by those truly concerned about the future and welfare of the Church.

To some, the "desacralization" that appeared once any changes at all were introduced into the old way of celebrating Mass has *meant* — "Vatican II." No matter that most of what the Council decreed or intended can be readily justified and indeed sounds very good on paper; hardly anybody has read the Council's documents to find out how it all reads on paper. The actual experience of the changeover to the New Order of the Mass thus prompted too many Catholics to begin asking some of the kinds of questions with which we have been obliged to deal at length in these pages.

At a time when the saying, "nothing is sacred any longer," had practically become a proverb, it suddenly seemed to many that — neither was the Church "sacred" any longer. This, of course, is not true. The Church, "with her marvelous propagation, eminent holiness and inexhaustible fruitfulness in everything that is good," remains, as the First Vatican Council taught, "a great and perpetual motive of credibility and an irrefutable testimony of her divine mission."[6]

As we have been at pains to demonstrate, all the anguished questions that have arisen about the Pope, the Council, and the Mass can be answered to the satisfaction of most Catholics; but wouldn't it have been preferable for all if these questions about the changes in Catholic worship and practice desired by the Council had never arisen?

This is merely another way of asking: wouldn't it have been preferable if the Council and the Holy See had been more carefully followed in the implementation of all the changes? Not all of the changes would necessarily have been *liked* any better by some, but at least some of the other radical questions about the licitness, validity, etc., of the *Novus Ordo* might not have arisen; and the exodus into numerous "little churches" might have been avoided.

A careful reading of the excellent collection of official conciliar and post conciliar Church liturgical documents, such as the ones contained in Austin Flannery's *Vatican II: The Conciliar and Post-Conciliar Documents,*[7] will readily satisfy most unprejudiced observers that the Council's ideas about the liturgy are not really so startling or untraditional; many of them constitute a return to *earlier* Church traditions, in fact; many others, such as a greater re-orientation back towards the scriptures and greater participation by the congregation, were recommended by Popes Pius X and Pius XII (See Question #6), were long overdue even then, and are surely now necessary for the renewed task of evangelization which is today especially the task of all Catholics. At the very least, the liturgical reforms envisaged by Vatican II ought to be studied in the Council's documents before they are condemned.

Still the fact remains that, in practice, too many of the Council's reforms have been implemented by people with secularized mentalities in a radically secularized atmosphere. What we have is not always so much "Vatican II," as it is a reflection of the more or less desacralized mentality of today. It is unfortunate that neither the bishops nor, sometimes, even the Roman Congregations themselves, have seemed to notice the effect this kind of liturgy has had, and is still having, on too many Catholics.

Nevertheless, for the record, it is necessary to record that both the Pope and the Roman Congregations, where they perceived that all was not well, more than once attempted to get the Council's liturgical reform back on the tracks in the post-conciliar years. No one can hold that Church authorities were simply oblivious to liturgical aberrations. As early as 1967, Pope Paul VI was saying:

> ". . .cause of concern and sorrow are the disciplinary irregularities in communal worship that have occurred in various places. They frequently are shaped to suit individual whims and often take forms that are wholly at odds with the precepts now in force in the Church. This greatly upsets many upright Church members. Moreover, these innovations are often interlaced with issues that endanger the peace and good order of the Church, issues that must be rejected. They are also harmful because they set an example that sows confusion in people's minds. In this connection, We would remind you of what the Constitution on the Sacred Liturgy has to say about the regulation of the liturgy: 'Regulation of the sacred liturgy depends solely on the authority of the Church' (#22).
>
> "We are even more anxious, however, to express Our hope that bishops will keep a close watch on such episodes, that they will maintain balance and harmony in the Church's liturgical worship and its religious life. Right now, in this post-conciliar period, these areas are objects of special concern and the most tender care.
>
> "We would make the same plea to religious orders, for at

present the Church expects them to aid this cause in a special way by their fidelity and example. We also urge the clergy and all the faithful not to give in to unbridled and free-wheeling experimentation, but rather to perfect and execute the rites prescribed by the Church. . . .

"An even greater source of sorrow is the inclination of some to deprive the liturgy of its sacred character—to 'desacralize' it (if we can even call it liturgy anymore). This necessarily leads to the desacralization of the Christian religion as well. This new outlook whose sordid roots are easy to discern, would destroy authentic Catholic worship. It leads to doctrinal, disciplinary and pastoral subversions of such magnitude that We do not hesitate to consider it deviant. We say this with sadness, not only because it evinces a spirit that runs counter to canon law and that is too caught up with novelty for its own sake, but also, because it necessarily involves the disintegration of religion. . . .

"This danger must be repulsed. Individuals, periodicals and institutions which may be under its spell must be won over again to the cause of the Church and its support. The norms and teachings of the Council must be defended."[8]

In 1970, a Roman Congregation, in a similar vein, issued a notice which specifically attempted to deal with the phenomenon of "desacralization":

"Liturgical reform is not synonymous with so-called *desacralization* and should not be the occasion for what is called the *secularization of the world*. Thus the liturgical rites must retain a dignified and sacred character.

"The effectiveness of liturgical actions does not consist in the continual search for newer rites or simpler forms, but in an ever deeper insight into the word of God and the Mystery which is celebrated. The presence of God will be ensured by following the rites of the Church rather than those inspired by a priest's individual preference" (Notice of the Sacred Congregation for Divine Worship, Third Instruction on the Correct Implementation of the Constitution of the Sacred Liturgy *Liturgiae Instaurationes,* September 5, 1970, #1).

We could quote many other examples of the attempts of the Pope and of the Holy See to deal with the problem of desacralization which was disfiguring the reform desired by the Council; but it must be conceded that attempts to deal with problems on the basis of "authority" alone are seldom successful if none or few of those subject to authority are prepared to follow it. Authority requires acceptance and obedience, if it is to function properly. Presumably, there remains the alternative of expelling from the Church those who do not accept authority and obey it, but, on the evidence, the number would mount up pretty drastically, on all sides, if the Holy See finally resorted to *that* policy!

We must never forget the obvious meaning of Our Lord's Parables of the Kingdom. Surely the Holy See cannot be singled out for blame just because Our Lord's own predictions about the presence of unholy members in His Holy Church prove to be true. The Holy See has tried to enforce discipline, and must sometimes patiently wait for its efforts to take effect. We will quote one more example of the continuing efforts made by the Holy See to remind everyone of the Church's true liturgical norms, if only to show that the Holy See did continue to try to deal with the problem, as it continues to do so today, and can be expected to do in the future:

> ". . .it is to be hoped that pastors of souls, rather than introduce novelties in the texts or rites of the sacred actions, will zealously lead the faithful to greater understanding of the character, the structure and the elements of the celebration and especially of the eucharistic prayer, so that they will take part in the celebrations more fully and with greater awareness. The power of the liturgy does not consist merely in the novelty and the variety of the elements, but rather in a more profound sharing in the mystery of salvation, present and active in the liturgical action. Only in this way can the faithful, professing the same faith and offering to God the same prayer, save themselves and their brethren" (Circular Letter on Eucharistic Prayers *Eucharistiae Participationem,* #19, Sacred Congregation for Divine Worship, April 27, 1973).

Before simply concluding from shock or dislike of the "changes" that the liturgical "fruits" from Vatican II have now ripened and in fact have rotted on the tree, and that nothing will do but to conclude that the Council and its "reforms" were all a ghastly mistake, we should remind ourselves: 1) that most of the "fruits" in question can be shown to have resulted from *not* following the Council's prescriptions rather than from following them; and that 2) a period of turbulence and confusion followed many Councils in the past—including Nicaea, Ephesus, Chalcedon, Lyons, Florence, and Trent.

The comprehensive *Cambridge Medieval History* notes the following about the Council of Nicaea, for example, the First General Council of the Church, which assembled in 325 A.D.:

> "The great experiment was not an immediate success: the Nicene council rather opened than closed the history of Arianism on the larger stage, and it was not till after the lapse of half a century that wisdom was seen to be justified of its own works, though the very keenness of the struggle made the long delayed and hardly won triumph more complete in the end.[9]

For any who will reflect for a moment, it was precisely during the period *following* the Council of Nicaea that the great St. Athanasius, the "Father of Orthodoxy," had to do his lifetime work in defense of the faith (See Question #19). Far from the work for orthodoxy having been done *by* the Council, it fell to the faithful, especially the laity, under the inspiring leadership of St. Athanasius, to uphold the decisions of the Council[10]; and, in this respect, Nicaea was not all that different from Vatican II. What if the faithful had concluded from the initial evident bad "fruits" of the Council of Nicaea that the Council itself was illegitimate? Where would St. Athanasius have been without the support of the faithful?

The battle was not against those who favored and upheld the Council of Nicaea but against those who didn't, whatever their pretention to do so. St. Athanasius' entire life was devoted to vindicating the decisions of the Council which he had attended as a young deacon. And the obstacles he faced were not so different from the obstacles we face today in getting accepted the true teaching of Vatican II in the place of the false and mythical "spirit of Vatican II" that some have propagated in their own interest in the post-conciliar period. St. Athanasius had to contend with exactly the same problem; he took note in one of his writings of those within the Church who were actually enemies of the Church and who, in his words, were "unwilling that the decrees of the Council should be enforced; they desire to enforce their own decisions; and they use the name of the Council. . . ."[11]

It is not a new thing in the Church, in other words, that those within the Church disloyal to her authentic teachings and rulings, should try to use "the name of the Council" for their own ends; it didn't start with Vatican II; this phenomenon goes all the way back to the First General Council of the Church at the beginning of the fourth century. Things similar to what we have experienced since Vatican II—and much worse—can be documented in the periods following many of the other general councils in the history of the Church.

The Council of Ephesus in Asia Minor, the Third General Council of the Church, ended in a hopeless deadlock, with two major factions of the Eastern bishops of the Church mutually excommunicating each other. Although the doctrinal issue was settled later between the two Patriarchs of Antioch and Alexandria, the bitter theological passions aroused led not only to the famous false "Robber Council," also held at Ephesus, at which the Pope himself (Pope St. Leo I) was "excommunicated," but also led, before a full twenty years had passed, to the convocation of still another legitimate general council to try to deal with the "fruits" of the one before.[12]

This latter convocation, the Council of Chalcedon, convened across the Bosphorus from Constantinople in 451 A.D., issued the cadenced, lucid, and majestic definition on the human and divine natures joined in one divine Person of Our Blessed Lord which has endured in the Church to this day: "Perfect in divinity and perfect in humanity, the same truly God and truly man, always the same composed of rational soul and body, the same one in being with the Father as to the divinity and one in being with us as to His humanity, like unto us in all things but sin (Cf. *Heb.* 4:15). . .begotten from the Father before all ages as to divinity and in the latter days for us and our salvation was born as to His humanity from Mary, the Virgin Mother of God."[13]

No Catholic can doubt, judging from this definition, that the Holy Spirit was truly present at the Council of Chalcedon—as the Holy Spirit was also present at Ephesus earlier in 431 at the Council where Mary's divine motherhood was defined. These doctrinal fruits are evident in the case of both of these Councils. Yet some of the other evident "fruits" of each of them did not quite as evidently stem from the Holy Spirit. From this we ought to perhaps learn a bit of caution when we begin talking about what the "fruits" of a particular council might be: men, even Catholic prelates, may regrettably exhibit "all-too-human" weaknesses, but God can bring good even out of *them*, though we sometimes have to give Him time

—and though He also wants *us* to help make reparation.

Following Chalcedon, large-scale schisms resulted among the Eastern-rite churches due to misunderstandings of conciliar teachings or resistance to them—again, a case of refusing to follow a council, not of following one. The "misunderstanding" following the Council of Chalcedon resulted in the propagation of the Monophysite heresy, in fact, which has endured for more than 1500 years, separating the Coptic, Ethiopian, Armenian and Jacobite churches from Catholic unity for most of those centuries. When we consider that the doctrinal or theological points at issue turn chiefly upon an "interpretation" of the theology of St. Cyril of Alexandria, we are entitled to hope that maybe Vatican II's laudable efforts in ecumenism may result in seeing if such "misunderstandings" cannot possibly be cleared up.

After the Council of Trent the dogmatic and disciplinary decrees of the Council which had met to reform the Church in head and members were widely ignored, for instance, by the parliament of the most powerful Catholic nation, France, which was to be later plagued by violent religious controversies over the spread of Jansenism and Gallicanism. After the Thirty Years War (1618-1648), the Church in nearly all the states of Europe had fallen victim to Royal Absolutism, and in the words of the historian Philip Hughes, "the year 1789 found the Catholic religion everywhere in chains, in the various European states, its vitality low indeed after generations of captivity to the Catholic kings." In the words of another historian commenting on the extraordinary vitality infused into the Body of the Church by the Council of Trent, "the apostasy from the Catholic Church in the sixteenth century was followed in the seventeenth and eighteenth centuries by wholesale apostasy from Christianity itself."[14]

It is not true, in other words, that the "fruits" of a council all have to be evidently good before we can judge that council to be good—for unbelief and apostasy in the world saw an unprecedented growth in the centuries following the Council of Trent, even though that Council accomplished what could be accomplished, given the situation. But we—and the Church—are still attempting to deal with the consequences of that widespread unbelief and apostasy from Christianity that has grown up in spite of the Tridentine reforms. Pope John XXIII called the Second Vatican Council in an attempt to begin to devise ways to deal with today's massive unbelief and paganism (See Question #1).

Even the First Vatican Council, which now seems to us so much a timeless part of the Church's Tradition, was in its own day regarded with considerable anxiety by some who feared for a Church increasingly exposed to the growing aggression of nationalistic and secularistic states. Reassuring one such "alarmist," John Henry Newman, in a private letter, admitted that it was a "serious precedent" that Vatican I should have defined the dogma of the infallibility of the Pope "without definite and urgent cause." There are those today who reproach Pope John XXIII for similarly having summoned a general council without, as these critics see it, what Newman called "a definite and urgent cause." Some of these critics not only feel vindicated by the confusion which has followed Vatican II; some of them even go so far as to imagine that this confusion somehow invalidates the acts of the Council, a notion we have shown to be without foundation in our answer to Question #2.

Cardinal Newman pointed out to his friend fearful of the possible bad effects of Vatican I, however, what we have established here, namely, that, in Newman's own words, "there has seldom been a Council without great confusion after it—so it was even with the first—so it was with the third, fourth, and fifth—and the sixth which condemned Pope Honorius" (See Question #22). In spite of that, Newman counseled his friend, basing his statement on his own vast knowledge of the history of the Church especially in her earlier centuries, "God will provide."[15] If necessary, God will make up for what men have done wrong. God does not hold us responsible for whatever may occur at or after one of the Church's councils (except for our docility towards it). God does not ask it of us to judge of any council's fruits when, in the nature of things, we cannot live long enough to evaluate them in full perspective.

It is essential that the words of Our Lord "By their fruits you shall know them" (*Lk.* 6:43-45) be applied with discernment. They certainly do not mean that the "learning Church" is assigned to sit in judgment on the "teaching Church."

In any case, the lessons of history indicate that a longer-range perspective is called for before we can justify a charge of evil "fruits" against the Second Vatican Council. We have to give the Council time. It still remains to be carried out. And with respect to the "discernment of spirits" underlying any valid application of the principle "By their fruits you shall know them" we should remember that the discernment carried out by the hierarchical Magisterium centered in Peter is to be preferred to that of any private judgment. Here the testimonies of both John Paul I and John Paul II, each of whom, at the beginning of his pontificate, unhesitatingly reaffirmed his loyalty to the Council and his intention of carrying out its program (See Question #1), assumes a very great importance. We must go forward with the Pope(s) we have, if we are going to remain truly Catholic.

That better fruits have not yet come from the conciliar reform— so many have: the picture is far from black- can be laid at the door of those who have failed to implement the liturgical reforms properly. Proper implementation of the reforms has also been interfered with by doctrinal deviations. That favorable results have been *slower* and less dramatic than we might have wished is but confirmation of Our Lord's Parable of the Leaven: "To what shall I compare the Kingdom of God? It is like leaven, which a woman took and buried in three measures of meal, till it was all leavened" (*Lk.* 13:20-21). Not only does leaven work slowly and silently, but it clearly depends upon a measure of necessary human cooperation (the kneading of the dough). Other parables of Our Lord would be equally appropriate to cite in this connection.

We have already mentioned that some members of the hierarchy have been less than realistic in measuring the extent to which liturgical aberrations and irregularities have scandalized many of their faithful. Bishops are not immune from pastoral failures in this or in other areas. However, such liturgical abuses and other evidences of desacralization are, we must repeat, clearly due to the *nonobservance* of the liturgical reforms officially decreed. They are in contradiction to the many statements in conciliar and post-conciliar documents insisting upon the precise observance of liturgical norms.

But in the face of all this as in the face of the other problems that will always confront us in this life, Christ still asks us for *faith*— and still asks us to take up His cross with regard to the liturgy too if that is what is involved. Christ did not tell us that our faith in Him and His promises was supposed to be based on how well things were going in His Church. On the contrary, in many different ways, our Lord made clear that His followers must expect the *kind* of setbacks and reverses that those who have tried to be loyal to Christ over the past few years have in fact suffered. And it does not matter in the least that we are made to suffer by things happening *within* the Church; it is still our obligation to keep on following Christ to the best of our ability. As a practical matter, this means following the Pope and the Council even if it means suffering for us. The witness of suffering still is highly meritorious for the faithful Catholic who in this manner "will complete what is lacking in Christ's afflictions for the sake of His Body, that is, the Church" (*Col.* 1:24).

Just as we concluded the answer to Questions #15 and #16 with quotations from St. John Bosco and Pope St. Pius X about the disposition which the Catholic faithful should adopt towards a Pope, so we may usefully conclude this section with a quotation from St. Francis de Sales on the attitude we Catholics should adopt towards a general council of the Church:

> ". . . at general councils there are many lively debates and a profound search for the truth through reasoning, theological argument and council interventions; however, once a subject has been debated, it is up to the council fathers, that is to say, the bishops, to decide—to reach a conclusion, to determine the mind of the council. Once their determination has been made, everyone should then acquiesce in it and accept it, not because of the arguments that were advanced in favor of the final determination, or the research which preceded it, but rather because of the authority of the Holy Spirit.
>
> "Invisibly presiding at general councils, the Holy Spirit it is Who really judges and determines by means of the mouths of those of His servants who have been established by Him as the Pastors of Christendom.
>
> "All the reasoning, theological argument and council interventions are made, as it were, in front of the Church; while the actual decisions and determinations of the council fathers are made in the sanctuary, where the Holy Spirit does speak through the mouths of the visible heads of the local Churches, just as Jesus Christ promised."[16]

Thus, St. Francis de Sales, a Doctor of the Church—who shows himself possessed of the simple faith of a child which Christ asks of all of us.

Question # 18

WHY CANNOT THE POPE ALLOW THE LATIN TRI-DENTINE MASS, FOR THOSE WHO PREFER IT, ALONGSIDE THE NEW ORDER OF THE MASS?

In the experience of the authors, no question is asked more frequently than this question by those who in one degree or another are concerned about or are tempted to reject the course the Church has been following since Vatican II. One encouraging thing about the way the question is framed is that the Pope's authority to decide which Mass or Masses may be celebrated seems to be implicitly recognized in it. This, after all, is the key issue of the whole traditionalist question.

To the question, strictly taken, then, of whether the Pope could allow the Tridentine Mass to be said alongside of the *Novus Ordo*, the answer would have to be that, for good and sufficient reasons, he could—as far as the simple question of which Mass he might allow is concerned. There are those who do not question the validity of the *Novus Ordo* but who value the beauty and venerable character of the Tridentine Mass and would like to see retained in the Church this great treasure, which was normative for the Church for so many centuries; they believe it ought to be restored even if not fully on a par with the New Order of Mass, at least it should be allowed now and then; certainly it should not be prohibited or "banned." According to this way of thinking, it seems scandalous to some that what the Church *required* for so many years could now be forbidden; so it is thought that perhaps the Tridentine Mass could be said at least on special occasions.

Now it seems clear that not only could the Pope allow a partial restoration of the Tridentine Mass in this fashion; Pope Paul VI did that very thing in giving an indult to the hierarchy of England and Wales to allow the celebration of Tridentine Masses on special occasions. Whether Pope John Paul II might extend that kind of privilege—or whether it would satisfy large numbers of traditionalists if he did—is a matter that remains unclear at the moment of writing. But for pastoral reasons and for the good of the Church the Pope certainly could allow the old Roman Missal to be used.

To the extent that he readmitted the Tridentine Mass as a regular "option" for the *Novus Ordo*, however, we must be clear in our minds about *what* the Pope would then be doing: he would be exempting those who chose to exercise their "option" of attending a Tridentine Mass from the liturgical reforms requested by a general council of the Church. Vatican Council II did decree, *inter alia*, that:

> "The rite of the Mass is to be revised in such a way that the intrinsic nature and purpose of its several parts, as well as the connection between them, may be more clearly manifested, and that devout and active participation by the faithful may be more easily achieved.
>
> "For this purpose the rites are to be simplified, due care being taken to preserve their substance. Parts which with the passage of time came to be duplicated, or were added with little advantage, are to be omitted. Other parts which suffered loss through accidents of history are to be restored to the vigor they had in the days of the holy Fathers, as may seem useful or necessary" (Constitution on the Sacred Liturgy *Sacrosanctum Concilium*, #50).

The revised Roman Missal published in 1969 represented the results of the Holy See's efforts to fulfil this mandate of the Council. To restore the use of the older, unrevised Roman Missal alongside the new, revised one would not only mean going back on what the Council, after long deliberation, desired as regards the liturgy; it could also re-inaugurate a new round of liturgical confusion among the great mass of the faithful. The New Order of the Mass in the vernacular is now what the faithful are accustomed to, just as they were accustomed to the Tridentine Mass in Latin when all the original "changes" began. If serious consequences have come from upsetting the habits of worship of the faithful without careful preparation and explanation—and the whole phenomenon of "traditionalism" to which this book has been addressing itself testifies to the seriousness of some of the consequences of liturgical change— then the possible consequences of still more changes, even those aimed at a restoration of the Tridentine Mass, would surely have to be carefully considered in the light of the Church's experience with the changes that have been made up to now. It could not be excluded that a restoration of the Tridentine Mass alongside the *Novus Ordo* could help split the unity of the Roman rite which the old Roman Missal of Pope St. Pius V originally did so much to bring about (See Question #4).

None of this is to say, however, that the Pope could not for pastoral reasons admit both the old and the new Missals—the old becoming a kind of separate "rite," as it were. There is no intrinsic reason, in the nature of things, why the old Missal could not be used alongside the new Missal; why the Tridentine Mass could not be permitted by Church authority as an alternate rite for those bishops, priests and laity so desiring it and requesting it of the Supreme Pontiff. This is a matter of Church discipline and government; and if the common good of the Church would seem to warrant such a departure from the traditional liturgical uniformity characteristic of the Roman rite, it could doubtless be considered and granted by the Roman Pontiff. Whether it will or not is another question.

We cannot leave this subject, however, without taking note of the fact that a request to allow the Tridentine Mass alongside the *Novus Ordo* was actually made to Pope Paul VI by Archbishop Marcel Lefebvre. One of the things that Archbishop Lefebvre requested of Pope Paul VI when the Archbishop visited the Pope in September, 1976, was this right to celebrate the Tridentine Mass alongside the *Novus Ordo*. "You would like to see recognized the right to celebrate Mass in various places of worship according to the Tridentine rite," the Pope responded to the Archbishop later, on October 11, 1976. "You wish also to continue to train candidates for the priesthood according to your criteria 'as before the Council,' in seminaries apart, as at Econe."

The answer that the Pope gave for being obliged to decline the request was an interesting one; he did not say that the Tridentine Mass could never be celebrated alongside the New Order of the Mass; but he pointed out that those who desire this appear to desire it on grounds that are incompatible with the loyalty to the Church required of Catholics. It is not merely a matter of preferring the old and disliking the new, sincerely believing that the old had a sacred character superior to the new; it involves the rejection of the new on the grounds that it is not "Catholic," that the supreme authority of the Catholic Church has attempted to impose on the faithful a rite contrary to Catholic Tradition; and this, in turn, involves the judgment that a Pope and a general council of the Church did, in fact, depart from Tradition. The slogan of at least some of the Traditionalists has been, in fact, "Give us back the Catholic Mass!"

The problem is not just liturgical, in other words: the problem is theological. The problem is not just "pastoral," it is doctrinal. It involves the faith itself and the necessity that Catholics accept *on* faith and *in* obedience what the competent authority in the Church legitimately teaches and decrees, in disciplinary as well as doctrinal matters. We have already shown that this is the attitude which, according to strict Catholic Tradition, Catholics must adopt towards the teachings and decisions of a general council of the Church (Question #2) and towards those of a Pope (Questions #3 and #8). We have further illustrated the *disposition* with which Catholics ought to accept the decisions of a Pope (Questions #15 and #16) and those of a general council (Question #17).

"What is indeed at issue," Pope Paul VI wrote to Archbishop Lefebvre:

> ". . . is the question—which must truly be called fundamental —of your clearly proclaimed refusal to recognize in its entirety, the authority of the Second Vatican Council and that of the Pope. This refusal is accompanied by an action that is orientated towards propagating and organizing what must indeed, unfortunately, be called a rebellion. This is the essential issue, and it is truly undeniable . . . .
>
> "A single bishop without a canonical mission does not have . . . the faculty of deciding in general what the rule of faith is or of determining what Tradition is. In practice you are claiming that you alone are the judge of what Tradition embraces. You say that you are subject to the Church and faithful to Tradition by the sole act that you obey certain norms of the past that were decreed by the predecessors of him to whom God has today conferred the powers given to Peter. That is to say, on this point also, the concept of 'Tradition' that you invoke is distorted."

Pope Paul VI's letter of October 11, 1976, from which this passage is taken, is of such importance in explaining the real issues and the attitude taken by Church authority with regard to the traditionalists that we are reprinting it *in toto* in Appendix IV. Anyone who believes that Church authority has been unjust towards the traditionalists owes it to himself to study carefully the complete text of this 1976 letter of Pope Paul VI to Archbishop Lefebvre; it is a document which, if it had become adequately known when it was first issued, could have precluded much of the confusion over the Archbishop Lefebvre case which has unfortunately prevailed.

For this is not just a matter of one Pope declining to accede to traditionalist desires because his own personal stewardship of the papacy is called into question by the requests made of him; this is a matter of Tradition and of the authority of the Catholic Church as it has always been understood in the true sense.

And this is at bottom a doctrinal question, not merely a disciplinary question; it involves the teaching of the Church on the obedience which all Catholics owe to the legitimate acts of the Church's divinely-constituted authority. Although the Council and the Holy See decreed and carried out far-reaching changes in the Church's life and worship (proving thereby, in fact, that such things *could* be changed), no Pope and no council will ever change Catholic *doctrine* on the nature of true authority in the Church and on the obedience of the faithful which is owed to it for the simple reason that they *cannot* change it.

The position that every Pope must take towards those who remove themselves from the authority of the Catholic Church and constitute themselves in some "little church" of their own is the position that Leo XIII took towards one of the "little churches" which found wanting the leadership of the Church in his day:

"Its members pretend that their sole preoccupation is to affirm the proper and original right of the Church, that they have nothing more at heart than to protect her liberty from every hostile action. . . .

"It is certainly true that no man of good sense will ever believe that some private individuals or some bishops have more at heart the rights and liberty of the Church than has the Holy See itself, the Mother and Mistress of all the Churches. Or that in order to procure this good, the Roman Church needs to be prodded by those who, in order to be and to be held as good Catholics, owe the Roman Church submission and obedience before all else. . . .

"Therefore, there can be no legitimate cause for these men, whoever were the first leaders of those concerned today, to be separated from the most holy communion of the Catholic world. Let them not rely on the upright quality of their conduct, not on their fidelity to discipline, not on their zeal in safeguarding teaching and stability in religion. Does not the Apostle

say plainly that without charity all this profiteth nothing?
(I *Cor.* 13:3). . . .

"From this it follows also that they cannot promise themselves any of the graces and fruits of the perpetual sacrifice and
of the sacraments which, although they are sacrilegiously administered, are nonetheless valid and serve in some measure
that form and appearance of piety which St. Paul mentions
and which St. Augustine speaks of at greater length : 'The form
of the branch,' says the latter with great precision, 'may still be
visible, even apart from the vine, but the invisible life of the root
can be preserved only in union with the stock. That is why the
corporal sacraments, which some keep and use outside the unity
of Christ, can preserve the appearance of piety. But the invisible
and spiritual virtue of true piety cannot abide there any more
than feeling can remain in an amputated member'" (Serm.
LXXI, in *Mt.*, 32).[1]

Those who have rejected the New Order of the Mass and the
authority of the Church to impose it may have sometimes preserved
"the appearance of piety"—but many of them have also thereby
cut themselves off from the Church. Although the Pope could restore
the old Roman Missal as a pastoral option, he could surely never
admit as the *reason* for doing it the belief that the Church has
established something less than "Catholic" in the *Novus Ordo*.

WHY HAS THERE BEEN SUCH TOLERANCE IN THE CHURCH FOR MODERNIST AND LIBERAL DISSENTERS AND SUCH SEVERITY TOWARDS ARCHBISHOP MARCEL LEFEBVRE AND OTHERS WHO PREFER THE TRIDENTINE MASS?

In July, 1976, Pope Paul VI suspended retired Archbishop Marcel Lefebvre *a divinis*, that is, from all priestly functions, after the latter had ordained thirteen seminarians at the Seminary he had founded in Econe, Switzerland, disobeying a specific order from the Holy Father that he *not* ordain them. Subsequently, Archbishop Lefebvre has ordained still other priests and deacons in defiance of the Pope, including some three dozen of them since the election of Pope John Paul II.[1] The Archbishop publicly declared that he was "encouraged" by the fact that Pope John Paul II did not immediately condemn these ordinations.[2]

In addition, against the wishes of other bishops—and in contravention of canon law, it must, sadly, be said—Archbishop Lefebvre several times has entered their dioceses in Europe, North America, and Latin America to administer various sacraments as well as to celebrate the Tridentine Mass for those refusing to accept the Pope's authority in the matter of the *Novus Ordo*. Although the Masses celebrated thus were no doubt "valid" because the Archbishop is validly ordained, they were clearly not "licit," as local ordinaries have often had to point out publicly.[3] Insofar as he has heard confessions where he had no jurisdiction, he—like the priests of other "little churches"—may *not* have conferred a valid absolution, since, in the case of confession the minister must have jurisdiction for validity, except in cases of danger of death.[4]

In addition to functioning without regard to the authority of the Pope, or the local bishop, or canon law, the Archbishop has also made it quite clear in his many writings, speeches and acts that he does not fully accept various decrees of the Second Vatican Council since he believes they embody what he considers to be doctrinal errors opposed to Catholic apostolic Tradition.

He has been quoted as saying: "The criterion of truth in the Church is Tradition. In doubtful cases, it is there we must look."[5] However, judging by his actions in ignoring the Pope and the Council, he seems to forget the important "Tradition" that Catholics are *subject* to the Pope and to councils of the Church. There is no instructed Catholic who can really plead ignorance of the *defined* doctrine of the Pope's supreme authority in the Church; assent to his teachings and obedience to his decrees are consequently owed to him by all Catholics, as we have already seen (Questions #3 and #8). All Catholics are similarly subject to the decisions of ecumenical councils, as we have also seen (Question #2). Indeed the great Pope Pius XII ventured to teach that it is Christ Himself, "Who, even if He is not seen presides over the councils of the Church and directs them with His light" (Encyclical *Mystici Corporis*, #50).

Thus, to accuse the Pope and an ecumenical council of promoting errors in faith is a position which is impossible to reconcile with professing the traditional Catholic faith. There can be no justification on traditional grounds for a Catholic bishop to defy the legitimate authority of the Roman Pontiff and to reject doctrines of an ecumenical council; no bishop doing it could possibly be acting for Him who was "obedient unto death, even death on a Cross" (*Phil.* 2:8). Moreover, in setting himself up as the judge of what belongs to the unchangeable Catholic Tradition and what does not, Archbishop Lefebvre is again usurping a role that properly belongs to the Church herself (See Questions #6 and #18).

Following the election of the Polish Cardinal Karol Wojtyla as Pope John Paul II, Archbishop Lefebvre, along with many other traditionalists, began to talk about accepting Vatican Council II "interpreted according to Catholic Tradition." He even claimed that in the meeting he had with Pope John Paul II in Rome in November, 1978, the Pontiff "approved" of this new formula of his.[6] However, unless the Archbishop admits that Tradition is authentically interpreted only by the authority of the Church, he has not really adopted any new position here; if he insists upon the right or prerogative of interpreting Tradition himself, according to his own private judgment, he will still be out of line, and nothing will turn out to have been settled by his adoption of this new formula.

It is possible to understand and to sympathize with a "reaction" against the errors and abuses that have become manifest within the Catholic Church in the post-conciliar years; however, the "reaction" of Archbishop Lefebvre and of some other traditionalists has surely been wide of the mark in ascribing these errors and abuses to the Second Vatican Council and to the Pope rather than to the individuals responsible for them. It is even possible to understand and sympathize with the view that too many of the errors and abuses that have surfaced have gone *uncorrected*; it has been a mystery to many of the faithful how much certain people, especially certain theologians, have been able to get away with in the post-conciliar years. How can the mass media notice that things have almost gotten out of hand in the Church—as in the *Life* magazine article of a few years ago entitled "The Pope's Unruly Flock"—while some members of the sacred hierarchy of the Church charged with correcting such situations apparently do not notice that things have almost gotten out of hand, or, at any rate, often show little sign, year after year, of wanting to do anything about what for the average instructed Catholic can only be scandalous? This has been a mystery for many of the faithful—but it does *not* justify any Catholic in removing himself from the legitimate authority of the hierarchy of the Church. After all, in what do errors and abuses consist, by whomever committed, but in teaching or acting apart from what the sacred hierarchy has decided?

Archbishop Lefebvre has been compared by some of his admirers to St. Athanasius, the great fourth century champion of orthodoxy against the Arians. But this great Doctor of the Church devoted his whole life to (and was persecuted for) *upholding* the teachings and rulings of the ecumenical Council of Nicaea (325 A.D.)—during a period when many, including many bishops, acceding to intense pressures from the Roman emperors and Roman society of the times, agreed in one degree or another to hold the Council as of no account. During the period following the Council of Nicaea, in fact, perhaps a majority of the Catholic bishops in the East, some under pressure from the state, came to depart in one degree or another from Nicene orthodoxy. This was the period of which St. Jerome remarked that the whole world woke and groaned to find itself Arian.[7] Yet assembled in a new general council, the Council of Constantinople which convened in 381, many of these same arianizing bishops ended up upholding Nicene orthodoxy after all—a striking example, indeed, that 1) turmoil can follow a general council and many can err or fall away, even bishops; but that 2) general councils do enjoy the protection of the Holy Spirit against heresy![8]

By not fully accepting the Second Vatican Council, Archbishop Lefebvre thus forgets that the inerrancy of general councils in those of their teachings confirmed by a Pope is one of the most important of all Catholic Traditions. St. Athanasius never challenged the authority of the reigning Popes of his time. Indeed, it was through the steadfast determination of the Roman Pontiffs that Athanasian orthodoxy finally triumphed over the heresies, deceptions and cruelties of the Arian party seeking to shred the Mystical Body of Christ.

St. Athanasius consistently sought the support of the Popes of his day in his battle for orthodoxy. At one point he appealed to Pope Saint Julius and even fled to Rome for refuge; he was vindicated by the latter, and they forged an alliance. Later on it was St. Athanasius who persuaded Pope St. Damasus to act against the Arians and his successor as Archbishop of Alexandria, his own brother Peter, was obliged to flee to Pope Damasus in Rome for refuge, just as, more than thirty years earlier, St. Athanasius had fled to Pope Julius for the same reason. (See also Question #18).[9]

Thus Archbishop Lefebvre's supporters can in no way liken him to a modern St. Athanasius; the analogy doesn't fit.

It has often been asked what is wrong with Archbishop Lefebvre's teaching seminarians exactly "as all seminarians were trained prior to Vatican II." The answer to this has to be that all Catholic seminarians before Vatican II were taught, e.g., the primacy of the Pope, the binding nature of the decisions of an ecumenical council, the ordinary jurisdiction of Catholic bishops within their own sees, the authority of the Church over both sacred Scripture and sacred Tradition, etc. All Catholic seminarians before Vatican II, in other words, were trained to be loyal to the Church with the Pope at the head of it, in the memorable words of Cardinal Journet (See Question #14). That is not the way Archbishop Lefebvre's seminarians have been trained; they are being trained in a "Church" not under the jurisdiction of the Pope; this is *not* "traditional" seminary training.

We are going over all this ground not to draw up an indictment against Archbishop Lefebvre. In fact, we have deliberately avoided mentioning the Archbishop to the extent possible in this work (although, needless to say, it has not been entirely possible) because we have wanted to focus on issues, not on personalities.

However, it has been necessary in a work on this subject to face the questions of Archbishop Lefebvre and to review the Archbishop's position if only in order to make the point, with respect to the Holy See's "severity" towards him, that, however he may have been provoked, the Archbishop has, unfortunately, committed some serious breaches of Catholic Church law and custom. Even his supporters

have to concede that. Whatever the solution to *l'affaire Lefebvre* —
and the authors still hope and pray for a reconciliation at the time of
writing—the Archbishop's true situation will have to be taken
into account. According to his own lights, his own position has been
a highly irregular one. Pope Paul VI was obliged to remark truly, if
sadly, "Our predecessors to whose discipline he presumes to appeal
would not have tolerated a disobedience as obstinate as it is pernicious for so long a period as we have patiently done" (Pope Paul VI,
Address to the Consistory of Cardinals, June 27, 1977).[10] However,
it is worthy of note that, while he lived, Pope Paul VI never resorted
to his ultimate canonical weapon: excommunication; nor, at the time
of this writing, has Pope John Paul II taken or even hinted at any
such action. Thus it is hard to argue that the Holy See has been unduly severe with him.

Where doubts about his treatment seem to arise in the minds of
many, however, these doubts do not so much concern the measures
which the Pope reluctantly and after considerable hesitation took
against Archbishop Lefebvre, tempering these measures, in the case
of both Paul VI and John Paul II, with a willingness to meet with the
Archbishop and discuss his case further. The doubts arise, rather,
from the belief that *while* the Holy See did finally move against
him, a traditionalist, it has consistently *failed* to move against the
modernists, the progressives and the dissenters "on the left." The
Holy See—like those bishops who are quick to issue statements
against traditionalist chapels but to ignore dissent against *Humanae
Vitae* among their priests and flocks—is seen by some to be following a double standard: severity towards the traditionalists, indulgence
towards the progressives. It is, of course, much more difficult to
maintain this thesis since the Holy See moved decisively in late 1979
to investigate the work of theologian Fr. Edward Schillebeeckx; and,
even more decisively, revoked Fr. Hans Küng's mandate to teach
theology. Nevertheless some still do maintain that Church authority
is consistently harder on the traditionalists than it is on the progressives. To the extent that such a double standard truly exists, it is
easy to understand how it would cause resentment.

Let us examine, then, this charge of a double standard, especially
as regards the actions of the Holy See (and those whom the Holy
See has been able to influence). We have remarked already that we
live in a period when it is surprising how much theologians speaking
against the Church's teachings can get away with. Nevertheless it
is not true that only dissenters on the "right" have been the object

of discipline by Church authorities; what is true is that until the cases of Fathers Schillebeeckx and Küng came along some of the cases of those on the "left" did not have the same media interest as the case of Archbishop Lefebvre and hence were not publicized to the same extent.

However, there was a great stir caused in Italy in 1975, for example, when the Vatican deposed the Archbishop of Ravenna, Salvatore Baldassarri, aged 68, the so-called "Red Archbishop," and appointed Monsignor Ersilio Tonini official Administrator for Ravenna to replace him; Archbishop Baldassarri had begun carrying on "a continuous dialogue with workers, visiting strikers and holding opinions in questions of celibacy and divorce diverging from those of the Vatican."[11] The Marxist theologian Fr. Giulio Girardi was similarly removed in 1975 from his teaching post by his Salesian superior and later suspended *a divinis* by the Holy See.[12]

A much more important case, in view of the rank of the ecclesiastic involved, concerned Don Giovanni Battista Franzoni, Abbot of the Roman Basilica of St. Paul's Outside the Walls. Abbot Franzoni was first suspended *a divinis* and later defrocked by his monastic superiors by order of the Pope for publicly promoting Marxist class warfare, rejecting the teaching of the Holy See on *Humanae Vitae*, and disputing the Church's doctrine on the indissolubility of marriage; a Vatican decree on August 4, 1976, reduced the ex-Abbot Franzoni to the lay state—a more severe punishment than Archbishop Lefebvre's suspension *a divinis*.

Again in 1975, under fire from the Vatican, the Swiss Dominican Stephan Pfürtner, O.P., who contradicted the Church's teaching on contraception, abortion, divorce and homosexuality, was similarly obliged to resign his prestigious post as professor of moral theology at the venerable Catholic University of Fribourg, Switzerland. He later applied for laicization.[13]

Other not well-publicized actions against leftist dissenters concerned, for example, the case of Bishop Francesco Tortora of Gerace-Rocco in Calabria who suspended *a divinis* the leftist pastor of San Rocco, Don Natale Bianchi, and put the whole parish under interdict. The Vicar-General of the Pope for the Diocese of Rome, took a similar action against the pastor of the Roman parish of the Nativity, Don Luigi Dalla Torre. Four Marxist professors, Frs. Brugnoli, Diaz-Alegria, Pin, and Tuffari were dismissed from the Jesuit Gregorian University in Rome. Cardinal Siri of Genoa and Cardinal Florit of

Florence also took decisive action against various priests and religious influenced by Marxist ideology.[14]

Much closer to home for North American Catholics, was the action of the Sacred Congregation for the Doctrine of the Faith which, in the summer of 1977, sent a letter to the Superior General of the Society of Jesus, the Rev. Pedro Arrupe, S.J., ordering the *Imprimi potest* removed from the book *The Church and the Homosexual* by Fr. John McNeil, S.J. The Sacred Congregation declared in its letter that:

> "We find it extraordinary that a book so clearly contradicting the moral teaching of the Church would be published a few days after the publication of *Persona Humana* [Vatican Declaration on Certain Questions Concerning Sexual Ethics], a document of this Congregation treating in part of the same question."[15]

In the summer of 1979, the Sacred Congregation for the Doctrine of the Faith similarly ruled that the controversial book *Human Sexuality*, a work originally commissioned by the Catholic Theological Society of America, contained fundamental errors and invited the five authors of the book to correct these errors. The views expressed in the book had also been criticized and disavowed by the U.S. bishops' committee on doctrine when the book first appeared.[16] In spite of this condemnation by Rome *and* the U.S. bishops' doctrine committee, this book *Human Sexuality* has in the minds of many served as a prime example of blatant, gross error going publicly uncorrected by the authorities of the Church. But, in some cases of this kind at least, it may simply be a matter of the time it takes for the authorities to get around to dealing with a particular book or theologian — Rome traditionally has been both cautious and deliberate in such matters — or with the fact that the media never publicize salutary acts of authority to the same extent as sensational dissent.

But other examples could nevertheless be given where Rome or those Rome has been able to prevail upon have disciplined progressivist or leftist priests and professors challenging Church discipline or doctrine. In July, 1977, a liberal Swiss newspaper even complained that the Pope was handling the "traditionalists" with kid gloves while being unduly harsh towards liberals![17]

Other examples could also be given of prelates in other countries who have courageously disciplined rebels against Catholic teaching. Pope Paul VI, for example, was unremitting in encouraging bishops to uproot the "epidemic of errors" diminishing the credibility of the Catholic Church before the world.

For example, in his December 8, 1970, Apostolic Exhortation to the Bishops of the World Commemorating the Fifth Anniversary of the Close of the Second Vatican Council, the Pope urged:

> "Dearly beloved brothers, let us not be reduced to silence for fear of criticism, which is always possible and may at times be well-founded. However necessary the function of theologians, it is not to the learned that God has confided the duty of authentically interpreting the faith of the Church: that faith is borne by the life of the people whose bishops are responsible for them before God. It is for the bishop to tell the people what God asks them to believe.
>
> "This demands much courage of each one of us. . . . This is not the time to ask ourselves, as some would have us do, whether it is really useful, opportune and necessary to speak; rather it is the time for us to take the means to make ourselves heard. For it is to us bishops that St. Paul's exhortation to Timothy is addressed: 'Before God and before Jesus Christ who is to be the judge of the living and the dead, I put this duty to you, in the name of his appearing and of his kingdom: proclaim the message and, welcome or unwelcome, insist on it. Refute falsehood, correct error, call to obedience—but do all with patience and with the intention of teaching. The time is sure to come when, far from being content with sound teaching, people will be avid for the latest novelty and collect themselves a whole series of teachers according to their own tastes; and then, instead of listening to the truth, they will turn to myths. Be careful always to choose the right course; be brave under trials; make the preaching of the Good News your life's work, in thoroughgoing service'" (II *Tim.* 4:1-5).

Nobody can say that Rome has either not kept the faith or has not been vigilant. In the years following the Council, a whole series of documents emanating from the Holy See and the Sacred Congregation for the Doctrine of the Faith witnesses to the Holy See's vigilance to preserve the integrity and purity of the faith "that comes to us from the Apostles."

Perhaps the most notable are the following: Encyclical *Mysterium Fidei*, September 3, 1965; Encyclical on Priestly Celibacy, June 24, 1967; Credo of the People of God, June 30, 1968; Encyclical *Humane Vitae*, July 25, 1968; Declaration on Safeguarding the Incarnation and the Most Holy Trinity from Some Recent Errors, February 21, 1972; Declaration in Defense of the Catholic Doctrine on the Church Against Certain Errors of the Present Day, *Mysterium Ecclesiae*, June 24, 1973; Declaration on Abortion, November 18, 1974; Declaration on Certain Questions Concerning Sexual Ethics *Persona Humana*, December 29, 1975; Declaration on the Question of the Admission of Women to the Ministerial Priesthood, October 15, 1976.

We may be confident that the Holy See will stay on the course that has been charted. Not too long after his election, Pope John Paul II told a group of American bishops making their *ad limina* visit to Rome that purity of doctrine and sound discipline would be priority aims of his pontificate:

> "This then is my own deepest hope today for the pastors of the Church in America, as well as for all the pastors of the universal Church: 'that the sacred deposit of Christian doctrine should be more effectively guarded and taught.' The sacred deposit of God's word, handed on by the Church, is the joy and strength of our people's lives. It is the only pastoral solution to the many problems of our day. To present this sacred deposit of Christian doctrine in all its purity and integrity, with all its exigencies and in all its power is a holy, pastoral responsibility; it is, moreover, the most sublime service we can render.
>
> "And the second hope that I would express today is a hope for the preservation of the great discipline of the Church—a hope eloquently formulated by John Paul I on the day after his election: 'We wish to maintain intact the great discipline of the Church in the life of priests and of the faithful, as the history of the Church, enriched by experience, has presented it throughout the centuries, with examples of holiness and heroic perfection, both in the exercise of the evangelical virtues and in service to the poor, the humble, the defenseless.'
>
> "These two hopes do not exhaust our aspirations or our prayers, but they are worthy of intense pastoral efforts and apostolic diligence. These efforts and diligence on our part are in turn an expression of real love and concern for the

flock entrusted to our care by Jesus Christ, the chief Shepherd.
. . . " (Address to the Bishops of the seventh Pastoral Region of
the U.S., November 9, 1978).

The Pope's letter to all bishops and priests of the Roman rite
upholding the discipline of celibacy in the Roman rite certainly
served to show that John Paul II meant business; reports of his
stricter standards for laicization showed the same thing.[18]
The Sacred Congregation for the Doctrine of the Faith followed
up on these words of the Holy Father by issuing in April, 1979, a
Declaration censuring a book by Fr. Jacques Pohier, a French Dominican, as containing "assertions manifestly at variance with Revelation
and the Magisterium of the Church." This Declaration indicated that
for nearly a year the Sacred Congregation had been trying to get
Fr. Pohier to "publicly correct his errors and to declare his entire
adhesion to the teaching of the Church," failing which the Declaration itself was being made public. Observers in France pointed out
that in the case of a similar Declaration regarding the errors of Fr.
Hans Küng, the Holy See had waited for years before finally making
its first judgment against the Swiss theologican public; it finally
appeared only on February 14, 1975, although the anti-Church
position of Fr. Küng had been publicly known since the late sixties.[19]
Thus it became clear that the tempo of such judgments was being
stepped up by Pope John Paul II.
This step-up in the tempo of actions against dissenting theologians
was, of course, dramatically confirmed by the Holy See's actions in
late 1979 concerning the by-then celebrated cases of Dutch theologian Fr. Edward Schillebeeckx and Swiss-born Tübingen theologian
Fr. Hans Küng. Fr. Schillebeeckx was merely summoned to Rome
for an investigation of some of the Christological opinions expressed
in his book, *Jesus, An Experiment in Christology*. Still it hardly seems
likely that the Holy See will not continue to press this case *if* the Sacred
Congregation for the Doctrine of the Faith finds that any of the
Dutch theologian's Christological views do not square with the faith
of the Church. What is documented in the case of Fr. Schillebeeckx
is that he certainly has dissented from authentic Church doctrine
on other matters; he belongs, for example, to a group of more than
a dozen Dutch and Belgium theologians who in September, 1968,
issued a statement severely critical of both the manner and the matter
of Pope Paul VI's encyclical *Humanae Vitae*.[20] It thus seems that the
Holy See is on the right track in singling him out for investigation,
especially in view of his prominence and reputation.

In the case of Fr. Hans Küng, however, the Holy See has symbolically but firmly grasped the whole prickly nettle of post-conciliar dissent and disloyalty. Fr. Küng has rather flamboyantly represented the prototype of this kind of dissent and loyalty—a theologian who insists on subjecting the teaching of the Church to *his* personal scrutiny rather than docilely accepting the ultimate judgment of the Church on his work—and who effectively takes his case not to his theological peers alone but directly to a mass reading audience and, indeed, to the mass media generally, thus disturbing and disorienting the faithful everywhere. Fr. Küng was obviously a prime target if there was ever to be effective ecclesiastical disciplinary action against anybody; it was thus no real surprise to anyone acquainted with the way the Church acts that the full weight of ecclesiastical censure eventually fell on him. The only surprise was the timing: on December 18, 1979, Fr. Küng's mandate to teach theology in the name of the Church was withdrawn; the Sacred Congregation for the Doctrine of the Faith officially declared that "Professor Hans Küng, in his writings, has departed from the integral truth of Catholic faith, and therefore he can no longer be considered a Catholic theologian nor function as such in a teaching role."[21]

For most observers of Catholic affairs this Declaration about Fr. Hans Küng was long overdue. What such observers perhaps forget is that the Holy See has always, historically, been slow and deliberate in such matters, lest any injustice be done. It is worth briefly reviewing the history of the Holy See's actions in the case of Fr. Küng because it brings out how the mills of Church authority, although they traditionally grind slowly, also grind exceedingly fine: there is more than hope, there is certainty, that legitimate Church authority will eventually get around to dealing with the other dissenters who have deformed and misrepresented the truth that Christ committed into the hands of His Church.

To review briefly the case of Fr. Hans Küng, then: over more than a decade both the Holy See and the German bishops reasonably, repeatedly, at first privately, and always charitably (as the tone of the final Vatican Declaration itself proves) tried to get Professor Küng even to discuss his views with them, the constituted authorities of the Church. As far back as 1967, Fr. Küng was courteously advised by the Sacred Congregation for the Doctrine of the Faith on the advisability of having discussions about his book *The Church*. The Congregation became even more concerned (understandably) after the publication in 1970 of Fr. Küng's book *Infallible? An Inquiry*.

But Fr. Küng systematically refused even to discuss his views with those who were, after all, only the competent authorities in the case; he seems to have been the one to have gone first to the press with his case, in July, 1971, after which the Congregation confirmed (*L'Osservatore Romano*, August 7, 1971) that letters had indeed been written to him about these two books.

After a lengthy exchange of letters between him and the Congregation, Fr. Küng still successfully managed to avoid being pinned down; but the Congregation still issued no outright condemnation of him. Instead on July 6, 1973, it issued its lucid Declaration in Defense of the Catholic Doctrine on the Church Against Certain Errors of the Present Day, *Mysterium Ecclesiae*. In this magisterial Declaration, Fr. Küng's name was not so much mentioned; the Church's challenged teachings were merely reaffirmed and clarified. It wasn't until February, 1975, that the Congregation finally issued a condemnation of some of the opinions in *The Church* and in *Infallible? An Inquiry*, finally mentioning Fr. Küng by name—without any discussion, again, because Fr. Küng always steadfastly refused to have any, protesting the Congregation's "procedures." Even then, the censure of certain of his opinions in the two books came in the most measured and restrained terms; Fr. Küng was reminded that "ecclesiastical authority [had] granted him permission to teach sacred theology in the spirit of the doctrine of the Church but not opinions that subvert this doctrine or call it into question."

Later, in 1977, the German bishops' conference did finally manage to organize a meeting of several hours with Hans Küng about some of his views; but the end result of discussing his views with him proved to be no more fruitful than not discussing them, as far as the authentic teachings of the Church were concerned; and so the German bishops too were obliged to issue a statement warning against some of the opinions in still another Küng book, *On Being a Christian*.

By this time, Fr. Küng had moved on to write still another book *Existiert Gott?* ("Does God Exist?"), in which, according to Joseph Cardinal Höffner, a "promise" Fr. Küng had made to clarify his views was not carried out. And in the Spring of 1979 he went on to restate, in even stronger terms, an opinion about the Church's so-called "indefectibility in truth" (rather than "infallibility") which he had been warned against holding or teaching in the 1975 Declaration of the Sacred Congregation for the Doctrine of the Faith.

In the face of such surely impertinent defiance, the German bishops and the Holy See no doubt decided they finally had to act even more strongly than they had to date in the case of Fr. Küng. It was only after more than a decade of this kind of defiance and ob-fuscation on Fr. Küng's part, in other words—Cardinal Höffner, in the statement he issued on behalf of the German bishops, was sadly obliged to speak of Fr. Küng's "flagrant violation" of conditions which he had presumably agreed to—that the Holy See finally issued its Declaration to the effect that Fr. Küng could no longer be con-sidered a Catholic theologian.

Throughout this entire period of more than a decade Fr. Küng was steadily given by Church authority the benefit of every doubt and plenty of time to pray and reflect on the course he was following. The fact of the matter, the inevitable conclusion, is that he him-self obviously did not *want* to go on being a Catholic theologian; he *insisted* on affirming non-Catholic opinions instead; and so the Holy See in removing his teaching faculties was merely taking official cognizance of an accomplished fact—a fact accomplished by Fr. Küng himself.[22]

The question might be asked why Church authority did not act sooner in the case of provocations so notorious as those offered to it by Professor Küng. The answer to this is that it is *part* of the authority possessed by the hierarchical Church to decide *when* it is necessary to move decisively, taking all factors into account. We Catholic faithful should be content that in the case of Fr. Hans Küng both the Holy See and the German bishops now have finally acted. Consistent with the Church's own explanation of her action in this case, we can be sure that she will not fail to continue to act in the same fashion in similar cases.

Indeed, in June, 1979, a new Apostolic Constitution on norms for ecclesiastical universities and faculties published by Pope John Faul II virtually insured that the Church will continue to act vigor-ously in cases of theological dissent similar to that of Hans Küng.

This new Apostolic Constitution, entitled *Sapientia Christiana*, has strict new rules that "in studying and teaching Catholic doctrine, fidelity to the Magisterium of the Church is always to be empha-sized" and that "those who teach disciplines concerning faith and morals must receive, after making their profession of faith, a canon-ical mission ... for they do not teach on their own authority but by virtue of the mission they have received from the Church." Institutions subject to these new regulations are required to pre-pare new statutes, to be approved by the Holy See, in which both provisions for hiring teachers — and firing them — must be spelled out in accordance with the strict new Roman norms. The issuance of this document surely marks at least a first necessary step in dealing with theological "dissent." Nobody reading through it will conclude that the Pope is anything but very serious in issuing it and requiring compliance to it by faculties under direct pontifical jurisdiction.[23]

Moreover, in fairness to Pope Paul VI, we should point out that this strict document, *Sapientia Christiana,* was virtually ready for promulgation at the time of his death. Its issuance was delayed by his death, and by the death of Pope John Paul I less than two months later. Pope John Paul II issued it as soon as practicable after his own pontificate was underway (in June, 1979, although it was officially dated April 15, 1979). Those who have been anxious that Rome should "crack down" should realize that this has always been only a matter of time; Rome always proceeds with great deliberation.

But there can be no doubt that Rome has continued and will continue to teach and discipline in her usual fashion—and to urge that the bishops of the world do the same. We *cannot* conclude, as far as the Holy See is concerned, that there is tolerance towards modernists and progressives combined with a severity towards traditionalists. There is not, in short, as far as the Holy See is concerned, any "double standard." In the present climate, many departures from the Church's doctrine and discipline may have been *tolerated* so far, but if they have been tolerated it has been on both the "right" and "left." And we should be clear in our minds that the authorities of the Church have the responsibility for deciding when and how they will exercise the disciplinary authority they have from Christ. It is not for the laity to "demand" action, but to give the legitimate Church authorities time and leeway to try to restore order in today's truly exceptional situation.

And if some especially notorious cases of "dissent" nevertheless continue to be unresolved as of this writing—that of Fr. Charles Curran at Catholic University in the United States comes to mind, (although there are press reports that he too is now finally under investigation by the Holy See)[24] —this does not mean that the Holy See has not told the bishops concerned and given the example.

Certainly, on the evidence, then, there is no justification for a traditionalist rebellion on the grounds that the Church has ceased to function—to teach the saving truths and purvey the life-giving sacraments required for our salvation and to correct those out of line. Faithful Catholics owe it to the Church to give her *time* to cope with all the problems that have arisen in this day of gross disobedience and indiscipline. The Popes have been working on the problem. Faithful Catholics must bear with the Church and not lightly accuse her of a "double standard." "If my mother is sick," Pope John Paul I advised, "if my mother by chance should become lame, I love her even more. It is the same in the Church. If there are —and there are — defects and shortcomings, our affection for the Church must never fail" (Address to a General Audience, "To Live the Faith," September 13, 1978).

Question # 20

EVERYTHING YOU HAVE SAID WOULD BE MORE PLAUS-IBLE IF IT HAD NOT BEEN SHOWN THAT VATICAN II CONTRADICTED THE CONSTANT TEACHINGS OF THE CHURCH IN ITS DECLARATION ON RELIGIOUS FREEDOM. WHAT ABOUT THAT?

We have already shown (Question #2) that the decisions of a general council of the Church, when ratified by a soverign Pontiff, are both protected from error as regards their doctrinal teaching and binding upon the faithful as regards their discipline. The Church recognizes no such thing as a "pastoral council" which might in some undefined way be "optional" for Catholics to follow or not to follow. A general council of the Church, in other words, would itself be the judge (subject to the final decision of the Pope) of what it would have to hold or teach in order to be consistent with previous Church teaching, whether ordinary or extraordinary.

To assert that a general council of the Church *could* contradict "the constant teaching of the Church" would really be to set oneself up as the judge of the Catholic Tradition and to forget what the Holy Office decided back in 1949, as we have already quoted (Question #6): "The Savior did not leave it to private judgment to explain what is contained in the deposit of faith, but to the doctrinal authority of the Church."[1] Short of a solemn definition of dogma, no teaching must presumably be accorded greater weight than that of a general council duly ratified by a Pope. Pope Paul VI confirmed that the teaching of the Second Vatican Council possessed at least "the authority of the supreme ordinary Magisterium" (General Audience, January 12, 1966). And the First Vatican Council taught that not only are solemn dogmatic definitions to be believed with "divine and Catholic faith" but also those things proposed by the Church "through her *ordinary* and universal teaching office" (emphasis added),[2] including, surely, those things decided by a general Church council, whether or not "dogmatically." It follows that the teachings of Vatican II are binding on the faithful.

Nor is it possible for those who dislike this conclusion to take refuge in the fact that Vatican II's teaching on religious freedom comes in a "mere" declaration of the Council instead of in a dogmatic constitution. For the "Tridentine" Profession of Faith issued by Pope Pius IV in 1564 requires acceptance and assent to everything "transmitted, defined, *and declared*" by an ecumenical council of the Church (emphasis added),[3] not just to those things solemnly defined. How it could be imagined that this Tridentine teaching would not apply also to a declaration of Vatican Council II is not at all clear. It simply cannot be shown that Vatican II is any less a general council of the Church than the other general councils which preceded it. However, we must look at the specific instance where Vatican II is most often said—*per impossibile*—to have taught contrary to the Church's earlier doctrinal teachings, that is, with regard to religious freedom.

First of all, then, what did Vatican II teach on this subject? Having ascertained this, we can then compare it with previous Church teachings on the same subject, especially those of Popes Pius IX and Leo XIII. Although we shall have to follow a somewhat winding road, we will eventually be able to satisfy ourselves that there is no real opposition between the Church of today and the Church of yesterday.

Vatican II taught, then, in essence, as follows:

> "The Vatican Council declares that the human person has a right to religious freedom. Freedom of this kind means that all men should be immune from coercion on the part of individuals, social groups and every human power so that, within due limits, nobody is forced to act against his convictions in religious matters in private or in public, alone or in associations with others. The Council further declares that the right to religious freedom is based on the very dignity of the human person as known through the revealed word of God and by reason itself. This right of the human person to religious freedom must be given such recognition in the constitutional order of society as will make it a civil right. . . .
>
> "It is through his conscience that man sees and recognizes the demands of the Divine law. He is bound to follow this conscience faithfully in all his activity so that he may come to God, who is his last end. Therefore he must not be forced to act

contrary to his conscience. Nor must he be prevented from acting according to his conscience, especially in religious matters. The reason is because the practice of religion of its very nature consists primarily of those voluntary and free internal acts by which a man directs himself to God. Acts of this kind cannot be commanded or forbidden by any merely human authority. . . .

"The freedom or immunity from coercion in religious matters which is the right of individuals must also be accorded to men when they act in community. Religious communities are a requirement of the nature of man and of religion itself.

"Therefore, provided the just requirements of public order are not violated, these groups have a right to immunity so that they may organize themselves according to their own principles . . ." (Vatican Council II, Declaration on Religious Liberty *Dignitatis Humanae*, #2, #3, #4).

Thus, according to the Council, human beings possess a right to religious freedom; they may not be forced to act against their beliefs nor may they be prevented—within the limits of public order—from acting on their conscientious religious beliefs. Moreover, this right extends to groups of persons, not just to individuals. In practice, this would mean that churches and religious communities other than the true Church of Christ, the Catholic Church, should be accorded recognition, toleration and protection by the state and, indeed, even by the Church herself.

It is this corollary of Vatican II's teaching on religious freedom that some believe contradicts earlier Church teachings: for if churches other than the true Church have rights to recognition, toleration and protection, would this not be tantamount to recognizing that "error has rights"? However, it seems quite clear from traditional Church teachings that error does not and cannot have "rights."

Pope Gregory XVI, for instance, in his encyclical *Mirari Vos*, in 1832, condemned what he called "the absurd and wrong view, or rather insanity, according to which freedom of conscience must be asserted and vindicated for everybody."[4] Pope Pius IX, in his encyclical *Qui Pluribus* in 1846, similarly included among errors against the Catholic faith the idea that "there is no difference between religions" or that "men can attain to eternal salvation by the practice of any religion whatever."[5] The same Pius IX issued still another encyclical in 1864, *Quanta Cura,* to which was attached the famous "Syllabus of Errors"; this was a list of the principal errors of the time which had in various ways been touched upon and censured by Pius IX in various of his allocutions, encyclicals and other documents. The Pope determined to have drawn up a compact list of the various opinions which he had in one degree or another condemned or censured to accompany the encyclical *Quanta Cura* for the easy reference of the bishops receiving that encyclical.

The "Syllabus of Errors" caused a sensation in its day and is still used to try to convict the Church of authoritarianism, illiberality or whatever other crime some wish to convict the Church of. However, a defense can be made that the condemned or censured propositions contained in the Syllabus all richly deserved to be censured or condemned, particularly when the context of most of these propositions is remembered.

The Church in Pius IX's day was mainly trying to defend herself against the aggressive new secularized and radical states of the day which were seeking to eliminate the Church's authority and influence over society with regard to such things as morality, religious discipline, education, the marriage bond, and so on. In many instances, civil governments did not scruple to confiscate the Church's lands and property, close her schools, and legislate to the effect that the children of the Church were no longer subject to her discipline. Understandably, Pius IX reacted to such proceedings — often, censure was the only weapon he possessed.

Specifically, on our present subject of religious liberty, some of the propositions condemned by him in the Syllabus of Errors included:

"Every man is free to embrace and profess that religion which, guided by the light of reason, he shall consider true" (#15).

"In the present day it is no longer expedient that the Catholic religion should be held as the only religion of the state, to the exclusion of all other forms of worship" (#77).

"Hence it has been wisely decided by law, in some Catholic countries, that persons coming to reside therein shall enjoy the public exercise of their own peculiar worship (#78).[6]

If such propositions as these were condemned by Pope Pius IX, how could Vatican II nevertheless teach that men have a right to religious freedom, or that non-Catholics have a civil right (which the state must respect) to profess and practice their own religion, individually, or collectively as non-Catholic churches?

Some who have asked these questions have pointed out that Pope Leo XIII also delivered a number of *dicta* which seem to support the apparent Catholic teaching to be inferred from the Syllabus; some of Leo XIII's teachings may further seem to call into question the teaching of Vatican II. For example, in his encyclical *Libertas Praestantissimum* issued in 1888, Leo XIII taught that of all man's obligations the "chiefest and holiest" is his duty to "worship God with devotion and piety." He specifically pointed out that what he called "liberty of worship":

> ". . .if considered in relation to the state, clearly implies that there is no reason why the state should offer any homage to God, or should desire any public recognition of Him; that no one form of worship is to be preferred to another, but that all stand on an equal footing, no account being taken of the religion of the people, even if they profess the Catholic faith. But, to justify this, it must needs be taken as true that the state has no duties toward God, or that such duties, if they exist, can be abandoned with impunity, both of which assertions are manifestly false."[7]

In his encyclical *Immortale Dei,* issued on November 1, 1885, Pope Leo XIII taught even more emphatically:

> "To hold. . .that there is no difference in matters of religion between forms that are unlike each other, and even contrary to each other, most clearly leads in the end to the rejection of all religion in both theory and practice. And this is the same thing as atheism, however it may differ from it in name. Men who really believe in the existence of God must, in order to be consistent with themselves and to avoid absurd conclusions, understand that differing modes of divine worship involving dissimilarity and conflict even on most important points cannot all be equally probable, equally good, and equally acceptable to God."[8]

These teachings from great nineteenth-century Popes all add up to the proposition that religious indifferentism on the part of individuals has been definitively condemned by the Church—which has also taught with equal definitiveness that the state has an obligation to favor and protect the true religion, unlike other religions which cannot claim the fullness of truth which is to be found only in the Catholic Church.

When Vatican II came along and taught that freedom to profess and practice any religion is a civil right for both individuals and such individuals gathered into their own churches, it seemed to some, in the light of what had been taught earlier, to be a clear case of the Church contradicting herself.

How can we surmount this apparent contradiction?

In the first place, we should carefully notice that nowhere in its formulation of the basic principles of religious freedom—either as summarily quoted above or as explained at length in the Declaration on Religious Freedom—does Vatican II really take issue with the truths declared by the earlier Popes; the Council simply proceeds to formulate and explain its own teaching on religious freedom. The Council thus does not in any way assert or suggest that "error has rights"; it only declares, what is in any case indisputable and entirely traditional in Church teaching, that *persons* have rights, "based on the very dignity of the human person as known through the revealed word of God and by reason itself."

It is not the specific intent of the Council to examine in depth in this particular Declaration the question of truth or error in religion. The Declaration reaffirms the belief of the Church that the "one true religion continues to exist in the Catholic and Apostolic Church" and says that "all men are *bound* to seek the truth, especially in what concerns God and his Church, and to embrace it and hold on to it as they come to know it" (#1; emphasis added). The Declaration *accepts*, in other words, the teachings we have quoted above from the great Popes of the nineteenth century. But the subject of this particular Declaration is different; it is talking about something else besides what Pius IX and Leo XIII were talking about.

The key to the solution of the apparent conflict between Vatican II's Declaration on Religious Liberty *Dignitatis Humanae* and Pope Pius IX and Leo XIII on religious freedom lies in our realization that the Council, and the nineteenth-century Popes, are *addressing themselves to different questions*. It is therefore not surprising, nor is it a contradiction in the true sense, that they come up with different answers. The Council is looking at the question of religious freedom from a totally different perspective than the one from which the nineteenth-century Popes looked at it.

These Popes were addressing themselves to naturalistic philosophies which held that men did not have any obligation to worship
the true God. Gregory XVI rightly styled this idea an "insanity." The
philosophies which claim to vindicate it are manifestly false, then
and now; what the other Popes said then on the same subject, samples
of which we have quoted above, was true then, and remains true now.

Similarly, with regard to questions of the relationship between
Church and state, the nineteenth-century Popes were addressing
themselves to a situation in which secularizing governments, ruling in
some cases over predominantly Catholic populations, were nevertheless determined to set at naught both the beliefs of their Catholic
peoples, the rights and responsibilities of the Church towards those
same Catholic peoples, and the responsibilities of the state towards
the true religion.

Much of what Popes Pius IX and Leo XIII taught in this regard
was done to try to stem the tide of secularization by reminding the
governments—especially of Catholic countries—of their responsibilities to their own peoples and to the Church—responsibilities
which their predecessor governments in these same countries had
recognized, at least in theory, and in some cases for centuries. The
new secularizing governments with which the Popes were trying to
cope were repudiating duties which Christian states had more or less
recognized since the time of the Emperor Constantine. The *purpose*
of all the papal teachings quoted above was thus to defend the role
of the Church and religion in a Christian commonwealth.

When Pius IX condemned the proposition that it was no longer
expedient that the Catholic religion should be held as the only religion of the state this was no doubt a valiant attempt on his part to
recall the governments of Catholic countries to their plain duty;
today, however, scarcely a government exists any longer in the world
that would recognize that it has any such duty to Catholics or to the
Church. This fact does not make Pius IX's teaching any less true; but
it does mean that there is no longer any situation in the world to
which Pius' particular teaching *applies*.

Similarly, when Leo XIII taught that indifferentism in religion
would inevitably lead to atheism, he not only taught truly; he was
quite a prophet as well! Indifferentism has indeed spread everywhere
in spite of all of his and of the Church's strenuous efforts generally;
and it has indeed led to atheism practically everywhere too, just as he
had prophesied that it would!

So there is nothing at all wrong with Leo XIII's teaching; it is as

true as ever; it even applies to individuals today with the same force
as it ever did. Once again, however, it doesn't apply to the conditions
of today as far as the state is concerned. It may be "manifestly false"
as doctrine—as it certainly is—that the "state has no duties towards
God"; but unless the state itself is willing to recognize those duties,
the Church is unable to compel the state to do so. This is, roughly
speaking, the situation the Church is faced with throughout the whole
world today. Not even in Ireland, Portugal, or Spain does there exist
any government which any longer seriously heeds the Church's
insistence that the state has a duty to uphold true morality and true
religion.

Spain, indeed, adopted a new constitution by a referendum as
recently as December, 1978. In this new constitution it is stipulated
that "there shall be no state religion." The former Spanish constitution, which reflected the traditional reality, said, of course, that
"the profession and practice of the Catholic religion, which is the
religion of the Spanish state, shall enjoy official support." But the
situation has changed, not the principle. A new concordat which Spain
signed with the Vatican in January, 1979, officially reflects the new
state of affairs, namely, that Catholicism is no longer officially
recognized by the Spanish government as the established religion of
Spain.[9]

And it was to this new state of affairs that has been developing over
the past century that Vatican II was principally addressing itself.
The Council in no way intended to deny or oppose the earlier teachings; it was simply constrained to recognize that we can only have
Christian commonwealths or Christian states where we first have
Christians in sufficient numbers and with sufficient political influence—a situation that not only does not obtain in any of the
frankly atheistic or Communist states of the East—including Pope
John Paul II's native Poland—but does not even obtain in any major
Western country today, since the Western countries are given over
to secular humanism every bit as much as the Eastern countries are
given over to Communism. Secularism at best, and Communism at
worst, have nearly everywhere triumphed for the moment, and it
was to this new situation that the Second Vatican Council had to
address itself. The Church has to carry on *her* divine mission even
though formerly Christian states may now have abandoned Christianity.

In adapting to this new situation, the Council was expressly responding to the task assigned to it when it was convoked by Pope

John XXIII who had said in his Opening Speech to the Council that "while the Church should never depart from the sacred patrimony of truth received from the Fathers ... at the same time she must ever look to the present, to the new conditions and new forms of life introduced into the modern world which have opened new avenues to the Catholic apostolate." This was precisely what the Council was doing in its teaching on religious liberty.

The Council's teaching that "the freedom or immunity from coercion in religious matters which is the right of individuals must also be accorded to men when they act in community" today applies, in fact, first of all, *to Catholics and the Catholic Church herself!* For the secularized state of today, again nearly everywhere throughout the world, is ever so much more likely to ignore and belittle the Church's teachings, and trample upon her rights and those of its own Catholic citizens, than ever to uphold these things as Popes Pius IX and Leo XIII correctly taught the state has an obligation to do. But the states of today do not recognize this obligation or they have jettisoned it if they ever did, and we are now faced with a situation which resembles that of the early Church—before the Emperor Constantine recognized Christianity as the religion of the state. Surely no one would hold that the teachings of Pius IX or Leo XIII were ever meant to apply under the rule of, for example, the Roman Emperors Nero or Domitian! We are back in such a pagan situation today. Legalized abortion and divorce—symbolic of the new pagan world in which we now live—have even come to Italy.

Vatican II's teaching on religious freedom has thus actually come providentially and prophetically in this new day of pagan tyrannies practiced by secularized states, whether Communist or otherwise.

For the doctrine that no man may be coerced in the matter of his religious beliefs, or prevented from acting upon them, is an eminently traditional doctrine, viewed from the angle from which the Council considered the matter. The Second General Council of Nicaea back in 787, the Seventh General Council of the Church, was surely recognizing precisely this same principle when it legislated in one of its canons about Jews pretending to be Christians, but secretly keeping the sabbath and other purely Jewish observances: "Such people must not be received into the communion, nor in prayer, nor in the Church," the Second Council of Nicaea declared. *"But let them be Hebrews openly, according to their own religion."* (Emphasis added).[10] In other words, the *rights* of Jews, as human persons, to worship according to their consciences, and not to be prevented from acting according to their consciences in religious matters—and even to have their own synagogues publicly recognized, tolerated and protected by the Christian emperor—all these rights of Jews were clearly affirmed even by this early council of the Church. Vatican II has thus done no more than to formulate and spell out this same constant right of persons to religious freedom that has always been there and which the Church in her official teaching has consistently recognized to be there (although the same cannot always be said of the policies of some Christian *states* in the past, or of some church-men accommodating themselves to such state policies in accordance with the "spirit of the times," such as it was).

St. Thomas Aquinas held in the *Summa Theologica* that "among the infidels there are some who have never accepted the Christian faith, such as Gentiles and Jews; and these should in no way be constrained to embrace the faith and profess belief. For belief depends upon the will."[11]

In another article of the *Summa*, St. Thomas taught the same principle as the Second Council of Nicaea, namely, that non-Catholic worship can be "openly" tolerated, "either on account of some good that ensues therefrom or because of some evil avoided . . . The Church . . . has tolerated the rites even of heretics and pagans," St. Thomas observes, "when unbelievers were very numerous."[12] Surely unbelievers have never been more numerous than they are today. Surely Vatican II was not out of line in wishing to bring out or emphasize those of the Church's teachings which apply to the situation we have in the world today.

Pope Pius XII, in a remarkable address delivered to the Tenth-International Congress of the Historic Sciences on September 7, 1955, explicitly recognized that the Church's teaching on religious liberty and the obligations of the state towards the true religion are to some degree contingent upon whether or not the state is "Christian" or itself recognizes any particular obligations to the Church or to its Catholic citizens who profess the true faith. Recognizing the truth of Leo XIII's teaching that the state and the Church are independent powers but that they cannot, for all of that, ignore one another, Pope Pius XII pointed out that this teaching "reflect[ed] the consciousness of the Church" throughout *most* of her history. But he specifically excepted the first "few centuries" of that history when the teaching simply did not apply—as it similarly cannot entirely apply in the case of our new pagan states of today.[13]

Indeed, the election of the Polish Pope John Paul II underlined the real intent and significance of Vatican II's Declaration on Religious Freedom. For Cardinal Wojtyla, as Archbishop of Cracow, functioning as a bishop under a Communist government, had gratefully received the Declaration from the Council—and as Cardinal Archbishop he characteristically invoked this Declaration precisely against the usurpations of the Communist government of Poland of the rights to worship of Catholics and of the Church!

In the address on "The Eucharist and Man's Hunger for Freedom" which Cardinal Wojtyla delivered to the International Eucharistic Congress in Philadelphia in 1976, the future Pope declared:

> "In our times, on the background of the maturing social and human consciousness, the principle of the freedom of the human spirit, of the freedom of conscience, of the freedom of religion has become much more evident. The Second Vatican Council has expressed it in many places and especially in the separate Declaration on Religious Freedom. But is this principle really respected everywhere? Do we never meet with the case of those who are underprivileged because of their religious convictions? May we not even speak today of actual persecutions of those who confess their religion, especially Christians, persecuted as they were in the first centuries after Christ?
>
> "This is what the Declaration on Religious Freedom says on the subject: 'Forms of government still exist under which, even though freedom of religious worship receives constitutional recognition, the powers of the government are engaged in the effort to deter citizens from professing religion and to make life difficult and dangerous for religious communities' (*Dignitatis Humanae*, #15).
>
> "And so today we bring to this great community of confessors of the Eucharistic Christ, gathered at the Eucharistic Congress in Philadelphia, the whole hunger for freedom which permeates contemporary man and all humanity. In the name of Jesus Christ we have the right and the duty to demand true freedom for men and for peoples. We therefore bring this hunger for real freedom and deposit it on this altar. Not only a man, a priest, a bishop, but Christ himself is at this altar, he who through our ministration offers his unique and eternal sacrifice."[14]

The future Pope John Paul II saw, in this passage, that the issue of religious freedom primarily involves coercion by the state. Since becoming Pope, John Paul II has gone above and beyond the call of duty both to affirm the principles of the Vatican II Declaration and to express his support of the document itself. He went out of his way to do both in his encyclical *Redemptor Hominis* (#17); he did the same in an "Appeal for Religious Freedom" addressed to the Secretary General of the United Nations Organization on December 11, 1978, on the occasion of the Thirtieth Anniversary of that body's "Universal Declaration of Human Rights."[15] The subject of religious freedom has been raised in other talks, homilies, or messages, which he has delivered; for example, John Paul II repeated the Council's definition of religious liberty when, in an address to Italian Catholic doctors delivered on December 28, 1978, he called for "respect, in legislation and in fact, of freedom of conscience, understood as the fundamental right of the person not to be forced to act contrary to his conscience or prevented from behaving in accordance with it."[16]

Finally, John Paul II made Vatican II's teaching on religious freedom the keystone of his entire message during his dramatic visit to Poland in June of 1979. As the *New York Times* reported: "John Paul II touched an even deeper nerve, the legitimacy of state power when he raised the question of normalization of relations between church and state in a speech before the Polish bishops. In specific Polish terms, he said, religious freedom does not mean simply freedom of worship, but *freedom for the church to take its total place in society*" (emphasis added).[17]

Not only is Vatican II's teaching on religious freedom compatible with past Church teachings, it has proved to be indispensable to the Church in enabling her to meet the challenge of trying to fulfill the mission confided to her by Christ in an age of Communist tyrannies.

Those who believe Vatican II's Declaration on Religious Freedom is opposed to the teaching of Popes Pius IX and Leo XIII are failing to interpret what these Popes taught in the light of this constant Church teaching against coercion in matters of religious belief. It was Pius IX himself who taught that "it must be held as certain that those who are in ignorance of the true religion, if this ignorance is invincible, are not subject to any guilt in this matter before the eyes of the Lord" and that "only when we have been released from the bonds of this body and shall 'see God as He is' (I *Jn.* 3:2) shall we understand how closely and wonderfully the divine mercy and justice are linked."[18]

Leo XIII, in the very encyclical *Immortale Dei* which some have held stands against Vatican II, taught that "the Church is also always very careful that nobody be forced to join the Catholic faith against his will, for, as Augustine wisely admonishes, 'only he who wills so can believe.'" Leo XIII did not believe that non-Catholic religions should have the *same* rights as the true religion, but he quite explicitly recognized, also in *Immortale Dei,* the right of persons to religious freedom, "for the sake of attaining a great good or of avoiding to cause evil,"[19] which Vatican II later spelled out.

Those who hold that Vatican II's Declaration on Religious Liberty *Dignitatis Humanae* contradicts earlier Church teachings on the subject thus need to study both this Vatican II document and the teachings of Popes Pius IX and Leo XIII more carefully and in their proper contexts. It is of great interest to those interested in the continuity of Church teachings that both *Immortale Dei* and *Libertas Praestantissimum* of Leo XIII are actually cited in the Vatican II documents as among the sources for Vatican II's teaching on religious freedom — so far from the Council contradicting these encyclicals! The Council but incorporated into this document an impressive doctrinal synthesis of the best elements of the Church's theological reflection across the centuries. It did so, moreover, having subjected the text of the Declaration on Religious Liberty to more revisions by the Fathers themselves than any other document of the Council. The sixth and final edition of the original schema was approved by a vote of 2308 to 70, and, when finally promulgated by Pope Paul VI, it was to the great applause of the Council Fathers.[20]

The principal objection of the 70 Council Fathers who voted against the document, incidentally, was not against its message as a whole. According to Fr. Ralph Wiltgen's lively account of the proceedings in *The Rhine Flows Into the Tiber,* they wanted the criterion determining the limits of religious freedom to be the "common good" and not the "just requirements of the public order," as specified in #4 of the Declaration. If this "correction" were made, these Fathers too indicated their willingness to vote for the Declaration.[21] In the event, the correction was not made, perhaps because of the evident absurdity of imagining today's modern secularistic or Communist states as *able* to make a judgment about "the common good" in the true Catholic understanding of that term — once again, the intent of the Declaration was to reaffirm the rights of persons, not to spell out the duties of states.

Dignitatis Humanae, Vatican II's Declaration on Religious Freedom, promulgated on December 7, 1965, is thus based on quite traditional doctrine concerning the inviolability of conscience, the freedom of the act of faith, and the demands of natural justice—all of which can be found, at least partially, elucidated in the writings of the Church's great doctors such as St. Thomas Aquinas, as we have already seen above. It is also, in fact, the very document in which the Council makes it unmistakably clear that conscience is not an absolute—the doctrine that Pope Gregory XVI and Pope Pius IX were really condemning—but rather that the traditional Catholic doctrine still obtains that:

> ". . . in forming their consciences the faithful must pay careful attention to the sacred and certain teaching of the Church. For the Catholic Church is by the will of Christ the teacher of truth. It is her duty to proclaim and teach with authority the truth which is Christ and, at the same time, to declare and confirm by her authority the principles of the moral order which spring from human nature itself" (*Dignitatis Humanae*, #14).

No indifferentism here! Rather, this is a ringing reaffirmation of both the truth of the teaching of the Church and of the natural law — and of the obligation to form one's conscience in accordance with them!

The Declaration on Religious Liberty further takes care to note that the core of its teaching concerning religious freedom, i.e., understanding religious freedom as "immunity from coercion in civil society" (#1), is but a fuller development of a teaching already found in the writings of earlier Popes.

Within the space of a couple of paragraphs in his great 1931 encyclical against Fascism in Italy, *Non Abbiamo Bisogno*, Pope Pius XI managed both to affirm the very right of persons to religious freedom later developed by Vatican II *and* to condemn again the false idea of the absolute liberty of a supposedly autonomous conscience— the idea rightly condemned by the nineteenth-century Popes:

> "We state, Venerable Brethren, the sacred and inviolable rights of the soul and of the Church, and this is the reflection and conclusion that more than any other concerns Us, as it is, than any other, more grave. Time and again, as is well known, We have expressed Our thoughts—or, better, the thoughts of the Holy Church—on these important and essential matters,

and it is not to you, Venerable Brethren, faithful masters in Israel, that it is necessary to say more. But We must add something for the benefit of those dear people committed to your care and whom as shepherds of souls, you nourish and govern by Divine mandate and who nowadays would almost never be able, save for you, to know the thoughts of the Common Father of their souls. We said sacred and inviolable rights of souls and of the Church because the matter concerns the rights of souls to procure for themselves the greatest spiritual good according to the teaching and under the formation work of the Church, of such a teaching and of such an unique work that it is constituted by Divine mandate in this supernatural order, established in the Blood of God the Redeemer, necessary and obligatory to all in order to participate in the Divine Redemption. It concerns the right of souls so formed to bring the treasures of the Redemption to other souls, thus participating in the activities of the Apostolic Hierarchy.

"And in consideration of this double right of souls, We are, as We stated above, happy and proud to wage the good fight for the liberty of consciences, though not indeed (as someone perhaps inadvertently, has quoted Us as saying) for the liberty of conscience which is an equivocal expression too often distorted to mean the absolute independence of conscience, which is absurd in a soul created and redeemed by God" (Encyclical *Non Abbiamo Bisogno*).

Here Pius XI clearly distinguishes between the false idea of an absolute "liberty of conscience," and the right and duty to worship God in accordance with the dictates of one's conscience. There was, in other words, an explicit distinction drawn in Church teachings between these ideas long before Vatican II. Hardly any Catholic before Vatican II was heard to object to the following passage of Pope John XXIII's famous 1963 encyclical *Pacem in Terris*, addressed to Catholics and to "all men of good will": "Also among man's rights is the right to be able to worship God in accordance with the right dictates of his own conscience, and to profess his religion *both in private and in public* (#14; emphasis added).

The great nineteenth-century pioneer of Catholic social teaching, Bishop Wilhelm von Ketteler, would doubtless have looked upon Vatican II's *Dignitatis Humanae* as but the logical fruition of his own insistence that: "The Church places so high a value on freedom of religion that she rejects as immoral and illegitimate any use of external force against those who are not her members."[22] Bishop von Ketteler in the nineteenth century was not saying anything too different from what St. Athanasius had already said in the fourth century when he remarked that "it is the part of true godliness not to compel but to persuade."[23] Vatican II recognized that as the special new task of the Church today, in a de-Christianized era. Our Lord Himself recognized our freedom to collaborate or not to collaborate in that task when He asked His disciples: "Will you also go away?" (*Jn.* 6:67). We too are *free* to go on questioning the Council's teachings or quibbling, but what is the point of doing so when there is so much to be done for Christ?

We may fittingly close this section by repeating Vatican II's own affirmation that its teaching on religious liberty is simply a new and necessary way of looking at a radically changed world not, in any sense, a "new" doctrine:

> "So while the religious freedom which men demand in fulfilling their obligation to worship God has to do with freedom from coercion in civil society, *it leaves intact the traditional teaching on the moral duty of individuals and societies towards the true religion and the one Church of Christ*" (*Dignitatis Humanae*, #1; emphasis added).

Guided by the Holy Spirit, the Second Vatican Council, like the prudent scribe instructed in the kingdom of heaven, has truly resembled that householder "who brings out of his treasure what is new and what is old" (*Mt.* 13:52).

Question # 21

BUT WHY DIDN'T VATICAN COUNCIL II
CONDEMN COMMUNISM?

The question would at first sight seem to have very little to do
with the subject of this book, but, in the experience of the authors,
no question is more frequently asked by traditionalists. The fact
that the Second Vatican Council did not explicitly condemn Communism seems to be an especially important reason in the minds
of many to distrust the Council which also instituted the liturgical
changes which have now become so familiar. Moreover, it is sometimes held that the Council was remiss in not condemning Communism even according to its own lights, since the Council aimed to
deal with contemporary problems, and what greater problem is there,
especially for the Church, than Communism?

In reply it must be pointed out, first of all, that one rather obvious
reason why Communism did not have to be singled out for explicit
condemnation by a general council of the Catholic Church was that
it had already been definitively condemned by the Church—in Pope
Pius XI's encyclical *Divini Redemptoris*. Its condemnation in this
encyclical has in no way been rescinded and still stands. The Council
did not have to repeat an action that had already been taken by the
Church. Vatican I similarly did not explicitly condemn Freemasonry
in its day, since there was no possibility of any doubt as to where
the Church stood on Freemasonry. Not even the Council of Trent
condemned a militant Islam in its day, although Islam posed a danger
to the Church then perhaps even as great as the danger posed by Communism today. Lack of specific condemnation has never meant
that that Church has relaxed her position on the evils she condemns;
it only means that she can be concerned with more than one subject
on different occasions.

It was an aim both of Pope John XXIII in convoking the Council
and of the Council itself in its acts to find a new and fresh approach
to the problems of the day. It was hoped that the Church could
be renewed in a way that would attract the millions of souls living

without Christ in the secularistic atheistic world of today (See Question #1). It was not believed that repeated condemnations of things already condemned would particularly assist in this renewal. Rather, it was hoped that the Church could be once again projected in her true essence as alone capable of fulfilling man's deepest longings, his desires for justice, peace and happiness. The Council wanted to reemphasize the true essence of the Church as the upholder of all natural values and legitimate human aspirations. In a sense, the original program of the Council was the same program which Pope John Paul II announced as *his* program at the beginning of his pontificate :

"The absolute and yet sweet and gentle power of the Lord responds to the whole depths of the human person, to his loftiest aspirations of intellect, will, and heart. It does not speak the language of force but expresses itself in charity and truth. . . .

"Brothers and sisters, do not be afraid to welcome Christ and accept His power . . . . Do not be afraid. Open wide the doors for Christ. To His saving power open the boundaries of states, economic and political systems, the vast fields of culture, civilization and development. Do not be afraid. Christ knows 'what is in man.' He alone knows it. . . .

". . . the whole Church . . . praying, meditating and acting in order that Christ's words of life may reach all people and be received by them as a message of hope, salvation and total liberation" (Homily at the Mass Marking the Beginning of His Pastoral Ministry, October 22, 1978).

The emphasis of Vatican II was intended to be positive—just as John Paul II sees his own pontificate in these terms, though he, of all possible Popes, can scarcely be imagined to be naive about Communism or "soft" on it. For these reasons as well as others— the rush to prepare the final text of the Pastoral Constitution on the Modern World *Gaudium et Spes* for promulgation, and the desire *not* to provoke further reprisals and persecution of already hard-pressed Catholics behind the Iron Curtain—a petition signed by 450 bishops to have Communism explicitly condemned by the Second Vatican Council was not acted upon at the Council. However, there could be no mistaking the *equivalent* condemnation of Communism in its contemporary ideological and political expression when the Council declared :

"Among the various kinds of present-day atheism, that one should not go unnoticed which looks for man's autonomy through his economic and social emancipation. It holds that religion, of its very nature, thwarts such emancipation by raising man's hopes in a future life, thus both deceiving him and discouraging him from working for a better form of life on earth. That is why those who hold such views, wherever they gain control of the state, violently attack religion, and in order to spread atheism, especially in the education of young people, make use of all means by which the civil authority can bring pressure to bear on its subjects.

"The Church, as given over to the service of both God and man, cannot cease from reproving, with sorrow yet with the utmost firmness, as she had done in the past, those harmful teachings and ways of acting which are in conflict with reason and with common human experience, and which cast man down from the noble state to which he is born" (Pastoral Constitution on the Church in the Modern World *Gaudium et Spes*, #20-21).

It is clear from these paragraphs that the Council renounced none of the Church's principles but rather reaffirmed them. The footnote attached to the last paragraph refers specifically to documents containing the Church's repeated condemnations of atheistic Communism, especially to Pope Pius XI's 1937 encyclical *Divini Redemptoris*, "On Atheistic Communism," which we have already referred to above and which is acknowledged to be one of the most succinct and trenchant analyses of Communism that has ever been written.

Moreover, if the Council did not condemn Communism explicitly by name, the Pope *did*—and while the Council was still sitting. We refer to Pope Paul VI's very first encyclical *Ecclesiam Suam*, issued in 1964, wherein the then Chief Shepherd of the Church declared to all the bishops of the Catholic world:

"Sad to say, there is a vast circle comprising very many people who profess no religion at all. Many, too, subscribe to atheism in one of its many different forms. They parade their godlessness openly, asserting its claims in education and politics, in the foolish and fatal belief that they are emancipating mankind from false and outworn notions about life and the world and substituting a view that is scientific and up-to-date.

"This is the most serious problem of our time. We are firmly convinced that the basic propositions of atheism are utterly false and irreconcilable with underlying principles of thought. They strike at the genuine and effective foundation for man's acceptance of a rational order in the universe, and introduce into human life a futile kind of dogmatism which, far from solving life's difficulties, only degrades it and saddens it. Any social system based on these principles is doomed to utter destruction. Atheism, therefore, is not a liberating force, but a catastrophic one, for it seeks to quench the light of the living God. We shall therefore resist this growing evil with all our strength, spurred by our great zeal for safeguarding the truth, inspired by our social duty of loyally professing Christ and His gospel, and driven by a burning, unquenchable love, which makes man's good our constant concern. We shall resist in the invincible hope that modern man may recognize the religious ideals which the Catholic faith sets before him and feel himself drawn to seek a form of civilization which will never fail him, but will lead on to the natural and supernatural perfection of the human spirit. May the grace of God enable him to possess his temporal goods in peace and honor and to live in the assurance of acquiring those that are eternal.

"It is for these reasons that We are driven to repudiate such ideologies as deny God and oppress the Church. *We repudiate them as Our predecessors did, and as everyone must do who firmly believes in the excellence and importance of religion. These ideologies are often identified with economic, social and political regimes; atheistic communism is a glaring instance of this.* Yet is it really so much we who condemn them? One might say that it is rather they and their politicians who are clearly repudiating us, and for doctrinaire reasons subjecting us to violent oppression. Truth to tell, the voice we raise against them is more the complaint of a victim than the sentence of a judge" (Encyclical *Ecclesiam Suam,* #99-100; emphasis added).

In light of the foregoing, the claim that has sometimes been made that Vatican II's teaching signified somehow a *rejection* of the Church's well-known condemnations of Communism as an ideological and politico-cultural system founded on atheism can only be dismissed as a misinterpretation of the actual teaching of the Church and of the Council. There can be no change in the Church's attitude towards the errors of atheistic Marxism. However, in the spirit of true Christianity, the Council did remind Catholics of the supernatural virtue of charity which must motivate them in any struggle, even against the evil and perversities of Communism:

> "Love and courtesy ... should not, of course, make us indifferent to truth and goodness. Love, in fact, impels the followers of Christ to proclaim to all men the truth which saves. But we must distinguish between the error (which must always be rejected) and the person in error, who never loses his dignity as a person even though he flounders amid false or inadequate religious ideas. God alone is the judge and searcher of hearts: he forbids us to pass judgment on the inner guilt of others.
>
> "The teaching of Christ even demands that we forgive injury, and the precept of love, which is the commandment of the New Law, included all our enemies: 'You have heard that it was said, "you shall love your neighbor and hate your enemy." But I say to you, love your enemies, do good to them that hate you; and pray for those who persecute and calumniate you'" (*Mt.* 5:43-44). (Pastoral Constitution on the Church in the Modern World *Gaudium et Spes,* #28).

In a sense, as we have already suggested in the answer to Question #1, we may say that Vatican II was looking *beyond* the present worldwide threat posed by the success of the Communist movement; Vatican II was looking to the fact that a more fundamental problem even than the socio-political and moral problem of Communism is the problem of *unbelief* which today exists among great masses of people on *both* sides of the Iron and Bamboo Curtains, and which is one of the root causes that enables Communism and other evils to flourish without principled opposition; and the Council's answer to this worldwide problem of unbelief, indeed the very purpose for which the Council deliberated and issued its teachings pertaining to the real world of today, was to reorient the attitude of Catholics towards the need for *evangelization*—the preaching of the Gospel again to our contemporary "faithless generation" (*Mk.* 9:19), the making of new Christians who will be the only solid foundation for the new Christian society which can one day be built upon the ruins of the ones which the Communists, like the other secularizers of today, may say they are trying to build but will not finally succeed in building because "without Me you can do nothing" (*Jn.* 15:5).

In considering how we Catholics should regard Communists, then, even while we know from the Church's teaching that the Communist *system* is evil, let us recall the words of the great Fr. Werenfried van Straaten, *O. Praem.*, founder of Aid to the Church in Need (formerly Iron Curtain Church Relief), who has worked tirelessly for the persecuted Church behind the Iron Curtain for over thirty years and has no illusions about the Communist system; yet Fr. Werenfried can still declare:

> "We are not advocates of a crusade against communism. Christ was a lover of peace. He sat at table with sinners and did not refuse Judas' kiss. That is why Pope John considered it unchristian to refuse the handshake of a communist. Communists too, even though they are the servants of Satan, have a right to expect us to return evil with good. If they slap us in the face they may expect in virtue of the gospel that we should turn the other cheek. We owe them a Christian answer because they can only recover the God they have lost by the witness of authentic Christianity."[1]

This is the kind of "answer" the Church—and Catholics—should be giving to the threat of Communism.

Question # 22

DIDN'T A POPE, AS WELL AS A GENERAL COUNCIL, ONCE CONDEMN THE ACTS OF ANOTHER POPE, POPE HONORIUS I? IS IT NOT AT LEAST POSSIBLE THAT POPE PAUL VI MIGHT SOMEDAY BE CENSURED IN A SIMILAR WAY FOR DARING TO CHANGE THE MASS?

The thought-process behind this question, asked with surprising frequency by traditionalists, seems to be: if a Pope was once actually condemned by a subsequent Pope—and by a general council of the Church as well, perhaps some day Pope John XXIII could be condemned for calling Vatican Council II or Pope Paul VI for carrying out the reforms decreed by the Council.

The question thus assumes that the two Popes would deserve to be condemned for calling the Council and carrying out its reforms. This is a pretty heady assumption. Indeed it is of interest in this connection that both Popes John Paul I and John Paul II immediately pledged at the beginning of their pontificates to continue to implement the decrees of the Council (See Question #1) and hence would already seem to be implicated also in any possible future censure.

As we have more than once had occasion to remark in these pages, the turbulence and confusion which have undeniably followed Vatican II cannot simply be characterized as the "bitter fruits" of the Council itself—as well assign as "bitter fruits" to the great Council of Nicaea, the model of all subsequent orthodox councils, the fact, which we have already remarked on (Questions #17 and #19), that perhaps a majority of Catholic bishops, at least in the East, fell away from Catholic orthodoxy for a longer or shorter time in the decades following the Council of Nicaea; this was, as we have also noted, precisely the situation to which the great St. Athanasius addressed his life's work.[1] But the defection from orthodoxy which followed the Council of Nicaea was scarcely the Council's own fault. We must not fall into the elementary logical fallacy which the scholastics designated *"post hoc, ergo propter hoc,"* "this follows that, therefore it was *caused* by that." Because something follows something else, it is *not* necessarily caused by it.

However, those who may think there is still some reason to "appeal" on traditional grounds against the things that have been changed in the Church since Vatican II to some future Pope or Council, should recall that the First Vatican Council *defined* that the acts of a supreme Pontiff are not subject to such an "appeal":

> ". . .the judgment of the Apostolic See, whose authority is unsurpassed, is not subject to review by anyone; nor is anyone allowed to pass judgment on its decision. Therefore, those who say that it is permitted to appeal to an ecumenical council from the decisions of the Roman Pontiff, as to an authority superior to the Roman Pontiff, are far from the straight path of truth."[2]

As with regard to the First Vatican Council's definition that the Roman Pontiff has supreme jurisdiction in matters of discipline and government—and not just "in faith and morals"—so with regard to this dogmatic teaching, we find the practice of many who profess to follow traditional Catholicism quite at variance with the traditional Church teaching on the matter! For probably the principal occupation and preoccupation of many traditionalists and traditionalist journals in the years following the Second Vatican Council have surely been to "review. . .the judgment of the Apostolic See," and to "pass judgment on its decision [s]."

Be that as it may, the question of the condemnation of Pope Honorius I arises with enough frequency to warrant our reviewing it briefly here so as to determine whether the question really has any relevance to the Church in the post-Vatican II years.

The bare facts are these:[3] a Patriarch of Constantinople in the seventh century, Sergius, hoping to reconcile the Monophysites who had rejected the Council of Chalcedon of 451, devised a formula to which he thought both Monophysites and Catholics could subscribe. The Monophysites thought that the Catholics were "dividing Christ" when they spoke of His two natures—a divine nature and a human nature—in one divine person. The reconciling formula of the Patriarch Sergius therefore avoided the question of "natures" altogether and spoke instead of there being in Our Lord only one source

of action, or will. That this theory, which came to be called Monothelitism, really amounted to Monophysitism in another guise was
not immediately apparent to all, although it was subsequently
brought out by Sophronius, a learned Egyptian monk who later
became Patriarch of Jerusalem.

But in his anxiety to promote his formula of reconciliation declar-
ing that there was one action, or will, in the person of Christ, the
Patriarch Sergius of Constantinople wrote to the Pope, who was
Honorius I, hoping to rally the authority of the latter behind the
hoped-for reconciliation with the Monophysites, who by then had
been separated from the Catholic Church for nearly two centuries.
In writing to Honorius, Sergius did not reveal that questions had
already been raised about his formula by Sophronius of Jerusalem.
Monsignor Philip Hughes describes the fateful response to the Patriarch's letter made by this Pope:

> "The reply of the Pope Honorius I (625-638), is curiously
> interesting, because he fails utterly to grasp the point of the
> patriarch's letter. Sergius had before him the Monophysite con-
> tention that since Catholics repudiated the phrase 'union in
> one nature,' they must believe that in Christ there are two
> beings united by a moral union. To disprove this he urges that
> Catholic belief accords to Christ Our Lord one only faculty
> of action. This point the pope wholly overlooks or, more truly,
> misunderstands. Not the singleness of the faculty but the unity
> in action between the divine and the human is the subject of
> the pope's reply. Certainly, Honorius answers, Christ always
> acted with the two natures in harmony, no conflict between
> them being possible, the unity of action being perfect. . .he
> agrees with Sergius that the question should be left where it
> stands [i.e., no further discussion of it permitted].
>
> "Obviously, Sergius and Honorius are at cross-purposes,"
> Monsignor Hughes continues. "They are not discussing the same
> thing at all. But the consequences of the misunderstanding
> could hardly have been more serious. . . ."[4]

Where Pope Honorius failed was in not noticing that a new heresy
was springing up and then not moving to censure it. It was not that
he was in any way compromised by the heresy itself; he just didn't
understand that Monothelitism was a new heresy in a new and particularly subtle form. The Patriarch Sergius had not, in any case,

explained the whole thing for his own reasons; and therefore the Pope's actions in forbidding further discussions made it difficult for the orthodox forces to bring out the objections to it.

A successor of Pope Honorius, Pope John IV (640-642) even protested to a later Patriarch of Constantinople that Honorius had been deliberately misled: The words of Honorius' fatal letter to Sergius "some have twisted to their own ends," John IV declared, "alleging Honorius to have taught that there is but one will to [Christ's] divinity and humanity which is indeed contrary to truth."[5]

"That Honorius held and taught the faith of Chalcedon is clear enough, despite the muddle," Monsignor Hughes summarizes. It is equally clear that he failed to grasp that a new question had arisen and was under discussion; clear, also, that he assisted the innovators by thus imposing silence alike on them and on their orthodox critics; clear, finally, that he definitely said, in so many words, that there is but one will in Christ"—referring, however, to the unity of action in Christ's two natures, human and divine.[6]

It was to be more than fifty years before the question was finally settled at the Third General Council of Constantinople in 681 (the Sixth General Council of the Church). By that time the whole issue had been thoroughly aired, not the least because the Byzantine Emperors more than once in those years tried to impose the Monothelite "reconciliation" on the Church—efforts which the successors of Honorius in the See of Peter, especially Pope St. Martin I (649-655), took the lead in resisting from the moment that it was clear that heresy was involved.

Included among the condemnations of those who had fostered the heresy which Constantinople III finally issued in 681 was the name of Pope Honorius "because in his writings to Sergius he followed his opinions and confirmed his impious teachings."[7] This was not entirely true to the facts, of course, as we have seen above, but when the acts of Constaninople III were sent to the reigning Pope to be confirmed, this Pope, Leo II (682-683), did confirm them, letting the condemnation of Honorius stand and waxing even more indignant than the Council had over his predecessor's failure to act nearly a half-century earlier.

Leo II explained in a letter to the bishops of Spain just what Pope Honorius I had done to deserve the condemnation both of a general council and of a subsequent Pope: Honorius "did not extinguish the fire of heretical teaching, as behooved one who exercised the authority of the apostles, but by his negligence blew the flames still higher."[7] In other words, he was censured not for anything he did but for what he failed to do.

It is thus clear that Pope Honorius in no way compromised the papal primacy or papal infallibility "by his negligence." A Pope is guarded from error in what he positively teaches. He *could*, of course, be remiss in failing to speak out in a timely manner. But this latter is all that is involved in the censure of Honorius I. A similar charge of failing to speak out against modernism or other errors and abuses cannot be brought against Paul VI, however. We have cited numerous instances in these pages where Paul VI, unlike Honorius, did speak out (Questions #11, #15, #17, #19 and #21).

If Pope Paul VI is to be calumniated as "another Honorius," it would be well to be honestly informed of the *specific heresy* (and one that is equivalent to the spread of the Monothelite dogma) he helped impose on the universal Church. None such can be brought forth.

Even non-Catholic historians have acknowledged that Honorius never positively taught heresy. He was condemned not as a formal heretic, but as a *"fautor haeresis,"* i.e., as one who unwittingly helped spread the heretical doctrine of one will and one energy. He "fanned it by his negligence," Pope Leo II explained, indicating the precise sense in which the condemnatory sentence of the Sixth Ecumenical Council was to be understood. Pope Hadrian II (867-872) in a letter read at the Eighth General Council was to stress further that such an unprecedented condemnation of a Pope by an ecumenical council was only possible because the *Apostolic See itself* had consented to it (a remarkable testimony, by the way, to the Roman See's "plenitude of power" in the Church).[8]

Thus, continuing to bring up the history of Honorius as if this case really applied to the Church in the post-conciliar era, is not legitimate. It resembles the use of the quotation from St. Paul's Epistle to the Galatians, cited with perhaps equal or greater frequency than the case of Honorius by some traditionalists, in which St. Paul remarks that he "opposed [Peter] to his face" (*Gal.* 2:11). And why? Because the first Pope had "acted insincerely" (*Gal.* 2:13) —in other words, because his *personal conduct* had been deserving of censure, not his exercise of the divine authority granted to him as the Prince of the Apostles by Jesus Christ. It is also noteworthy that Paul thus "opposed" Peter to his face; that is to say, in person, not by stirring up absent third persons against him, as is done today in speeches, articles, books, and letters by many of those who justify themselves by reference to St. Paul's example. It is also worthy of note in this connection that St. Paul was not self-appointed to the task of establishing Christian policy towards the Gentiles, but he was himself God's specially appointed Apostle to the Gentiles, recognized as such by St. Peter. St. Paul was "sent" in a way that those who appoint themselves to criticize the Pope or the Council are surely not "sent."

To pretend to be defending "Catholic Tradition" by publicly opposing or publicly criticizing the visible head of the Church and guarantor of that Tradition is a most singular way of proceeding, especially when carried out by those who have no claim, as St. Paul did, to be special vessels of election (See Question #23).

The Honorius case seems, rather, to have been dredged up by the enemies of the Church in order to oppose the absolutely central Catholic "Tradition" of the Roman primacy. If the Honorius case is the worst indictment that can be brought against this Tradition, the enemies of the Church should properly be conceding how *good* the "track-record" of the Popes has been.

Henri Daniel-Rops is among those orthodox Catholic historians who believed that even the whole Honorius issue was blown far out of proportion at Constantinople III by the desire of the Greeks "to depreciate the authority of Rome."[9] Even the mild-mannered Monsignor Philip Hughes raises his voice slightly when commenting on how "controversial archeologists, straining every resource to embarrass the champions of the Roman primacy, turned to the record of the Sixth General Council and with more ingenuity than good faith tried to put on the decrees a meaning they were never meant to bear."[10]

What does it all mean to us today, in the aftermath of Vatican II? The authors are not really sure why the case is brought up so persistently by traditionalists if it is not, as we suggested at the beginning of this article, to imply that Popes John XXIII and Paul VI might similarly fall under a condemnation at some time in the future, just as the unfortunate Pope Honorius I did.

But it has not been shown what they could conceivably be condemned for. The Council was carried through with the virtually unanimous participation of the Catholic bishops of the whole world. In any case, the judgment of a council or a future Pope on the conduct of any predecessor would be a wholly different thing than a similar judgment rendered by private persons, say, in the columns of some traditionalist paper, who may imagine they are defending Catholic Tradition but who, in doing so, often curiously end up using the same accusations and allegations as the enemies of "the Roman primacy," which is to say, the enemies of the Church. This is a singular way to defend Catholic Tradition.

Supposing the conduct of some Pope to be truly deserving of condemnation, for "his negligence" or whatever, his official acts as Pope would nevertheless in no way be rendered invalid. Nothing that Pope Honorius I said or did during his papacy was in any way affected by the censure he received fifty years later at the hands of Constantinople III and his successor, Leo II. Certainly, disobedience to his authority during his reign by any of the faithful presuming to anticipate the official judgment of the Church would in no way whatsoever have been justified. Even those who might believe John XXIII or Paul VI to be deserving of a similar judgment could not adduce that belief as reason for not obeying their authority or that of their successors. The case of Honorius simply does not *apply* to the situation in the Church today.

Perhaps what really applies to a case like this is the saying of Our Lord: "Let the dead bury their dead" (*Mt.* 8:22).

Question # 23

YET OUR FAITH IS CLEARLY UNDER ATTACK TODAY. MUST WE NOT FIGHT BACK AGAINST ALL THE HERESY AND INFIDELITY? DIDN'T ST. ROBERT BELLARMINE TEACH THAT IT WAS LICIT TO RESIST EVEN A PONTIFF WHO ATTACKED SOULS?

When the question comes up of how we "fight" in and for the Church of God, many people make two fundamental mistakes:

1) They regard the Church as primarily a political-type organization in which the weapons of politics — pressure, exposure, and the like — are seen as appropriate also in the Church; and 2), on the analogy of democratic politics where the system *provides* for "throwing the rascals out" when they do not follow the popular will, they challenge the authorities of the Church directly as if these authorities were office-holders under a democratic system.

Neither of these reactions is really appropriate for a Catholic with regard to the Church. As regards the first reaction, that we must exert pressures on the authorities of the Church and expose their negligences and lapses, we must remember that "we are not contending against flesh and blood, but against principalities, against the powers. . .against the spiritual hosts of wickedness in the heavenly places *(Eph.* 6:12)," i.e., ultimately against evil spirits; and that spiritual, not political, weapons are what are most required in such a spiritual battle.

As regards the idea that Church authorities might be challenged and even removed from office by means of popular pressures, as if they were Congressmen or a President confronted with a Watergate cover-up or something of the sort, we must remember that the Church is not founded upon a democratic principle of government by the people but upon the principle of a divinely established authority from the top down, from Christ through the Pope and bishops down to the faithful. In establishing His Church upon His apostles, Christ said: "He who hears you hears Me, and he who rejects you rejects Me, and he who rejects Me rejects Him who sent Me" (*Lk.* 10:6).

When it is asked how we "fight" those who are sowing error and confusion in the Church, what is forgotten are the words of Our Lord that only "*if my kingdom were of this world*, my servants would fight" (*Jn.* 18:36); but His Kingdom is *not* of this world and hence we are not obligated to "fight" in the political sense suggested by the question—not if we are truly reflecting on what it means to be a servant of Christ.

Witness to our faith and bear fruit in our lives, yes; but "fight"? This does not mean that we ought not to proclaim Catholic truth and refute error with whatever means we dispose of to do so, or respectfully to draw the attention of Church authorities to certain errors or abuses. But we lay people have not been appointed to rule in the Church as though it were our responsibility to call a halt to the errors and abuses that we might see. The Church, as established by Christ, is ruled by a sacred hierarchy, whose members "the Holy Spirit has made . . . guardians, to feed the Church of the Lord" (*Acts* 20:28). The faithful are enjoined to "obey your prelates and be subject to them" (*Heb.* 13:17).

The manner in which the Church has been set up is not changed just because she is undergoing a crisis. She has undergone many crises in her long history and has eventually triumphed over them all. No doubt the same will be true of the present crisis. It is part of our *faith* that the "gates of hell" will not prevail (Cf. *Mt.* 16:18). God has permitted today's error and confusion for reasons best known to Himself; He will bring good out of it. It is not our duty to take active charge of correcting errors or abuses in the Church but rather, first of all, to try to be better Catholics and better examples ourselves, *especially* today, when there are so many bad examples!

Let us take a look at the teaching of St. Robert Bellarmine, that it would be licit to "resist" even a Pontiff who attacked souls. This is usually quoted as follows:

> "Just as it is licit to resist the Pontiff who attacks the body, so also it is licit to resist him who attacks souls, or who disturbs the civil order, or above all, him who tries to destroy the Church. I say that it is licit to resist him by not doing what he orders and by impeding the execution of his will; it is not licit, however, to judge him, to punish him or depose him, for these are acts proper to a superior."[1]

The first thing that has to be said about this opinion of St. Robert Bellarmine is that for it to apply at all in the case of the changes in the Church it would have to be shown that a Pontiff was in fact, "attacking souls"; otherwise it would not apply.

We have been able to show, in our replies to all the questions raised about the Mass and the reforms of Vatican II that by no stretch of the imagination was Pope Paul VI "attacking souls." Nor have his successors been doing so in continuing his policies. So the quotation, in fact, does not apply to our post-conciliar situation as far as the Pope is concerned. Though it is one of the quotations most frequently encountered in traditionalist literature, it really begs the question.

When we examine the context in which St. Robert Bellarmine was writing, we find that it has even *less* applicability than at first sight. The quotation is taken from one of St. Robert's replies to a long series of objections to the authority of the Pope drawn from various Protestant authors. The main point at issue in St. Robert's discussion is that the Pope has no superior on earth. As a human being he may have every frailty that flesh is heir to, of course, and so St. Robert Bellarmine, for the sake of argument, entertains many hypothetical possibilities, some of them even frivolous, to show that none of them really impinges upon or annuls the Pope's *authority*.

The particular question St. Robert Bellarmine is addressing himself to in the reply from which the above quotation is taken is the Protestant allegation that the Pope "murders souls by his own evil example." In reply, St. Robert concedes that one might resist a Pontiff who really was assaulting the body or soul but goes on to specify that, in the case of the Pope, considering the authority he possesses in his office, one could only "resist" him in a passive and negative way, that is, by "not doing what he orders," by abstaining from following his orders; but not by taking any positive action against him.

It is ironic that a passage from St. Robert Bellarmine which was written with the express intention of defending the unique and unsurpassed authority of the Pope is invoked today to undermine that authority. In no way can this passage justify not attending the New Order of the Mass, for instance, since the condition of the Pontiff "attacking souls" doesn't obtain. In any case, those who do not attend the *Norvus Ordo*—"not doing what he orders"—usually don't stop with such passive resistance; they go on to do exactly what St. Robert Bellarmine says it is *not* licit to do: they go on to "judge" the Pope and "punish" him, e.g., they attack the authority he had to revise the Roman Missal in the way that he revised it.

This approach reverses St. Robert Bellarmine's teaching to say exactly the opposite of what he taught.

When we go on to consider the further question of the faithful "fighting" in the Church for what they want, even rebelling or murmuring against the mandates of legitimate Church authority, we encounter a rather solid Catholic tradition against the very idea of it. This is true even when it is conceded, as it has to be conceded today, that there *are* evils to be fought against. But then we cannot lose sight of one plain fact of being a Catholic that, as Pope Leo XIII taught, "there are in the Church two grades, very distinct by their nature: the shepherds and the flock, that is to say, the rulers and the people. It is the function of the first order to teach, to govern, to guide men through life, to impose rules; the second has the duty to be submissive to the first, to obey, to carry out orders, to render honor."[2] Thus a Catholic is not justified in fighting *against* the hierarchy. The very nature of the hierarchical structure of the Church requires respect and deference from the Catholic for his prelates. "Honor thy father. . . ." This does not mean that the faithful, especially the laity, do not have any *rights* in the Church. On the contrary, as Pope Pius XII taught:

> "The layman has a right to receive from the priest every spiritual good, so that he may realize the salvation of his soul and attain Christian perfection: when the fundamental rights of the Christian are at stake he may assert his needs; it is the meaning and the very goal of the life of the Church which is here at stake, as well as the responsibility before God of the priest no less than of the layman."[3]

But even though all the faithful have rights there are limits on what they can say or do, even when real objective evils arise, because, after all, the faithful are not in charge of the Church; the pastors are, and Christ set it up that way. What the laity may do, even when they legitimately "assert their needs," is somewhat limited by the very hierarchical structure of the Church.

The Second Vatican Council nevertheless went on to make definitive the rights the laity do enjoy in the Church:

> "Like all Christians, the Laity have the right to receive in abundance the help of the spiritual goods of the Church, es-

pecially that of the word of God and the sacraments from the pastors. To the latter the laity should disclose their needs and desires with that liberty and confidence which befits children of God and brothers of Christ. By reason of the knowledge, competence or preeminence which they have the laity are empowered — indeed sometimes obliged — to manifest their opinion on those things which pertain to the good of the Church. If the occasion should arise this should be done through the institutions established by the Church for that purpose and always with truth, courage and prudence and with reverence and charity towards those who, by reason of their office, represent the person of Christ" (Dogmatic Constitution on the Church *Lumen Gentium*, #37).

Now this teaching is hardly a mandate for "fighting" in the sense of demanding that one's views prevail in the Church as if she were merely some kind of a political entity rather than the Mystical Body of Christ. The Council specifies that a Christian spirit should prevail in whatever representations may be made to the hierarchy. Indeed the Council goes on to teach that, once they have made known their needs "with truth, courage and prudence and with reverence and charity," the laity may then properly commend the issue to the providence of God:

> "Like all Christians, the Laity should promptly accept in Christian obedience what is decided by the pastors who, as teachers and rulers of the Church, represent Christ. In this they will follow Christ's example who, by his obedience unto death, opened the blessed way of the liberty of the sons of God to all men. Nor should they fail to commend to God in their prayers those who have been placed over them, who indeed keep watch as having to render an account of our souls, that they may do this with joy and not with grief" (*Ibid.*).

Lest it seem "untraditional" to some thus to say that the Catholic faithful are required by the Catholic faith itself to be not only obedient but docile to the Church authorities placed over them, and not to contest and "fight" them, we hasten to quote earlier Church pronouncements which show that this teaching has, in fact, been constant and consistent.

Pope Pius IX, for example, in 1854, taught as follows:

"We beg you urgently to be each day more ardent in your love for religion, to employ your zeal for the maintenance of peace, and not only never to undertake anything against the Church or against your pastors—as those are accustomed to do who have severed themselves from Catholic unity—but still more to lend the support of your counsel and your efforts so that the Catholic Church will grow and prosper among you, and all will be animated by those sentiments of respect, devotion, and docility, which they ought to have, whether towards the authority of Peter and his successors the Roman Pontiffs, divinely charged by Christ Our Lord to feed—that is to say, to rule and govern—the Church in its entirety, or to the sacred and venerable authority which bishops have over their own flocks. . . ."[4]

The teachings of Leo XIII in the same vein are almost too numerous to mention, but we quote one from the year 1885:

"By certain indications it is not difficult to conclude that among Catholics—doubtless as a result of current evils—there are some who, far from satisfied with the condition of 'subject' which is theirs in the Church, think they are allowed to examine and judge after their own fashion, the acts of authority. A misplaced opinion, certainly. If it were to prevail, it would do very grave harm to the Church of God, in which, by the manifest will of her Divine Founder, there are to be distinguished in the most absolute fashion two parties: the teaching and the taught, the Shepherd and the flock, among whom there is one who is the head and the Supreme Shepherd of all.

"To the shepherds alone was given all power to teach, to judge, to direct; on the faithful was imposed the duty of following their teaching, of submitting with docility to their judgment, and of allowing themselves to be governed, corrected, and guided by them in the way of salvation. Thus, it is an absolute necessity for the simple faithful to submit in mind and heart to their own pastors, and for the latter to submit with them to the Head and Supreme Pastor."[5]

Here is another one from Leo XIII dating from the year 1888:

"No, it cannot be permitted that laymen who profess to be Catholic should go so far as openly to arrogate to themselves in the columns of a newspaper, the right to denounce, and to find fault, with the greatest license and according to their own good pleasure, with every sort of person, not excepting bishops, and think that with the single exception of matters of faith they are allowed to entertain any opinion which may please them and exercise the right to judge everyone after their own fashion."[6]

Indeed, as we have already seen in the reply to Question #3, Pope Pius IX *condemned* in his encyclical *Quanta Cura* the proposition that "without sinning and without at all departing from the profession of the Catholic faith, it is possible to refuse assent and obedience to those decisions and decrees of the Apostolic See whose declared object is the general good of the Church and its rights and discipline, provided only that such decisions do not touch upon dogmas of faith or morals."[7]

The general principle that the Catholic faithful have an obligation of docility and obedience to the sacred hierarchy in everything pertaining to our holy religion is thus blindingly clear. No Catholic could possibly deny this principle. Problems arise today because in the midst of the present crisis, given the confusion that is endemic in the Church, some Catholics perceive the hierarchy itself as not upholding the faith and discipline of the Church; the post-Vatican II changes themselves are thought to be the causes of the proliferation of error and abuses throughout the post-conciliar Church. The temptation is to assume that traditional Church teachings about the need for docility and obedience to the hierarchy, no matter how clearly and firmly they may have been established in the Tradition—as we have seen that they have been established— simply cannot *apply* to our unique post-conciliar situation. Extraordinary times call for extraordinary measures. So it is argued. No Catholic who cares about the faith can simply remain passive and docile in the face of action by a hierarchy which itself is held to undermine the faith and discipline of the Church or—a much more plausible hypothesis—of *inaction* and *permissiveness* on the part of the hierarchy which is harmful to the Church. By this latter is meant that the hierarchy is considered to be merely looking on while others, be they dissenting theologians, liturgical innovators, "liberated" priests or nuns, sex educators, "new" catechists opposed to teaching doctrine, or whatever, enjoy the "freedom of the Church" to carry on their activities uncorrected; indeed average Catholics are often left unenlightened and uncorrected when they show by their plain words and actions (or in the results of the latest poll) that *they* now think they can pick and choose among the doctrines and disciplines of the Church.

This is the situation some of the faithful think they *see* today in the Church. And there is evidence, available to anyone, that their eyes are not always deceiving them. So they ask: where are the bishops? Where, indeed, is the Pope? *How* can anyone simply be "docile" towards leaders seen as not doing their jobs?

So the question is asked, and so the whole traditionalist phenomenon which we have been examining in these pages arises as one — mistaken — answer to it.

The two authors do not share this unduly pessimistic view about the post-conciliar Popes and hierarchy, as the present book testifies. We have shown throughout the book that the official enactments of recent Popes or the Second Vatican Council cannot be stigmatized as the cause of the present crisis of the Church. The real cause has been primarily disobedience to Church authority. We have demonstrated in particular in the answer to Question #19, that the Holy See, especially, throughout the entire period of the present crisis, has continued to function as Christ promised. Rome cannot be blamed for the crisis. Unexpected as the crisis was, the Holy See has nevertheless consistently tried to face up to it. And it is simply common sense, whoever or whatever is to blame, to realize that the authorities of the Church, not only in Rome but at every level, now have to be allowed both time and elbow room, if they are to be able to deal effectively with a crisis of the magnitude of the present one. In short, public criticisms, exposés, recriminations, reproaches, confrontations, or other forms of "pressure" on the Holy See or the sacred hierarchy over the present problems of the Church are hardly what is called for. Human nature being what it is, these things will only be resented. They can even be temporarily mistaken for the real "problem," and may thus even delay the solution to some of the problems the traditionalists may be correct in recognizing but wrong in their method of resolving.

This having been said, however, the fact still remains that if the laity, according to traditional Catholic doctrine, have a duty to be obedient and docile to the hierarchy, as we have shown, the hierarchy, according to that same traditional Catholic doctrine, has a duty which it too must carry out; it has an obligation not merely to teach authentic doctrine and establish disciplinary and liturgical norms in some formal or official way; it also has an obligation to *enforce* both orthodoxy and discipline on the part of everybody within the Church. The members of the hierarchy must enforce both doctrine and discipline — thus says the second half of the scriptural quotation we already cited earlier exhorting the faithful to obey their prelates — "as men who will have to give an account" (*Heb.* 13:17). However much the Church today may *prefer,* in Pope John XXIII's famous phrase, "to make use of the medicine of mercy rather than that of severity,"[8] the latter is surely *not* to be excluded if proved necessary. This is inherent in the fact that the Church has been given *authority.*

In the context, Pope John was in any case referring to the stance the Church should adopt towards the *world,* to try to win it over, since honey attracts more readily than vinegar, as St. Francis de Sales so aptly observed. Pope John's words thus cannot be used as the justification for any indulgence or laxity towards those *within the Church* who reject, in whatever degree, the Church's legitimate teaching and discipline.

This is not merely "traditional" Catholic doctrine. Vatican Council II, in its Dogmatic Constitution on the Church *Lumen Gentium,* taught that "episcopal consecration confers. . .the *duty* of teaching and *ruling*" (#21); "all the bishops have the obligation of fostering and safeguarding the unity of faith and of *upholding the discipline* which is common to the whole Church" (#23); that "the bishops are heralds of the faith. . .teachers endowed with the authority of Christ. . .and with watchfulness *they ward off whatever errors threaten their flock*" (#25); that "bishops have a sacred right and a duty before the Lord of legislating for and of *passing judgment* on their subjects, as well as of *regulating everything* that *concerns the good order* of divine worship. . ." (#27; emphasis added throughout).

These passages establish beyond any doubt that Vatican II envisaged a continuation of firm discipline among the committed faithful. Pope John's "medicine of mercy" was not primarily intended to apply here. Has this been fully understood by the hierarchy since the Council?

It is no part of the intention of the authors to charge the members of the hierarchy, or any individuals among them, with being derelict or remiss in carrying out or enforcing the Church's teachings in the post-conciliar period. We make no assertions about this. It is sufficient for our purposes here that the hierarchy has been *perceived* as being deficient in this regard by at least some of the faithful. The very existence of a traditionalist movement bears witness to this unhappy fact. That the hierarchy can itself thus be perceived today as being in the wrong, even if only occasionally, even if only on one single point, creates an obvious problem for the faithful Catholic. What *is* a Catholic supposed to do, if, for example, his bishop, the prelate he is supposed to obey, turns out to be out of line himself on some Catholic doctrine or basic Church practice?

First of all, from all that has been said and quoted from Church teachings above, we can immediately reply that it is not the duty or the function of the faithful, on their own, to *correct* a wayward prelate. Pope Leo XIII made this very clear as far back as 1888:

> "If by chance there should be in the ranks of the episcopate a bishop not sufficiently mindful of his dignity and apparently unfaithful to one of his sacred obligations, in spite of this he would lose nothing of his power, and, so long as he remained in communion with the Roman Pontiff, it would certainly not be permitted to anyone to relax in any detail the respect and obedience which are due his authority. On the other hand, to scrutinize the actions of a bishop, to criticize them, does not belong to individual Catholics, but concerns only those who, in the sacred hierarchy, have a superior power; above all, it concerns the Supreme Pontiff, for it is to him that Christ confided the care of feeding not only all the lambs, but even the sheep."[9]

Pope Leo XIII returned to this point again two years later in his encyclical *Sapientiae Christianae,* issued in 1890:

> "Among the prelates, indeed, one or other there may be affording scope to criticism either in regard to personal conduct or in reference to opinions by him entertained about points of doctrine; but no private person may arrogate to himself the office of judge which Christ our Lord has bestowed on that one alone whom He placed in charge of His lambs and of His sheep."[10]

The import of these traditional papal teachings is unmistakable:

correction of bishops is reserved to the Pope. Leo XIII recognized, of course, that the faithful possess a "right of appeal" over the head of a possibly wayward bishop, a right that Vatican II's Dogmatic Constitution on the Church *Lumen Gentium,* as we have quoted it above, would surely allow. Even in allowing such a "right of appeal" for the faithful, however, Leo XIII evidently excludes the kind of harsh public criticism of a bishop or bishops which some traditionalists have considered themselves fully entitled to make in the past few years:

> "When the faithful have grave cause for complaint," Leo XIII said, "they are allowed to put the whole matter before the Roman Pontiff, provided always that, safeguarding prudence and the moderation counseled by concern for the common good, they do not give vent to outcries and recriminations which contribute rather to the rise of divisions and ill-feeling, or certainly increase them."[11]

The first point is clear, then: it is not the duty of the laity to correct delinquent prelates if any such are to be found. A second point is equally clear, one that can almost be taken as axiomatic for a Catholic, and that is that the only standard or criterion by which an individual bishop *could* be judged to be out of line would be whether he adhered in his teaching and acts to the doctrine and discipline established by the Roman Pontiff. "In order that the episcopate itself might be one and undivided," Vatican I taught, "and that the whole multitude of believers might be preserved in unity of faith and communion by means of a closely united priesthood, [Christ] placed St. Peter at the head of the other apostles."[12] The Most Reverend Jerome Hamer, O.P., Secretary of the Sacred Congregation for the Doctrine of the Faith, told the United States bishops assembled for their annual meeting in November, 1978, that it is always *presupposed* that a "bishop's teaching is carried out 'in communion with the Roman Pontiff,' in other words, within hierarchical communion and in accordance with its norms."[13]

But what if, in fact, it is not? What if a bishop's teaching, even on a single point, does not accord with a known teaching of the Pope? Or, what if, silent or inaccessible himself, a bishop allows others the freedom of the Church to teach or preach at variance with what the Holy See's teaching is known to be? Or what if a bishop sanctions or allows practices in the doctrinal realm at variance with what the Holy See's teaching is known to be? Or what if a bishop sanctions or allows practices in the disciplinary realm at variance with what Rome has decreed? Supposing any of these "ifs" were actually verified, it is obvious that a problem would be created for the Catholic desirous of following the Church—a problem would be created for him almost *in the degree* that he desired to follow the Church.

The practical problem that really, and acutely, arises is this: to what extent must a Catholic *obey* the directives of a bishop who is himself out of line with what the Holy See has enjoined? This is an acutely serious problem for some of the faithful who believe their prelates *are* out of line, and, whether or not they are correct in their judgment, they sometimes go further and join a traditionalist "little church" as the only practical alternative to living under a bishop who is considered out of line.

Usually the problem is not quite so clear-cut. Certainly no bishop could be held to be out of line for having instituted, for example, the *Novus Ordo*. The bishop was certainly obliged to do this and was wholly in line with the Holy See in doing so. There are other cases which are more real, however, and which also, inevitably, create problems for the conscientious Catholic—problems which may bring him to be tempted by the traditionalist response.

Let us take the case of, say, a diocesan policy mandating or allowing First Communion before First Confession when the reverse order represents the true discipline of the Holy See in this matter, as has been clear beyond all doubt ever since the publication of the General Catechetical Directory in 1971. Or let us imagine a diocesan catechetical program mandating deficient religion texts and perhaps forbidding other texts admittedly orthodox; or a diocesan program in so-called "sex education" failing to respect traditional Catholic teachings about chastity, modesty, marriage and the regulation of births. There might be cited further the problem of episcopal tolerance of priests or theologians publicly taking positions at variance with known Church doctrine; or a similar tolerance of such liturgical aberrations contrary to the established discipline of the Holy See as Communion in the hand (before it was authorized), "self-service" from the chalice, the use of "altar girls," Communion from "extraordinary ministers" while vested celebrants benignly sit in the sanctuary, dialogue homilies preached by the people, liturgical dancing, etc., etc.

It would be hard to deny that such things as these are sometimes to be encountered today. And while we can grant that it is the responsibility of the members of the hierarchy to handle these problems in the manner they believe most suitable—to correct or, possibly, withhold correction temporarily to avoid greater evils—even granting this, the point that we are making here is that if tolerance of abuses becomes a policy of *laissez-faire,* for whatever period of time, this is bound to have an effect on some of the faithful.

When the average Catholic faithful encounter unCatholic manifestations of whatever kind in Catholic parishes or Catholic schools, they almost inevitably conclude that these things could not be going on without the express sanction of the bishop, whether this is in fact true or not. In that case, some may quickly go on to conclude further that what they are encountering is in contradiction to the Catholic Church which they have always known; what they are seeing itself has to be heretical; the Pope and bishops and the Council are what is wrong; so they reason. Catholics who react this way are the natural recruits for the various "little churches" still offering Tridentine Masses which at least preserve the *appearance* of the Church which they have always known. It is regrettable to have to make this point, but we here touch upon one of the principal *reasons* for the rejection of the Second Vatican Council and the *Novus Ordo,* i.e., the fact that the post-conciliar Church has sometimes been allowed to appear to be no longer entirely "One, Holy, Catholic, and Apostolic."

The authors do not for a moment accept this proposition that the Church no longer bears her traditional marks. We only point to the fact that some Catholics have come to believe it in the midst of the post-conciliar confusion and ambiguity.

Other Catholics are aware that whatever aberrations may have occurred are not what the Council or post-conciliar Church really called for but indeed go against what they called for. Nevertheless, these Catholics too can face a problem which may sometimes become a real problem of conscience: to what extent can they go along with or obey things which apparently have the sanction, or at least the tolerance, of the bishop, by the very fact that they are going on, but which do not accord with what the Holy See has enjoined? Is a bishop who sanctions or allows such things still entitled to the obedience of the faithful subject to him? Do the faithful have to follow him when he is apparently not following the Pope?

The answer to this question can be summed up by saying that such a bishop continues to be entitled to obedience in *everything that he does legitimately command.* If he should happen to command or mandate one or more things that are not legitimate, we could in *that or in those cases only,* follow St. Robert Bellarmine's principle, enunciated above, of "not doing what he orders"; in other words, we could decline to follow a command or mandate in a case where we had certain knowledge that a positive action would be against Church discipline or the faith. To take some concrete examples: we could decline to enroll our children in a deficient school program which could harm their faith or morals; or we could remove them from such a program; or, aware of the Roman discipline, we could respectfully request First Confession before First Communion for our children against a contrary diocesan practice. Other examples easily come to mind along the same lines.

However, in thus, negatively, "not doing what he orders" in such concrete instances as these, we could *not* legitimately go on to conclude from the fact that a bishop might have lapsed in this or that point, or have sanctioned or allowed something at variance with what we know with certainty the mind of Rome to be, that such a bishop was no longer, in effect, a real bishop, or that no further obedience of any kind was owed to him. For we would still be obliged to obey him as our bishop in all other respects.

Let us suppose that a bishop permitted dissenters from the encyclical *Humanae Vitae* to teach or preach in his diocese, promoted or allowed general absolution contrary to Vatican norms, mandated questionable religion texts, and permitted his religion teachers to prepare children to receive First Communion before First Confession. Knowing the true teaching or discipline of the Pope on all these matters, we would be obliged to follow the Pope instead of the bishop *in these particular matters* —and to the extent that they impinged personally on us or those for whom the Church says we are responsible. But so long as we remained under his episcopal jurisdiction we would be obliged to follow him in all other respects in which presumably he would be teaching and acting in accord with the Holy Father—unless and until the Holy Father himself declared that he was no longer in communion with the Holy See.

It is not for the faithful to make this latter determination in a general sense. Even when, as may be the case in more than one diocese today, "the faithful have grave cause for complaint," in the words of Leo XIII, quoted above, and even when we might be allowed "to put the whole matter before the Roman Pontiff," it would still not devolve upon us to make the determination ourselves that a Catholic bishop had ceased to be a Catholic bishop and to withdraw ourselves from regular parish or sacramental life within a diocese, as some traditionalists have done. Errors and abuses are assuredly very serious, especially whenever they might actually be sanctioned or tolerated by a bishop, but they certainly do not excuse us from attending the *Novus Ordo* Masses which *have* been lawfully established in all the dioceses of the United States in accordance with the current discipline approved by the Bishop of Rome.

It has been necessary to spell out some of these distinctions because so many Catholics have taken the existence of errors and abuses as justifying an exodus into "little churches" where the Tridentine Mass is still said as it was before 1960. This is not the case; abuses do not justify disobedience. We have accordingly spelled out here the principles of the obedience that is still certainly owed by Catholics to their local Ordinary in spite of whatever blemishes might be present in his diocese. What we have said here accords with the principles of obedience to authority laid down by St. Thomas Aquinas which we have already quoted in the reply to Question #8, namely, that we must obey a lawful superior in all those respects in which he *is* our superior—unless we are obliged to obey a higher power in a different sense.[14] In his *Letter to the Duke of Norfolk,* John Henry Newman brought out the same principles of obedience when he said, in effect, that we must obey a superior in all that which he *has the authority to command.*[15]

Our bishop is empowered to teach the faith of Christ and to impose Church discipline in accord with the mind of Rome; and where he is doing this we always owe him our assent and obedience. But he does not have any authority to teach or permit to be taught by those under him what could in any point be shown to be a non-faith or an anti-faith or anything less than the faith, or to impose any discipline upon us contrary to the one approved by the Roman Pontiff. As St. Paul taught, Church authority has been given for "building up," not for "destroying" (cf. II *Cor.* 10:8).

Archbishop Jerome Hamer, O.P., Secretary of the Sacred Congregation for the Doctrine of the Faith, has also, again, said:

> "The religious assent of intelligence and will (Cf. *Lumen Gentium* #25) that the faithful owe to the authentic teaching of their own bishop (teaching in Christ's name, in the area of faith and morals, in communion with the head of the Church), cannot be expected, far less demanded, for the free opinions that this same bishop would like to propose."[16]

It is on this whole question that a great deal of confusion has reigned in the post-conciliar period. On the one hand, errors and abuses have sometimes been allowed to parade as if they were the real reforms of Vatican II. On the other hand, traditionalists have capitalized on these real errors and abuses as a pretext and justification for going back to the Tridentine Mass without the necessary sanction of the hierarchical Church.

Indiscriminate "fighting back against all the heresy and infidelity," as our present question puts it, will not improve the present undesirable situation in the Church. While Catholics may and must uphold truth by whatever means available, St. Robert Bellarmine's principle makes it very clear that it is illegitimate for them to "fight" their prelates; they can only "resist" them negatively — assuming a very real cause to do so exists — by "not doing what they command," not by taking any positive action against them. This is the Pope's responsibility. What the laity can best do to help ameliorate the present situation in the Church is to dedicate themselves to that *renewal* of the Church which the Second Vatican Council in fact called for. To paraphrase Chesterton, it is not that the Council has been tried and found wanting; it hasn't yet been tried. It is high time it was tried after all the false starts of the past few years.

To that subject we must now turn, in the answer to our next — and final — question.

Question # 24

WHAT, THEN, CAN WE DO IN THE MIDDLE OF THE "CRISIS IN THE CHURCH?"

What we can do in the middle of the "crisis in the Church"—all of us, whether laity, religious, priests or even bishops — is easy to state but hard to do. It is always hard to get that camel through the eye of that needle!

Let us state in four simple propositions what we can and must do:

1. Keep the faith;
2. Follow the Pope;
3. Find out what the Council really said; and
4. Do it.

"Keep the Faith." No matter what crisis ever overtakes the Church, we must remember that as far as we, individually, are concerned, our goal remains to escape the temptations of the world, the flesh and the devil, sanctify ourselves with the help of the graces given to us in the sacraments, especially the Holy Eucharist, and get to heaven. No matter what others may be doing, we still must keep our eyes on *our* goal: it is our first responsibility not to "save the Church" but, in the words with which St. Ignatius of Loyola almost always closed his letters to his Jesuits, to "seek to know God's most holy will and perfectly fulfill it."

To the extent that we keep our faith in Christ's word, mediated to us through the Church, and do it, He will see to it that what we do will *also* be for the good of the Church, in the measure that it is given to us to help the Church. We have a responsibility also to deepen our knowledge of the Catholic faith as taught by the Church's living Magisterium right down to and including the present. We must meditate on it, even seek a greater and deeper understanding of what it requires of us, and, of course, always defend and spread it to the best of our ability.

It is also good to recall that although we have been *promised* that in this world we will have "tribulation," Our Lord and Savior yet bids us to "be of good cheer, I have overcome the world" (*Jn.* 16:-33). In Him and His Church we must therefore continue to have precisely, *faith,* not because things are going well with the Church, but whether or not they are going well. Those who cite the current tribulations of the Church as "evidence" that her current rulers have led her away from Christ into error cannot really have very much of the child's faith that Christ in fact asks of all of us.

"For such is the power of great minds, such the light of truly believing souls," Pope St. Leo the Great said back in the fifth century, "that they put unhesitating faith in what is not seen with the bodily eye; they fix their desires on what is beyond sight. Such fidelity could never be born in our hearts, nor could anyone be justified by faith, if our salvation lay only in what was visible."[1] The Church has only survived down through the ages on the basis of faith such as this.

"Follow the Pope." In the course of this work, the authors have brought forward arguments and evidence showing that the questions about the Church and the Mass which the traditionalists started asking in the post-conciliar period were all mostly answered at the time by the Pope. The Pope explained what he was doing at almost every step of the way for those who had "ears to hear" (*Mt.* 11:15). But too many were not listening to what the Pope said; instead they were listening to other voices giving *their* interpretation of what the Pope meant or what the Catholic Tradition was. A book like this would have been unnecessary if Catholics had been doing what everybody knows Catholics are supposed to do, namely, follow the Pope. If we will do that in the future, the kinds of questions we have had to answer here will not even arise.

The advice of John Henry Cardinal Newman given to perplexed Catholics more than a century ago needs to be repeated today:

> "In the midst of our difficulties I have one ground of hope, just one stay, but, as I think, a sufficient one, which serves me in the stead of all other argument whatever, which hardens me against criticism, which supports me if I begin to despond, and to which I ever come round, when the question of the possible and the expedient is brought into discussion. It is the decision of the Holy See; St. Peter has spoken, it is he who has enjoined that which seems to us so unpromising. He has spoken and has a claim on us to trust him. He is no recluse, no solitary student,

no dreamer about the past, no doter upon the dead and gone, no projector of the visionary. He for eighteen hundred years has lived in the world; he has seen all fortunes, he has encountered all adversaries, he has shaped himself for all emergencies. If ever there was a power on earth who had an eye for the times, who has confined himself to the practicable, and has been happy in his anticipations, whose words have been facts, and whose commands prophecies, such is he in the history of ages, who sits from generation to generation in the Chair of the Apostles, as the Vicar of Christ, and the Doctor of His Church.

"These are not words of rhetoric, gentlemen, but of history. All who take part with the Apostle are on the winning side. He has long since given warrant for the confidence which he claims. From the first he has looked through the wide world of which he has the burden; and, according to the need of the day and the inspirations of his Lord, he has set himself now to one thing, now to another; but to all in season, and to nothing in vain."[2]

"Find Out What the Council Really Said." Because of the "crisis" which has overtaken the Church in the post-conciliar years, every Catholic now owes it to himself to find out what the Second Vatican Council was all about. There has been a general council only about once in a century in the history of the Church, and we should assume that through the Council held in our lifetime, the Holy Spirit has not troubled the world for nothing. Every Catholic should procure a copy of the Council's documents to read and study — especially those of us who are of the laity — to learn of the special call made to the laity by this Council.[3]

For the laity, the Council declared, are "called by God that, being led by the spirit of the Gospel, they may contribute to the sanctification of the world" (Vatican Council II, Dogmatic Constitution on the Church *Lumen Gentium,* #31). "All of Christ's followers. . .are invited and bound to pursue holiness," the Council further declared (*Ibid.* #42); this means that the laity too are called to further the renewal called for by the Council which Pope Paul termed an inner, personal, moral renewal. The apostolate of lay people is exercised, the Second Vatican Council still further says, "when they work at the evangelization and sanctification of men," an apostolate "which calls for concerted action" (Decree on the

Apostolate of Lay People *Apostolicam Actuositatem*, #2, 18).

It is this kind of true Catholic action that we must now undertake, nourished by the true voice of the Council. "What the Spirit said to the Church through the Council of our time, what the Spirit says in this Church to all the Churches (Cf. *Rev.* 2:2)", Pope John Paul II declared in his first encyclical *Redemptor Hominis* (#3)—as we have already had occasion to note (Question #1)—"cannot lead to anything else—in spite of momentary uneasiness—but a still more mature solidity of the whole salvific mission." Above all, John Paul II believes we must *trust* the Council.

"And Do It." The whole People of God, then—with the Catholic laity very much included—must now pursue the authentic renewal of the faith and the apostolate of the evangelization and sanctification of men called for by the Council: "The apostolate of the laity is a sharing of the salvific mission of the Church. Through Baptism and Confirmation all are appointed to this apostolate by the Lord Himself" (*Lumen Gentium* #33). By the Lord Himself! This is all the more true because the present crisis of faith which threatens all Christians living in a post-Christian society cannot be met successfully until professing Catholics really *live* the faith as the Church preaches and teaches it in her official doctrine and the acts of her authentic Magisterium. It is already past time for many Catholics in the United States and Canada (not to mention those in other decadent Western societies) to get back to the fundamental need for reconversion to Christ and evangelization of a paganized world.

Such a spiritual transformation in Christ is a necessary pre-condition for restoring internal peace within the Church, for reintegrating our separated brethren into the unity of the Church, and for forming those individual Christians who might again constitute the basis for a new kind of Christian society. The lay apostolate itself—as the Church has expounded so clearly in our time—demands the development of the cultivated lay man and woman, i.e., those who have achieved the spiritual and intellectual maturity which John Henry Newman, again, described so beautifully:

> "I want a laity, not arrogant, not rash in speech, not disputatious, but men who know their religion, who enter into it, who know just where they stand, who know what they hold, and what they do not; who know their creed so well that they can give an account of it, who know so much of history that they can defend it. I want an intelligent, well-instructed laity;

I am not denying you are such already, but I mean to be severe, and, as some would say, exorbitant in my demands. I wish you to enlarge your knowledge, to cultivate your reason, to get an insight into the relation of truth to truth, to learn to view things as they are, to understand how faith and reason stand to each other, what are the bases and principles of Catholicism."[4]

The Second Vatican Council's Decree on the Apostolate of the Laity *Apostolicam Actuositatem* envisages exactly this kind of layman who will readily undertake his necessary role as "evangelizer" of the modern world.

No one can mistake the earnestness with which the Second Vatican Council has called upon the laity to play their full role in the life and mission of the Church. The tasks are immense —from the task of defending Catholic truth against the current assaults of some even within the Church, to handing down the Catholic faith as parents and primary educators of their children. Again, "the laity are called by God. . .being led by the spirit of the Gospel, so that they can work for the sanctification of the world from within, in the manner of leaven" (*Lumen Gentium*, #31). Thus the laity are *sent*.

A lay apostolate is called for which will inflame hearts with the love of Christ and zeal for His cause. In keeping the flame of faith alive in our own hearts, there can be no substitute for firm doctrinal instruction for ourselves and our children. Above all, as we have noted already, we must listen carefully to the voice of the Vicar of Christ who from the indefectible Chair of Peter continues to feed the sheep and lambs of the flock of Christ with those certainties anchored in the revealed Word of God.

We do not need to listen to those voices which are "legion" and which revel in their own personal views; we must not listen to those who attack the Pope and the bishops in communion with him, and thus attack our faith. When our obedience to the Holy See or our faith in the validity and doctrinal integrity of the Holy Sacrifice of the Mass (as celebrated by priests in communion with that Holy See) is undermined by publications, writings and authors spreading not only half-truths but even errors, it is spiritually foolhardy to keep drinking such poison.

Are not these words of Cardinal Newman, whom we have had to call upon so often for help in these pages, again very much to the point concerning temptations against faith in our own time?

"And so again, when a man has become a Catholic, were he to set about following a doubt which has occurred to him, he has already disbelieved. *I* have not to warn him against losing his faith, he is not merely in danger of losing it, he has lost it; from the nature of the case he has already lost it; he fell from grace at the moment when he deliberately entertained and pursued his doubt. No one can determine to doubt what he is already sure of; but if he is not sure that the Church is from God, he does not believe it. It is not I who forbid him to doubt; he has taken the matter into his own hands when he determined on asking for leave; he has begun, not ended, in unbelief; his very wish, his purpose, is his sin. I do not make it so, it is such from the very state of the case. You sometimes hear, for example, of Catholics falling away, who will tell you it arose from reading the Scriptures, which opened their eyes to the 'unscripturalness,' so they speak, of the Church of the living God. No; Scripture did not make them disbelieve (impossible); they disbelieved *when* they opened the Bible; they opened it in an unbelieving spirit, and for an unbelieving purpose; they would not have opened it, had they not anticipated— I might say, hoped—that they should find things there inconsistent with Catholic teaching. They begin in self-will and disobedience, and they end in apostasy. This, then, is the direct and obvious reason why the Church cannot allow her children the liberty of doubting the truth of her word."[5]

The authors have now reached the end of their arduous labors, and, in doing so, it is sad to reflect how many today might consider the answers to the questions to which we have addressed ourselves mistaken because we have not been able to ratify the traditionalist position; or how many others might consider the questions themselves not worth bothering about. We, however, prefer the attitude of Fr. John A. Hardon, S.J., author of *The Catholic Catechism*,[6] who has said that he considers all the labor that goes into the making of a book eminently worth it if he can thereby influence one single reader and confirm his faith. We too have aimed principally to confirm the faith of Catholics that God does not lie. The Church is still the Church and "the gates of hell" will not prevail. We think it fitting to conclude with another quotation of the great Pope Pius XI, who says in a single paragraph much of what we, too, have labored to express:

"Every true and lasting reform stems, in the last analysis, from holiness, from men impelled by the fire of love of God and neighbor. By their courageous readiness to hear every one of God's appeals, and to realize it first in their own lives, they have been in a position, by reason of their humility and the awareness of their own vocation, to bring light and renewal to their times. But where reforming zeal has not sprung from personal purity, but was the expression and explosive manifestation of passion, it has disturbed instead of clarifying; destroyed rather than raised up; it has been not seldom the starting point of errors worse than the evils it expected or intended to remedy. Certainly, the Spirit of God breatheth where He will. From the very stones He can raise up those who will prepare the way for his designs. He chooses the instruments of his will according to his plans and not according to the plans of men. But He who founded the Church and called it into being in the mighty wind of Pentecost will not destroy the bases of that institute of salvation willed by Himself. The one who is moved by the spirit of God has spontaneously the appropriate interior and exterior attitude toward the Church, that sacred fruit on the tree of the Cross, that pentecostal gift of God's Spirit to a world in need of leadership."[7]

KNOW THE OFFICIAL DECREES OF THE HOLY SEE WITH REGARD TO THE LITURGICAL RENEWAL!

Vatican Council II, The Conciliar and Post Conciliar Documents, by Austin Flannery, O.P. $4.95

Letter of Pope John Paul II to All the Bishops of the Church "On the Mystery and Worship of the Eucharist," *Dominicae Cenae*
$.35

Sacred Congregation for the Sacraments and Divine Worship. "Instruction Concerning Worship of the Eucharistic Mystery," *Inaestimabile Donum* $.25

All Three Documents: $5.00

Please add $1.00 for postage and handling.

Order from:

CATHOLICS UNITED FOR THE FAITH
222 North Avenue — Box S
New Rochelle, N.Y. 10801

Appendix I

APOSTOLIC CONSTITUTION *MISSALE ROMANUM* OF POPE PAUL VI

(In view of all the controversy which has surrounded both this Apostolic Constitution revising the Roman Missal, and, especially, some of the translations of it which have appeared, we have elected to reprint here an original translation. This translation was made from the text of the Apostolic Constitution officially promulgated in the Acta Apostolica Sedis, *#4, April 30, 1969, in accordance with Canon IX of the Code of Canon Law. It is thus a direct translation from the Latin version recognized as binding by the Church.)*

APOSTOLIC CONSTITUTION

The Roman Missal, revised according to the decree of the Second Vatican Ecumenical Council, is promulgated.

PAUL, BISHOP, SERVANT OF THE SERVANTS OF GOD, FOR A PERPETUAL RECORD:

The Roman Missal, promulgated by Our Predecessor St. Pius V in 1570, according to the decree of the Council of Trent, is universally accepted to be among the many wonderful and useful fruits which that Holy Synod brought to the universal Church of Christ. For four centuries, not only did the priests of the Latin rite use it as the norm according to which they offered the Eucharistic Sacrifice, but preachers of the holy Gospel introduced it into almost all lands. Moreover, countless saintly men copiously nourished their piety towards God by drawing from it both readings of the Holy Scriptures and prayers, most of which were arranged in definite order by St. Gregory the Great.

But since that time study of the sacred liturgy began to grow and to gain vigor more widely among Christian people. This, in the opinion of Our Predecessor of venerable memory, Pope Pius XII, seemed to be a most favorable indication of the providence of God towards the men of this age and also an indication of a salutary passing of the Holy Spirit through His Church. Furthermore, it seemed to clearly manifest that the formulas of the Roman Missal should be somewhat revised, and enriched by certain additions. This same Predecessor of Ours began this work by revising the Easter Vigil and the Order of Holy Week, which constituted the first step towards adapting the Roman Missal to the new mentality of the present time.

The recent Second Vatican Ecumenical Council laid the foundation for a general revision of the Roman Missal by issuing the Constitution beginning with the words *Sacrosanctum Concilium*. It decreed that "the texts and rites should be so arranged that they express more clearly the sacred realities which they signify"; that "the Order of the Mass (*Ordo Missae*) should be so revised that the proper nature (*ratio*) of the individual parts and their mutual connection may be expressed more clearly, and the pious and active participation of the faithful may be facilitated"; further, that "the treasures of the Bible should be more fully opened up, so that the table of God's Word may be more richly prepared for the faithful"; and finally, that "a new rite of concelebration should be prepared and inserted into the Pontifical and the Roman Missal."

However, such a revision of the Roman Missal must in no way be thought to have been introduced hastily; for, beyond all doubt, advances made in liturgical studies over the last four centuries did prepare the way for it. After the Council of Trent, the careful examination of old codices from the Vatican Library and other places contributed not a little to that revision of the Roman Missal, as is confirmed by the Apostolic Constitution *Quo Primum* of Our Predecessor St. Pius V. Certainly, since that time, very old additional liturgical sources have been found and published, and the liturgical formulas of the Oriental Church have been studied in greater depth. This was done so that, as many desired, such riches of doctrine and of piety should no longer be committed to dark archives, but on the contrary, by being brought into the light, should illumine and nourish the minds and souls of Christians.

Now, however, in order that We may outline at least the general features of the new composition of the Roman Missal we draw attention first to the *General Instruction,* which We used as a preface to the book, and which sets forth the new norms for celebrating the Eucharistic Sacrifice, both with regard to the rites to be performed and to the proper duties of each one present and participating; and also with regard to the material things and necessary special arrangements for the celebration of divine worship.

One must judge the principal new characteristic of this revision to be found in the Eucharistic Prayer, as it is called. For, although in the Roman rite the first part of this Prayer, i.e., the Preface, has employed various formulas down through the centuries, its other part, which used to be called the Canon of Action, assumed an unchanging form throughout that time (although it has been in existence since the fourth to the fifth centuries) while the Oriental Liturgies, on the contrary, admitted certain variations into their Anaphoras. Now, however, besides the fact that the Eucharistic Prayer has been greatly augmented by an abundance of Prefaces, either taken from the ancient tradition of the Roman Church or now newly composed—by which the proper parts of the mystery of salvation may be more clearly manifested, and more and richer motives for giving thanks may be furnished—We have ordained that three new Canons be added to this Eucharistic Prayer. However, both for pastoral reasons, as they are called, and so that concelebration may be facilitated, We have ordered that the words of the Lord be one and the same in every formula of the Canon. Accordingly, We will that in each Eucharistic Prayer that formula be pronounced thus: over the bread: "ACCIPITE ET MANDUCATE EX HOC OMNES: HOC EST ENIM CORPUS MEUM, QUOD PRO VOBIS TRADETUR"; and over the chalice: "ACCIPITE ET BIBITE EX EO OMNES: HIC EST ENIM CALIX SANGUINIS MEI, NOVI ET AETERNI TESTAMENTI, QUI PRO VOBIS ET PRO MULTIS EFFUNDETUR IN REMISSIONEM PECCATORUM. – HOC FACITE IN MEAM COMMEMORATIONEM. The words "The mystery of faith" (MYSTERIUM FIDEI), however, have been taken out of the context of the words of Christ the Lord. Pronounced by the priest, they constitute as it were an occasion for an acclamation of the faithful.

With regard to the Ordinary of the Mass, "while rightly preserving their substance, the rites have been made more simple." For those things were omitted "which with the passage of time came to be duplicated or were added with but little advantage," particularly with respect to the rite of offering the bread and wine, and with respect to the rite of the breaking of the bread and the communion.

In keeping with this aim, "some things are being restored to the previous norm of the holy Fathers which injuries sustained at various times had cut off," such as the Homily, the General Prayer or Prayer of the Faithful, and the penitential rite or rite of reconciliation with God and brethren, which belong to the beginning of the Mass. As was fitting, the revision has restored the importance of all these things.

In accordance with what was also ordered by the Second Vatican Council, "that within a specified period of years the more preeminent parts of the Sacred Scriptures should be read to the People," the whole body of Readings to be read on Sundays has been arranged in a three-year cycle. Moreover, whenever feast days occur, it is proposed that other readings of the Epistle and Gospel be chosen, whether from the Old Testament, or, in Paschal Time, from the Acts of the Apostles. By this procedure the continuous process of the mystery of salvation manifested by the revealed word of God is more clearly illustrated. This great abundance of biblical readings by which the preeminent parts of the Sacred Scriptures are presented to the faithful on feast days is truly completed by the addition of the remaining parts of the Sacred Books, which are read on the non-feast days.

All these things have been wisely arranged in order to stimulate more and more in Christ's faithful such a hunger for the word of God that, led by the Holy Spirit, the people of the New Testament might seem as it were to be impelled towards the perfect unity of the Church. These matters being thus settled, We have, indeed, great confidence that both priests and faithful will prepare their souls with more holiness for the Lord's Supper, and that, meditating more deeply on the Sacred Scriptures, they will daily be more richly nourished by the words of the Lord. Briefly, then, let it follow, in accordance with the admonition of the Second Vatican Council, that the sacred writings be regarded by all as a definite perennial source of spiritual life, as the principal foundation (*agrumentum*) of the Christian doctrine handed down, and, indeed, as the quintessence of all theological training.

In this revision of the Roman Missal, however, not only have the three parts of which We have spoken up to now been changed — i.e., the Eucharistic Prayer, the Order of the Mass and the Order of Readings — but also other parts have likewise been examined and considerably altered, i.e., the Proper of Seasons, the Proper of the Saints, the Common of the Saints, Ritual Masses, and Votive Masses, as they are called. In these changes a certain special diligence has been employed with regard to the prayers, which have not only been increased in number, as a new response to the new requirements of these times, but also the oldest prayers have been restored to accord with the ancient texts. From this it came about that for each day of the principal liturgical seasons, namely, Advent, Christmas, Lent, and Easter, a different daily prayer has been added.

As for the rest, although the text of the Roman Gradual, at least as regards the chant, will not have been changed, nevertheless, both the Responsorial Psalm, about which St. Augustine and St. Leo the Great often made mention, and also the Introit and Communion Antiphons to be used in non-sung Masses, have been revised where suitable.

Finally, it now seems good to Us to conclude with an important point about the things which We have set forth here concerning the new Roman Missal. Since Our Predecessor St. Pius V promulgated the original edition of the Roman Missal, it has represented to the Christian people, as it were, an instrument of liturgical unity and likewise a monument of genuine religious worship in the Church. By no means do We wish differently; although, in accordance with the prescription of the Second Vatican Council, We have admitted into the new Missal "legitimate variations and adaptations," We nevertheless trust that nothing will be otherwise, but that this also will be accepted by Christ's faithful as an aid to proving and confirming the mutual unity of all, so that by its strength, in so many different languages, one and the same prayer of all will ascend everywhere, more fragrant than incense, to the Heavenly Father, through our High Priest, Jesus Christ, in the Holy Spirit.

What We have commanded by this Constitution of Ours will begin to take effect from the thirtieth day of next November, this year, that is, from the First Sunday of Advent.

We will, moreover, that these statutes and prescriptions of Ours be firm and efficacious both now and in the future, notwithstanding, as far as is necessary, Apostolic Constitutions and Ordinances issued by Our Predecessors, and other prescriptions, even those worthy of special mention and derogation.

Given at Rome, at the See of St. Peter, the third day of the month of April, Holy Thursday, in the year 1969, the sixth of Our Pontificate.

Appendix II

TWO GENERAL AUDIENCES OF POPE
PAUL VI ON THE MASS

(Pope Paul VI explained to the world at the time he instituted the official changes in the form of the Mass by revising the Roman Missal the reasons this was being done; his public explanation was principally contained in two of his General Audiences, those of November 19, 1969, and November 26, 1969. Both of these addresses are reprinted below.)

"THE MASS IS THE SAME"

Address of Pope Paul VI to a General Audience, November 19, 1969

Our Dear Sons and Daughters:

1.—We wish to draw your attention to an event about to occur in the Latin Catholic Church: the introduction of the liturgy of the new rite of the Mass. It will become obligatory in Italian dioceses from the First Sunday of Advent, which this year falls on November 30. The Mass will be celebrated in a rather different manner from that in which we have been accustomed to celebrate it in the last four centuries, from the reign of St. Pius V, after the Council of Trent, down to the present.

2.—This change has something astonishing about it, something extraordinary. This is because the Mass is regarded as the traditional and untouchable expression of our religious worship and the authenticity of our faith. We ask ourselves, how could such a change be made? What effect will it have on those who attend Holy Mass? Answers will be given to these questions, and to others like them, arising from this innovation. You will hear the answers in all the Churches. They will be amply repeated there and in all religious publications, in all schools where Christian doctrine is taught. We exhort you to pay attention to them. In that way you will be able to get a clearer and deeper idea of the stupendous and mysterious notion of the Mass.

3.—But in this brief and simple discourse We will try only to relieve your minds of the first, spontaneous difficulties which this change arouses. We will do so in relation to the first three questions which immediately occur to mind because of it.

4.—How could such a change be made? Answer: It is due to the will expressed by the Ecumenical Council held not long ago. The Council decreed: "The rite of the Mass is to be revised in such a way that the intrinsic nature and purpose of its several parts, as also the connection between them, can be more clearly manifested, and that devout and active participation by the faithful can be more easily accomplished.

5.—"For this purpose the rites are to be simplified, while due care is taken to preserve their substance. Elements which, with the passage of time, came to be duplicated, or were added with but little advantage, are now to be discarded. Where opportunity allows or necessity demands, other elements which have suffered injury through accidents of history are now to be restored to the earlier norm of the Holy Fathers" (*Sacrosanctum Concilium* #50).

6.—The reform which is about to be brought into being is therefore a response to an authoritative mandate from the Church. It is an act of obedience. It is an act of coherence of the Church with herself. It is a step forward for her authentic tradition. It is a demonstration of fidelity and vitality, to which we all must give prompt assent.

7.—It is not an arbitrary act. It is not a transitory or optional experiment. It is not some dilettante's improvisation. It is a law. It has been thought out by authoritative experts of sacred Liturgy; it has been discussed and meditated upon for a long time. We shall do well to accept it with joyful interest and put it into practice punctually, unanimously and carefully.

8.—This reform puts an end to uncertainties, to discussions, to arbitrary abuses. It calls us back to that uniformity of rites and feeling proper to the Catholic Church, the heir and continuation of that first Christian community, which was all "one single heart and a single soul" (*Acts* 4:32). The choral character of the Church's prayer is one of the strengths of her unity and her catholicity. The change about to be made must not break up that choral character or disturb it. It ought to confirm it and make it resound with a new spirit, the spirit of her youth.

9.—The second question is: What exactly are the changes?

10.—You will see for yourselves that they consist of many new directions for celebrating the rites. Especially at the beginning, these will call for a certain amount of attention and care. Personal devotion and community sense will make it easy and pleasant to observe these new rules. But keep this clearly in mind: Nothing has been changed of the substance of our traditional Mass. Perhaps some may allow themselves to be carried away by the impression made by some particular ceremony or additional rubric, and thus think that they conceal some alteration or diminution of truths which were acquired by the Catholic faith for ever, and are sanctioned by it. They might come to believe that the equation between the law of prayer, *lex orandi* and the law of faith, *lex credendi,* is compromised as a result.

11.—It is not so. Absolutely not. Above all, because the rite and the relative rubric are not in themselves a dogmatic definition. Their theological qualification may vary in different degrees according to the liturgical context to which they refer. They are gestures and terms relating to a religious action—experienced and living—of an indescribable mystery of divine presence, not always expressed in a universal way. Only theological criticism can analyze this action and express it in logically satisfying doctrinal formulas. The Mass of the new rite is and remains the same Mass we have always had. If anything, its sameness has been brought out more clearly in some respects.

12.—The unity of the Lord's Supper, of the Sacrifice on the cross of the re-presentation and the renewal of both in the Mass, is inviolably affirmed and celebrated in the new rite just as they were in the old. The Mass is and remains the memorial of Christ's Last Supper. At that Supper the Lord changed the bread and wine into His Body and His Blood, and instituted the Sacrifice of the New Testament. He willed that the Sacrifice should be identically renewed by the power of His Priesthood, conferred on the Apostles. Only the manner of offering is different, namely, an unbloody and sacramental manner; and it is offered in perennial memory of Himself, until His final return (cf. De la Taille, *Mysterium Fidei,* Elucd. IX).

13.—In the new rite you will find the relationship between the Liturgy of the Word and the Liturgy of the Eucharist, strictly so called, brought out more clearly, as if the latter were the practical response to the former (cf. Bouyer). You will find how much the assembly of the faithful is called upon to participate in the celebration of the Eucharistic sacrifice, and how in the Mass they are and fully feel themselves "the Church." You will also see other marvellous features of our Mass. But do not think that these things are aimed at altering its genuine and traditional essence.

14.—Rather try to see how the Church desires to give greater efficacy to her liturgical message through this new and more expansive liturgical language; how she wishes to bring home the message to each of her faithful, and to the whole body of the People of God, in a more direct and pastoral way.

15.—In like manner We reply to the third question: What will be the results of this innovation? The results expected, or rather desired, are that the faithful will participate in the liturgical mystery with more understanding, in a more practical, a more enjoyable and a more sanctifying way. That is, they will hear the Word of God, which lives and echoes down the centuries and in our individual souls; and they will likewise share in the mystical reality of Christ's sacramental and propitiatory sacrifice.

16.—So do not let us talk about "the new Mass." Let us rather speak of the "new epoch" in the Church's life. With Our Apostolic Benediction.

(Reprinted from the English edition of *L'Osservatore Romano*, November 27, 1969).

"CHANGES IN MASS FOR GREATER APOSTOLATE"

Address of Pope Paul VI to a General Audience, November 26, 1969

Our Dear Sons and Daughters:

1.—We ask you to turn your minds once more to the liturgical innovation of the new rite of the Mass. This new rite will be introduced into our celebration of the holy Sacrifice starting from Sunday next which is the first of Advent, November 30. [This was for Italy.]

2.—A new rite of the Mass: a change in a venerable tradition that has gone on for centuries. This is something that affects our hereditary religious patrimony, which seemed to enjoy the privilege of being untouchable and settled. It seemed to bring the prayer of our forefathers and our saints to our lips and to give us the comfort of feeling faithful to our spiritual past, which we kept alive to pass it on to the generations ahead.

3.—It is at such a moment as this that we get a better understanding of the value of historical tradition and the communion of the saints. This change will affect the ceremonies of the Mass. We shall become aware, perhaps with some feeling of annoyance, that the ceremonies at the altar are no longer being carried out with the same words and gestures to which we were accustomed—perhaps so much accustomed that we no longer took any notice of them. This change also touches the faithful. It is intended to interest each one of those present, to draw them out of their customary personal devotions or their usual torpor.

4.—We must prepare for this many-sided inconvenience. It is the kind of upset caused by every novelty that breaks in on our habits. We shall notice that pious persons are disturbed most, because they have their own respectable way of hearing Mass, and they will feel shaken out of their usual thoughts and obliged to follow those of others. Even priests may feel some annoyance in this respect.

5.—So what is to be done on this special and historical occasion? First of all, we must prepare ourselves. This novelty is no small thing. We should not let ourselves be surprised by the nature, or even the nuisance, of its exterior forms. As intelligent persons and conscientious faithful we should find out as much as we can about this innovation. It will not be hard to do so, because of the many fine efforts being made by the Church and by publishers. As We said on another occasion, we shall do well to take into account the motives for this grave change. The first is obedience to the Council. That obedience now implies obedience to the Bishops, who interpret the Council's prescription and put them into practice.

6.—This first reason is not simply canonical—relating to an external precept. It is connected with the charism of the liturgical act. In other words, it is linked with the power and efficacy of the Church's prayer, the most authoritative utterance of which comes from the Bishop. This is also true of priests, who help the Bishop in his ministry, and like him act *in persona Christi* (cf. *St. Ign. ad Eph.* I, V). It is Christ's will, it is the breath of the Holy Spirit which calls the Church to make this change. A prophetic moment is occurring in the mystical body of Christ, which is the Church. This moment is shaking the Church, arousing it, obliging it to renew the mysterious art of its prayer.

7.—The other reason for the reform is this renewal of prayer. It is aimed at associating the assembly of the faithful more closely and more effectively with the official rite, that of the Word and that of the Eucharistic Sacrifice, that constitutes the Mass. For the faithful are also invested with the "royal priesthood"; that is, they are qualified to have supernatural conversation with God.

8.—It is here that the greatest newness is going to be noticed, the newness of language. No longer Latin, but the spoken language will be the principal language of the Mass. The introduction of the vernacular will certainly be a great sacrifice for those who know the beauty, the power and the expressive sacrality of Latin. We are parting with the speech of the Christian centuries; we are becoming like profane intruders in the literary preserve of sacred utterance. We will lose a great part of that stupendous and incomparable artistic and spiritual thing, the Gregorian chant.

9.—We have reason indeed for regret, reason almost for bewilderment. What can we put in the place of that language of the angels? We are giving up something of priceless worth. But why? What is more precious than these loftiest of our Church's values?

10.—The answer will seem banal, prosaic. Yet it is a good answer, because it is human, because it is apostolic.

11.—Understanding of prayer is worth more than the silken garments in which it is royally dressed. Participation by the people is worth more—particularly participation by modern people, so fond of plain language which is easily understood and converted into everyday speech.

12.—If the divine Latin language kept us apart from the children, from youth, from the world of labor and of affairs, if it were a dark screen, not a clear window, would it be right for us fishers of souls to maintain it as the exclusive language of prayer and religious intercourse? What did St. Paul have to say about that? Read chapter 14 of the first letter to the Corinthians: "In Church I would rather speak five words with my mind, in order to instruct others, than ten thousand words in a tongue" (I *Corinthians* 14:19).

13.—St. Augustine seems to be commenting on this when he says, "Have no fear of teachers, so long as all are instructed" (P.L. 38, 228, *Serm.* 37; cf. also *Serm.* 229, p. 1371). But, in any case, the new rite of the Mass provides that the faithful "should be able to sing together, in Latin, at least the parts of the Ordinary of the Mass, especially the Creed and the Lord's Prayer, the Our Father" (*Sacrosanctum Concilium* n. 19).

14.—But, let us bear this well in mind, for our counsel and our comfort: the Latin language will not thereby disappear. It will continue to be the noble language of the Holy See's official acts; it will remain as the means of teaching in ecclesiastical studies and as the key to the patrimony of our religious, historical and human culture. If possible, it will reflourish in splendour.

15.—Finally, if we look at the matter properly we shall see that the fundamental outline of the Mass is still the traditional one, not only theologically but also spiritually. Indeed, if the rite is carried out as it ought to be, the spiritual aspect will be found to have greater richness. The greater simplicity of the ceremonies, the variety and abundance of scriptural texts, the joint acts of the ministers, the silences which will mark various deeper moments in the rite, will all help to bring this out.

16.—But two indispensable requirements above all will make that richness clear: a profound participation by every single one present, and an outpouring of spirit in community charity. These requirements will help to make the Mass more than ever a school of spiritual depth and a peaceful but demanding school of Christian sociology. The soul's relationship with Christ and with the brethren thus attains new and vital intensity. Christ, the victim and the priest, renews and offers up his redeeming sacrifice through the ministry of the Church in the symbolic rite of his last supper. He leaves us his body and blood under the appearances of bread and wine, for our personal and spiritual nourishment, for our fusion in the unity of his redeeming love and his immortal life.

17.—But there is still a practical difficulty, which the excellence of the sacred renders not a little important. How can we celebrate this new rite when we have not yet got a complete missal, and there are still so many uncertainties about what to do?

18.—To conclude, it will be helpful to read to you some directions from the competent office, namely the Sacred Congregation for Divine Worship. Here they are:

"As regards the obligation of the rite:

1) For the Latin text: Priests who celebrate in Latin, in private or also in public, in cases provided for by the legislation, may use either the Roman Missal or the new rite until November 28, 1971.

If they use the Roman Missal, they may nevertheless make use of the three new anaphoras and the Roman Canon, having regard to the provisions respecting the last text (omission of some saints, conclusions, etc.). They may moreover recite the readings and the prayer of the faithful in the vernacular.

If they use the new rite, they must follow the official text, with the concessions as regards the vernacular indicated above.

2) For the vernacular text. In Italy, all those who celebrate in the presence of the people from November 30 next, must use

the *Rito della Messa* published by the Italian Episcopal Conference or by another National Conference.

On feast days readings shall be taken: — either from the Lectionary published by the Italian Center for Liturgical Action, or from the Roman Missal for feast days, as in use heretofore.

On ferial days the ferial Lectionary published three years ago shall continue to be used.

No problem arises for those who celebrate in private, because they must celebrate in Latin. If a priest celebrates in the vernacular by special indult, as regards the texts, he shall follow what was said above for the Mass with the people; but for the rite he shall follow the *Ordo* published by the Italian Episcopal Conference.

19.—In every case, and at all times, let us remember that "the Mass is a Mystery to be lived in a death of Love. Its divine reality surpasses all words. . . It is the Action par excellence, the very act of our Redemption, in the Memorial which makes it present" (Zundel). With Our Apostolic Benediction.

(Reprinted from the English edition of *L'Osservatore Romano,* December 4, 1969)

Appendix III

APOSTOLIC CONSTITUTION *QUO PRIMUM*
OF POPE ST. PIUS V

From the very first, upon Our elevation to the chief Apostleship, We gladly turned our mind and energies and directed all our thoughts to those matters which concerned the preservation of a pure liturgy, and We strove with God's help, by every means in our power, to accomplish this purpose. For, besides other decees of the sacred Council of Trent, there were stipulations for Us to revise and re-edit the sacred books: the Catechism, the Missal, and the Breviary. With the Catechism published for the instruction of the faithful, by God's help, and the Breviary thoroughly revised for the worthy praise of God, in order that the Missal and Breviary may be in perfect harmony, as is fitting and proper — for it is most becoming that there be in the Church only one appropriate manner of reciting the Psalms and only one rite for the celebration of Mass — We deemed it necessary to give our immediate attention to what still remained to be done, viz., the re-editing of the Missal as soon as possible.

Hence, We decided to entrust this work to learned men of our selection. They very carefully collated all their work with the ancient codices in Our Vatican Library and with reliable, preserved or emended codices from elsewhere. Besides this, these men consulted the works of ancient and approved authors concerning the same sacred rites; and thus they have restored the Missal itself to the original form and rite of the holy Fathers. When this work had been gone over numerous times and further emended, after serious study and reflection, We commanded that the finished product be printed and published as soon as possible, so that all might enjoy the fruits of this labor; and thus, priests would know which prayers to use and which rites and ceremonies they were required to observe from now on in the celebration of Masses.

Let all everywhere adopt and observe what has been handed down by the Holy Roman Church, the Mother and Teacher of the other churches, and let Masses not be sung or read according to any other formula than that of this Missal published by Us. This ordinance applies henceforth, now, and forever, throughout all the provinces of the Christian world, to all patriarchates, cathedral churches, collegiate and parish churches, be they secular or religious, both of men and of women — even of military orders — and of churches and chapels without a specific congregation in which conventual Masses are sung aloud in choir or read privately in accord with the rites and customs of the Roman Church. This Missal is to be used by all churches, even by those which in their authorization are made exempt, whether by Apostolic indult, custom, or privilege, or even if by oath or official confirmation of the Holy See, or have their rights and faculties guaranteed to them by any other manner whatsoever.

This new rite alone is to be used unless approval of the practice of saying Mass differently was given at the very time of the institution and confirmation of the church by the Apostolic See at least 200 years ago, or unless there has prevailed a custom of a similar kind which had been continuously followed for a period of not less than 200 years, in which cases We in no wise rescind their above-mentioned prerogative or custom. However, if this Missal, which we have seen fit to publish, be more agreeable to these latter, We grant them permission to celebrate Mass according to its rite, provided they have the consent of their bishop or prelate or their whole Chapter, everything else to the contrary notwithstanding.

All other of the churches referred to above, however, are hereby denied the use of other missals which are to be discontinued entirely and absolutely; whereas, by this present Constitution, which will be valid henceforth, now, and forever, We order and enjoin that nothing must be added to Our recently published Missal, nothing omitted from it, nor anything whatsoever be changed within it under the penalty of Our displeasure.

We specifically command each and every patriarch, administrator, and all other persons of whatever ecclesiastical dignity they may be, be they even cardinals of the Holy Roman Church, or possessed of any other rank or preeminence, and We order them in virtue of holy obedience to chant or to read the Mass according to the rite and manner and norm herewith laid down by Us, hereafter, to discontinue and completely discard all other rubrics and rites of other missals, however ancient, which they have customarily followed;

and they must not in celebrating Mass presume to introduce any ceremonies or recite any prayers other than those contained in this Missal.

Furthermore, by these presents, in virtue of Our Apostolic authority, We grant and concede in perpetuity that, for the chanting or reading of the Mass in any church whatsoever, this Missal is hereafter to be followed absolutely, without any scruple of conscience or fear of incurring any penalty, judgment, or censure and may freely and lawfully be used. Nor are superiors, administrators, canons, chaplains and other secular priests, or religious, of whatever order or by whatever title designated, obliged to celebrate the Mass otherwise than as enjoined by Us. We likewise declare and ordain that no one whosoever is to be forced or coerced to alter this Missal, and that this present document cannot be revoked or modified, but remain always valid and retain its full force —notwithstanding the previous constitutions or edicts of provincial or synodal councils, and notwithstanding the practice and custom of the aforesaid churches, established by long and immemorial prescription—except, however, if of more than two hundred years' standing.

It is Our will, therefore, and by the same authority, We decree that after We publish this constitution and the edition of this Missal, the priests of the Roman Curia are, after thirty days, obliged to chant or read the Mass according to it; all others south of the Alps, after three months; and that those beyond the Alps either within six months or whenever the Missal is available for sale. Wherefore, in order that the Missal be preserved incorrupt throughout the whole world and kept free of flaws and errors, the penalty for nonobservance for printers, whether mediately or immediately subject to Our dominion, and that of the Holy Roman Church, will be forfeiting of their books and a fine of one hundred gold ducats, payable *ipso facto* to the Apostolic Treasury. Further, as for those located in other parts of the world, the penalty is excommunication *latae sententiae* [i.e., imposed by an ecclesiastical tribunal], and such other penalties as may in Our judgment be imposed; and We decree by this law that they must not dare or presume either to print or to publish or to sell, or in any way to accept books of this nature without Our approval and consent, or without the express consent of the Apostolic Commissaries of those places, who will be appointed by Us. Said printer must receive a standard Missal from the aforementioned Apostolic Commissary to serve as a model for subsequent copies, which, when made, must be compared with the standard Missal and agree faithfully with it and in no wise vary from the Roman Missal of the large type.

Accordingly, since it would be difficult for this present pronouncement to be sent to all parts of the Christian world and simultaneously come to light everywhere, We direct that it be, as usual, posted and published at the doors of the Basilica of the Prince of the Apostles, also at the Apostolic Chancery, and on the street at Campo Flora; furthermore, We direct that printed copies of this same edict signed by a notary public and made official by an ecclesiastical dignitary possess the same indubitable validity everywhere and in every nation, as if Our manuscript were shown there.

Therefore, no one whosoever is permitted to alter this letter or heedlessly to venture to go contrary to this notice of Our permission, statute, ordinance, command, precept, grant, indult, declaration, will, decree, and prohibition. Should anyone, however, presume to commit such an act, he should know that he will incur the wrath of Almighty God and of the Blessed Apostles Peter and Paul.

Given at St. Peter's in the year of the Lord's Incarnation, 1570, on the 14th day of July of the Fifth year of Our Pontificate.

Appendix IV

POPE PAUL VI'S LETTER TO
ARCHBISHOP MARCEL LEFEBVRE

(This letter was sent to Archbishop Marcel Lefebvre one month after he visited the Pope on September 11, 1976. The archbishop had rejected parts of the Vatican II decrees and some of the subsequent post-conciliar enactments of the Holy See and had been the object of widespread publicity as he celebrated Tridentine Masses in various parts of Europe. In June, 1976, the archbishop had defied a direct order from the Pope not to ordain seminarians at the seminary he founded in Ecône, Switzerland. In this letter, the Pope told the archbishop that while pluralism in the church is legitimate, it must be a licit pluralism rooted in obedience. The Pope said the archbishop, rather than practicing obedience, had propagated and organized a rebellion. This, he added, "is the essential issue" in the archbishop's regard. In this letter, the Pope outlined his conditions for rectifying matters, including a call for a declaration from the archbishop affirming adherence to Vatican II, a declaration that, among other things, retracts accusations or insinuations levelled against the Pope. The text of the Pope's letter has been taken from Origins, NC Documentary Service, December 16, 1976.)

When We received you in audience on last September 11 at Castelgandolfo, We let you freely express your position and your desires, even though the various aspects of your case were already well known to Us personally. The memory that We still have of your zeal for the faith and the apostolate, as well as of the good you have accomplished in the past at the service of the church, made Us and still makes Us hope that you will once again become an edifying subject in full ecclesial communion. After the particularly serious actions that you have performed, We have once more asked you to reflect before God concerning your duty.

We have waited a month. The attitude to which your words and acts publicly testify does not seem to have changed. It is true that

We have before Us your letter of September 16, in which you affirm: "A common point unites us: the ardent desire to see the cessation of all the abuses that disfigure the church. How I wish to collaborate in this salutary work, with Your Holiness and under Your authority, so that the church may recover her true countenance."

How must these few words to which your response is limited—and which in themselves are positive—be interpreted? You speak as if you have forgotten your scandalous words and gestures against ecclesial communion—words and gestures that you have never retracted! You do not manifest repentance, even for the cause of your suspension *a divinis*. You do not explicitly express your acceptance of the authority of the Second Vatican Council and of the Holy See—and this constitutes the basis of the problem—and you continue in those personal works of yours which the legitimate authority has expressly ordered you to suspend. Ambiguity results from the duplicity of your language. On Our part, as We promised you, We are herewith sending you the conclusion of Our reflections.

1. In practice you put yourself forward as the defender and spokesman of the faithful and of priests "torn apart by what is happening in the church," thus giving the sad impression that the Catholic faith and the essential values of tradition are not sufficiently respected and lived in a portion of the people of God, at least in certain countries. But in your interpretations of the facts and in the particular role that you assign yourself, as well as in the way in which you accomplish this role, there is something that misleads the people of God and deceives souls of good will who are justly desirous of fidelity and of spiritual and apostolic progress.

Deviations in the faith or in sacramental practice are certainly very grave, wherever they occur. For a long period of time they have been the object of Our full doctrinal and pastoral attention. Certainly one must not forget the positive signs of spiritual renewal or of increased responsibility in a good number of Catholics, or the complexity of the cause of the crisis: the immense change in today's world affects believers at the edge of their being, and renders ever more necessary apostolic concern for those "who are far away."

But it remains true that some priests and members of the faithful mask with the name "Conciliar" those personal interpretations and erroneous practices that are injurious, even scandalous, and at times sacrilegious. But these abuses cannot be attributed either to the Council itself or to the reform that have legitimately issued therefrom, but rather to a lack of authentic fidelity in their regard. You want to convince the faithful that the proximate cause of the crisis is more than a wrong interpretation of the Council and that it flows from the Council itself.

Moreover, you act as if you had a particular role in this regard. But the mission of discerning and remedying the abuses is first of all Ours; it is the mission of all the bishops who work together with Us. Indeed We do not cease to raise Our voice against these excesses: Our discourse to the consistory of last May 21 repeated this in clear terms. More than anyone else We hear the suffering of distressed Christians, and We respond to the cry of the faithful longing for faith and the spiritual life. This is not the place to remind you, brother, of all the acts of Our pontificate that testify to Our constant concern to ensure for the church fidelity to the true tradition, and to enable her with God's grace to face the present and future.

Finally, your behavior is contradictory. You want, so you say, to remedy the abuses that disfigure the church; you regret that authority in the church is not sufficiently respected; you wish to safeguard authentic faith, esteem for the ministerial priesthood and fervor for the eucharist in its sacrificial and sacramental fullness. Such zeal would, in itself, merit our encouragement, since it is a question of exigencies which, together with evangelization and the unity of Christians, remain at the heart of Our preoccupations and of Our mission.

But how can you at the same time, in order to fulfill this role, claim that you are obliged to act contrary to the recent Council in opposition to your brethren in the episcopate, to distrust the Holy See itself—which you call the "Rome of the neo-modernist and neo-Protestant tendency"—and to set yourself up in open disobedience to Us? If you truly want to work "under Our authority," as you affirm in your last private letter, it is immediately necessary to put an end to these ambiguities and contradictions.

2. Let us come now to the more precise requests which you formulated during the audience of September 11. You would like to see recognized the right to celebrate Mass in various places of worship according to the Tridentine rite. You wish also to continue to train candidates for the priesthood according to your criteria, "as before the Council," in seminaries apart, as at Ecône. But behind these questions and other similar ones, which We shall examine later on in detail, it is truly necessary to see the intricacy of the problem: and the problem is theological. For these questions have become concrete ways of expressing an ecclesiology that is warped in essential points.

What is indeed at issue is the question —which must truly be called fundamental—of your clearly proclaimed refusal to recognize in its whole, the authority of the Second Vatican Council and that of the Pope. This refusal is accompanied by an action that is oriented towards propagating and organizing what must indeed, unfortunately, be called a rebellion. This is the essential issue, and it is truly untenable.

Is it necessary to remind you that you are Our brother in the episcopate and moreover—a fact that obliges you to remain even more closely united to the See of Peter—that you have been named an assistant at the papal throne? Christ has given the supreme authority in his church to Peter and to the apostolic college, that is, to the Pope and to the college of bishops *una cum Capite.*

In regard to the Pope, every Catholic admits that the words of Jesus to Peter determine also the charge of Peter's legitimate successors: ". . .whatever you bind on earth will be bound in heaven" (*Mt.* 16:19); ". . .feed my sheep" (*Jn.* 21:17); ". . .confirm your brethren" (*Lk.* 22:32). And the First Vatican Council specified in these terms the assent due to the sovereign pontiff: "The pastors of every rank and of every rite and the faithful, each separately and all together, are bound by the duty of hierarchical subordination and of true obedience, not only in questions of faith and morals, but also in those that touch upon the discipline and government of the church throughout the entire world. Thus, by preserving the unity of communion and of profession of faith with the Roman pontiff, the church is a single flock under one pastor. Such is the doctrine of Catholic truth, from which no one can separate himself without danger for his faith and his salvation" (Dogmatic Constitution *Pastor Aeternus,* Ch. 3, DZ 3060).

Concerning bishops united with the sovereign pontiff, their power with regard to the universal church is solemnly exercised in the ecumenical councils, according to the words of Jesus to the body of the apostles: ". . .whatever you bind on earth shall be bound in heaven" (*Mt.* 18:18). And now in your conduct you refuse to recognize, as must be done, these two ways in which supreme authority is exercised.

Each bishop is indeed an authentic teacher for preaching to the people entrusted to him that faith which must guide their thoughts and conduct and dispel the errors that menace the flock. But, by their nature, "the charges of teaching and governing. . .cannot be exercised except in hierarchical communion with the head of the

college and with its members" (Constitution *Lumen Gentium,* 21;
cf. also 25). *A fortiori,* a single bishop without a canonical mission
does not have *in actu expedito ad agendum,* the faculty of deciding
in general what the rule of faith is or of determining what tradition
is. In practice you are claiming that you alone are the judge of what
tradition embraces.

You say that you are subject to the church and faithful to tradition by the sole fact that you obey certain norms of the past that
were decreed by the predecessor of him to whom God has today
conferred the powers given to Peter. That is to say, on this point
also, the concept of "tradition" that you invoke is distorted.

Tradition is not a rigid and dead notion, a fact of a certain static
sort which at a given moment of history blocks the life of this active
organism which is the church, that is, the mystical body of Christ. It
is up to the Pope and to councils to exercise judgment in order to
discern in the traditions of the church that which cannot be renounced without infidelity to the Lord and to the Holy Spirit—the
deposit of faith—and that which, on the contrary, can and must be
adapted to facilitate the prayer and the mission of the church
throughout a variety of times and places, in order better to translate
the divine message into the language of today and better to com-
municate it, without an unwarranted surrender of principles.

Hence tradition is inseparable from the living magisterium of the
church, just as it is inseparable from sacred scripture. "Sacred tradition, sacred scripture and the magisterium of the church. . .are so
linked and joined together that one of these realities cannot exist
without the others, and that all of them together, each in its own
way, effectively contribute under the action of the Holy Spirit to
the salvation of souls" (Constitution *Dei Verbum,* 10).

With the special assistance of the Holy Spirit, the popes and the
ecumenical councils have acted in this common way. And it is precisely this that the Second Vatican Council did. Nothing that was
decreed in this Council, or in the reforms that we enacted in order to
put the Council into effect, is opposed to what the 2,000-year-old
tradition of the church considers as fundamental and immutable. We
are the guarantor of this, not in virtue of Our personal qualities but
in virtue of the charge which the Lord has conferred upon Us as legitimate successor of Peter, and in virtue of the special assistance that
He has promised to Us as well as to Peter: "I have prayed for you
that your faith may not fail" (*Lk.* 22:32). The universal episcopate
is guarantor with us of this.

Again, you cannot appeal to the distinction between what is dogmatic and what is pastoral to accept certain texts of this Council and to refuse others. Indeed, not everything in the Council requires an assent of the same nature: only what is affirmed by definitive acts as an object of faith or as a truth related to faith requires an assent of faith. But the rest also forms part of the solemn magisterium of the church to which each member of the faithful owes a confident acceptance and a sincere application.

You say moreover that you do not always see how to reconcile certain texts of the Council, or certain dispositions which We have enacted in order to put the Council into practice, with the wholesome tradition of the church and in particular with the Council of Trent of the affirmations of Our predecessors. These are for example: the responsibility of the college of bishops united with the sovereign pontiff, the new *Ordo Missae*, ecumenism, religious freedom, the attitude of dialogue, evangelization in the modern world. . . .

It is not the place, in this letter, to deal with each of these problems. The precise tenor of the documents, with the totality of its nuances and its context, the authorized explanations, the detailed and objective commentaries which have been made, are of such a nature to enable you to overcome these personal difficulties. Absolutely secure counsellors, theologians and spiritual directors would be able to help you even more, with God's enlightenment, and We are ready to facilitate this fraternal assistance for you.

But how can an interior personal difficulty —a spiritual drama which We respect —permit you to set yourself up publicly as a judge of what has been legitimately adopted, practically with unanimity, and knowingly to lead a portion of the faithful into your refusal? If justifications are useful in order to facilitate intellectual acceptance — and We hope that the troubled or reticent faithful will have the wisdom, honesty and humanity to accept those justifications that are widely placed at their disposal —they are not in themselves necessary for the assent of obedience that is due to the Ecumenical Council and to the decisions of the Pope. It is the ecclesial sense that is at issue.

In effect you and those who are following you are endeavoring to come to a standstill at a given moment in the life of the church. By the same token you refuse to accept the living church, which is the church that has always been: you break with the church's legitimate pastors and scorn the legitimate exercise of their charge. And so you claim not even to be affected by the orders of the Pope, or by the suspension *a divinis*, as you lament "subversion" in the church.

Is it not in this state of mind that you have ordained priests without dimissorial letters and against Our explicit command, thus creating a group of priests who are in an irregular situation in the Church and who are under grave ecclesiastical penalties? Moreover, you hold that the suspension that you have incurred applies only to the celebration of the sacraments according to the new rite, as if they were something improperly introduced into the church, which you go so far as to call schismatic, and you think that you evade this sanction when you administer the sacraments according to the formulas of the past and against the established norms (cf. I *Cor.* 14:40).

From the same erroneous conception springs your abuse of celebrating the Mass called that of St. Pius V. You know full well that this rite had itself been the result of successive changes, and that the Roman Canon remains the first of the eucharistic prayers authorized today.

The present reform derived its *raison d'être* and its guidelines from the Council and from the historical sources of the liturgy. It enables the laity to draw greater nourishment from the word of God. Their more active participation leaves intact the unique role of the priest acting in the person of Christ. We have sanctioned this reform by Our authority, requiring that it be adopted by all Catholics.

If, in general, We have not judged it good to permit any further delays or exceptions to this adoption, it is with a view to the spiritual good and the unity of the entire ecclesial community, because, for Catholics of the Roman rite, the *Ordo Missae* is a privileged sign of their unity. It is also because, in your case, the old rite is in fact the expression of a warped ecclesiology, and a ground for dispute with the Council and its reforms under the pretext that in the old rite alone are preserved, without their meaning being obscured, the true sacrifice of the Mass and the ministerial priesthood.

We cannot accept this erroneous judgment, this unjustified accusation, nor can We tolerate that the Lord's Eucharist, the sacrament of unity, should be the object of such divisions (cf. I *Cor.* 11:18), and that it should even be used as an instrument and sign of rebellion.

Of course there is room in the church for a certain pluralism, but in licit matters and in obedience. This is not understood by those who refuse the sum total of the liturgical reform; nor indeed on the other hand by those who imperil the holiness of the real presence of the Lord and of his sacrifice. In the same way there can be no question of a priestly formation which ignores the Council.

We cannot therefore take your requests into consideration, because it is a question of acts which have already been committed in rebellion against the one true church of God. Be assured that this severity is not dictated by a refusal to make a concession on such and such a point of discipline or liturgy, but, given the meaning and the extent of your acts in the present context, to act thus would be on Our part to accept the introduction of a seriously erroneous concept of the church and of tradition. This is why, with the full consciousness of Our duties, We say to you, brother, that you are in error. And with the full ardor of Our fraternal love, as also with all the weight of Our authority as the successor of Peter, We invite you to retract, to correct yourself and to cease from inflicting wounds upon the church of Christ.

3. Specifically, what do We ask of you?

A.—First and foremost, a declaration that will rectify matters for Ourself and also for the people of God who have a right to clarity and who can no longer bear without damage such equivocations.

This declaration will therefore have to affirm that you sincerely adhere to the Second Vatican Ecumenical Council and to all its documents—*sensu obvio*—which were adopted by the Council fathers and approved and promulgated by Our authority. For such an adherence has always been the rule, in the church, since the beginning, in the matter of ecumenical councils.

It must be clear that you equally accept the decisions that We have made since the Council in order to put it into effect, with the help of the departments of the Holy See; among other things, you must explicitly recognize the legitimacy of the reformed liturgy, notably of the *Ordo Missae,* and our right to require its adoption by the entirety of the Christian people.

You must also admit the binding character of the rules of canon law now in force which, for the greater part, still correspond with the content of the Code of Canon Law of Benedict XV, without excepting the part which deals with canonical penalties.

As far as concerns Our person, you will make a point of desisting from and retracting the grave accusations or insinuations which you have publicly levelled against Us, against the orthodoxy of Our faith and Our fidelity to Our charge as the successor of Peter, and against Our immediate collaborators.

With regard to the bishops, you must recognize their authority in their respective dioceses by abstaining from preaching in those dioceses and administering the sacraments there: the eucharist, confirmation, holy orders, etc., when these bishops expressly object to your doing so.

Finally, you must undertake to abstain from all activities (such as conferences, publications, etc.) contrary to this declaration, and formally to reprove all those initiatives which may make use of your name in the face of this declaration.

It is a question here of the minimum to which every Catholic bishop must subscribe: this adherence can tolerate no compromise. As soon as you show Us that you accept its principle, We will propose the practical manner of presenting this declaration. This is the first condition in order that the suspension *a divinis* be lifted.

B.—It will then remain to solve the problem of your activity, of your works, and notably of your seminaries. You will appreciate, brother, that in view of the past and present irregularities and ambiguities affecting these works, We cannot go back on the juridical suppression of the Priestly Fraternity of St. Pius X. This has inculcated a spirit of opposition to the Council and to its implementation such as the Vicar of Christ was endeavoring to promote.

Your declaration of November 21, 1974, bears witness to this spirit; and upon such a foundation, as Our commission of cardinals rightly judged, on May 6, 1975, one cannot build an institution or a priestly formation in conformity with the requirements of the church of Christ. This in no way invalidates the good element in your seminaries, but one must also take into consideration the ecclesiological deficiencies of which We have spoken and the capacity of exercising a pastoral ministry in the church of today. Faced with these unfortunately mixed realities, We shall take care not to destroy but to correct and to save as far as possible.

This is why, as supreme guarantor of the faith and of the formation of the clergy, We require you first of all to hand over to Us the responsibility of your work, and particularly for your seminaries. This is undoubtedly a heavy sacrifice for you, but it is also a test of your trust, of your obedience and it is a necessary condition in order that these seminaries, which have no canonical existence in the church, may in the future take their place therein.

It is only after you have accepted the principle that We shall be able to provide in the best possible way for the good of all the persons involved, with the concern for promoting authentic priestly vocations and with respect for the doctrinal, disciplinary and pastoral requirements of the church. At that stage, We shall be in a position to listen with benevolence to your requests and your wishes and, together with Our departments, to take in conscience the right and opportune measures.

As for the illicitly ordained seminarians, the sanctions which they have incurred in conformity with Canon 985,7 and 2374 can be lifted, if they give proof of a return to a better frame of mind, notably by accepting to subscribe to the declaration which We have asked of you. We count upon your sense of the church in order to make this step easy for them.

As regards the foundations, houses of formation, "priories" and various other institutions set up on your initiative or with your encouragement, We likewise ask you to hand them over to the Holy See, which will study their position, in its various aspects, with the local episcopate. Their survival, organization and apostolate will be subordinated, as is normal throughout the Catholic Church, to an agreement which will have to be reached, in each case, with the local bishop—*nihil sine Episcopo*—and in a spirit which respects the declaration mentioned above.

All the points which figure in this letter and to which We have given mature consideration, in consultation with the heads of the departments concerned, have been adopted by Us only out of regard for the greater good of the church. You said to Us during our conversation of September 11: "I am ready for anything, for the good of the church." The response now lies in your hands.

If you refuse—*quod Deus avertat*—to make the declaration which is asked of you, you will remain suspended *a divinis*. On the other hand, Our pardon and the lifting of the suspension will be assured you to the extent to which you sincerely and without ambiguity undertake to fulfill the conditions of this letter and to repair the scandal caused. The obedience and the trust of which you will give proof will also make it possible for Us to study serenely with you your personal problems.

May the Holy Spirit enlighten you and guide you towards the only solution that would enable you on the one hand to rediscover the peace of your momentarily misguided conscience but also to ensure the good of souls, to contribute to the unity of the church which the Lord has entrusted to Our charge and to avoid the danger of a schism.

In the psychological state in which you find yourself, We realize that it is difficult for you to see clearly and very hard for you humbly to change your line of conduct: is it not therefore urgent, as in all such cases, for you to arrange a time and a place of recollection which will enable you to consider the matter with the necessary objectivity?

Fraternally, We put you on your guard against the pressures to which you could be exposed from those who wish to keep you in an untenable position, while We Ourself, all your brothers in the episcopate and the vast majority of the faithful await finally from you that ecclesial attitude which would be to your honor.

In order to root out the abuses which we all deplore and to guarantee a true spiritual renewal, as well as the courageous evangelization to which the Holy Spirit bids us, there is needed more than ever the help and commitment of the entire ecclesial community around the Pope and the bishops. Now the revolt of one side finally reaches and risks accentuating the insubordination of what you have called the "subversion" of the other side; while, without your own insubordination, you would have been able, brother, as you expressed the wish in your last letter, to help Us, in fidelity and under Our authority, to work for the advancement of the church.

Therefore, dear brother, do not delay any longer in considering before God, with the keenest religious attention, this solemn adjuration of the humble but legitimate successor of Peter. May you measure the gravity of the Hour and take the only decision that befits a son of the church. This is Our hope, this is Our prayer.

From the Vatican, October 11, 1976
    PAULUS PP. VI

FOOTNOTES AND REFERENCES

(These notes are confined to listing sources and hence the reader uninterested in such things can skip over them without loss. The authors believe that their sources did need to be shown, however, for those who are interested in knowing what these sources are. In order to cut down on the notes, however, quotations from the Holy Scriptures or from current official documents of the Church such as papal encyclicals or Vatican II documents, available in many editions or in diverse publications such as THE POPE SPEAKS or the English edition of L'OSSERVATORE ROMANO, are generally shown in parentheses in the text immediately following the passage quoted, and no further source is mentioned. Older Church documents, not contained in current compilations, or not easily available, are indicated here with the source given; non-official sources are also generally shown.)

INTRODUCTION

1. "Is the Church Declining?" Summary of a Study by a National Opinion Research Center (NORC) research team, *Origins*, NC Documentary Service, April 8, 1976, page 670.

2. All the Council's documents, like many of the major post-conciliar documents of the Holy See implementing the reforms of the Council, can be found in *Vatican Council II: The Conciliar and Post Conciliar Documents*, Austin Flannery, O.P., General Editor, Costello Publishing Co., Northport, New York, 1975. Available in paperback for $3.95 from C.U.F., 222 North Avenue, New Rochelle, New York 10801.

3. Quoted in *Our Sunday Visitor*, September 19, 1978.

4. Schuler, Msgr. Richard, *"Basta,"* quoted in Newsletter, St. Francis of Assisi Chapter, Catholics United for the Faith, Shipbottom, New Jersey, January, 1979.

5. Quoted in *Timor Domini* (Switzerland), May, 1978.

6. The Text of the Vatican I Dogmatic Constitution *Dei Filius*, April 24, 1870, can be found in *Documents of Vatican Council I*, 1869-1870, selected and translated by John F. Broderick, S.J., The Liturgical Press, Collegeville, Minnesota, 1971, pages 37-52.

QUESTION #1

1. The text of *Testem Benevolentiae* on Americanism, dated January 22, 1899, is to be found in Ellis, John Tracy (ed.), *Documents of American Catholic History*, Henry Regnery Company, Chicago (Regnery Logos Edition), 1967, Vol. II, pages 537 ff.

2. *Ibid.,* page 540.

3. The English text of Pope John XXIII's "Opening Speech to the Council" can be found in Abbott, Walter M., S.J. (Gen. Ed.), *The Documents of Vatican II*, Very Rev. Msgr. Joseph Gallagher (Translation Editor), America Press, New York, 1966, pages 710-719.

4. Pope Pius XII, Apostolic Constitution *Sacramentum Ordinis*, November 30, 1947. In *The Church* (Papal Teachings), selected and arranged by the Benedictine Monks of Solesmes. Translated by Mother E. O'Gorman, R.S.C.J., St. Paul Editions, Boston, 1962, page 638.

5. See Newman, John Henry Cardinal, *Via Media*, Christian Classics, Westminster, Maryland, 1978, Vol. I, pages 229-230.

6. See Hughes, Philip, *The Church in Crisis : A History of General Councils*, Hanover House, a Division of Doubleday and Company, Garden City, New York, 1961, page 218.

QUESTION #2

1. The text of Pope John XXIII's *Humanae Salutis* (December 25, 1961) can be found in Abbott, *op. cit.*, Note #3, Question #1, above, pages 705-709.

2. Pope Pius IX, Apostolic Letter *Aeterni Patris*, June 29, 1868, convoking the episcopate to the Ecumenical Council of the Vatican, in *The Church, op. cit.*, Note #4, Question #1, above, page 193.

3. Text of *Dei Filius* in Broderick, *op. cit.*, Note #6, Introduction, above, pages 37-52.

4. Hughes, Philip, *op. cit.*, Note #6, Question #1, above, pages 33-36.

5. *Ibid.*, pages 181 and 239.

6. *Ibid.*, page 176 and page 240.

7. Wojtyla, Karol (Pope John Paul II), *Sources of Renewal, The Implementation of Vatican II*, Harper & Row, San Francisco, 1979, pages 16-17.

8. Pope Pius IX, (1) Letter *Dolendum Profecto*, March 12, 1870, to Dom Gueranger, Abbot of Solesmes; (2) Letter *Inter Gravissimas*, October 28, 1870, to the German Episcopal Assembly at Fulda. In *The Church, op. cit.*, Note #4, Question #1, above, pages 202 and 219-220.

9. Pope Leo XIII, Letter *Sicut Acceptum*, April 29, 1889, to the Archbishop of Munich. In *The Church, op. cit.*, Note #4, Question #1, above, page 282.

10. Ott, Ludwig, *Fundamentals of Catholic Dogma*, Edited in English by James Canon Bastible, D.D., and translated from the German by Patrick Lynch, Ph.D., B. Herder Book Company, St. Louis, Missouri, 1954, page 298.

11. Cited by Hughes, *op. cit.*, Note #6, Question #1, above, page 14.

12. *Ibid.*, page 15.

13. Quoted in Ward, Wilfred, *The Life of John Henry Cardinal Newman*, Longmans, Green, and Company, New York, 1912, Vol. II, page 240.

14. Quoted in Fliche, Augustin and Martin, Victor (Eds.), *Histoire de l'Eglise Depuis Les Origines Jusqu'à Nos Jours*, Bloud and Gay, Paris, 1948, Vol. 4, page 182.

15. See *The Christian Faith in the Doctrinal Documents of the Catholic Church*. Edited by J. Neuner, S.J., and J. Dupuis, S.J., Christian Classics, Inc., Westminster, Maryland, 1975, pages 21-24. The Council of Trent's teaching that the Catholic bishops are the successors of the apostles is to be found in the same volume, chiefly, page 468.

16. Pope Pius IX, Letter *Tuas Libenter*, December 21, 1863, to the Archbishop of Munich. In *The Church, op. cit.*, Note #4, Question #1, above, page 173.

QUESTION #3

1. See Neuner and Dupuis, *op. cit.*, Note #14, Question #2, above, page 463.

2. Quoted in Hughes, *op. cit.*, Note #6, Question #1, above, page 64.

3. For the full text of the Vatican I Dogmatic Constitution *Pastor Aeternus*, July 18, 1870, see Broderick, *op. cit.*, Note #6, Introduction, above, pages 53-63.

4. This text from the Council of Trent is taken from Neuner and Dupuis, *op. cit.*, Note #14, Question #2, above, pages 353-354.

5. From *Ibid.*, pages 218-219.

6. Pope Pius IX, Encyclical *Quartus Supra* to the Armenians, January 6, 1873. In *The Church, op. cit.*, Note #4, Question #1, above, page 226.

7. Bellarmine, St. Robert, in *De Rom. Pont.*, iv, 2. Cited in Newman, John Henry Cardinal, *An Essay on the Development of Christian Doctrine*, Christian Classics, Westminster, Maryland, 1968, page 87.

8. Quoted in Ward, *op. cit.*, Note #12, Question #2, above, page 193.

QUESTION #4

1. Jungmann, Rev. Joseph A., S.J., *The Mass of the Roman Rite: Its Origins and Development.* Translated by Rev. Francis A. Brunner, C.SS.R.; revised by Charles K. Riepe. Christian Classics, Westminster, Maryland, 1974, page 105.

2. *The Catholic Encyclopedia.* In Fifteen Volumes. New York, Robert Appleton Company, 1911. Volume X, page 357.

3. Jungmann, *op. cit.*, Note #1, to this Question, above, page 106.

4. Quoted in Dunne, George H., S.J., *Generation of Giants*, University of Notre Dame Press, Notre Dame, Indiana, 1962, pages 164-165.

5. Pope Pius X, Apostolic Constitution *Divino Afflatu*, November 1, 1911, in Seasoltz, R. Kevin, *The New Liturgy: A Documentation 1903-1965*, New York, Herder and Herder, 1966, pages 22-26.

6. See *Magnum Bullarium Romanum, Tomus Quintus, Pars Tertia*, Roma, 1746, *An. Ch.* 1570, page 116.

7. Pope Pius XII, Decree *Maxima Redemptionis*, (by the Sacred Congregation of Rites), November 16, 1955, excerpt in *The Liturgy* (Papal Teachings), selected and arranged by the Benedictine Monks of Solesmes; translated by the Daughters of St. Paul, St. Paul Editions, Boston, Massachusetts, 1962, pages 468-470; full text in Seasoltz, *op. cit.*, Note #5, to the Question, above, pages 209-218.

8. Pope John XXIII, *Rubricarum Instructum*, July 25, 1960, quoted in *The Liturgy*, Note #7, Question #4, above, pages 565-566.

9. Wiltgen, Ralph M., S.V.D., *The Rhine Flows Into the Tiber*, New York, Hawthorne Books, 1967, pages 45-46.

10. See Note on the Obligation to Use the New Roman Missal *Conferentiarum Episcopalium*, 28 October, 1974, in Flannery, *op. cit.*, Note #2, Introduction, above, pages 281-282.

11. See Bouscaren, T. Lincoln, S.J., and Ellis, Adam C., S.J., *Canon Law: A Text and Commentary*. Third Revised Edition. The Bruce Publishing Company, Milwaukee, Wisconsin, 1957, page 35.

12. *Ibid.*

13. Quoted by Flanagan, Fr. John W., S.T.L., D.C.L., in *Catholic Priest's Association Newsletter*, Vols. 1 and 2, 1973, page 48.

14. Gregory XVI, *Studium Pio*, August 16, 1842, to the Archbishop of Rheims. In *The Liturgy, op. cit.*, Note #7, Question #4, above, pages 121-122.

15. See "Mass, Liturgy of the," in *op. cit.*, Note #2, Question #4, above, Volume IX, page 798.

16. See the work cited in Note #1 to this Question, above.

QUESTION #5

1. See *Conferentiarum Episcopalium*, Note on the Obligation to Use the New Roman Missal, Note #10, Question #4, above.

2. See *Ibid.*

3. For the text of *Indulgentiarum Doctrina*, see Flannery, Gen. Ed., *op. cit.*, Note # 2, Introduction, above, pages 62-79, especially page 78; for the text of *Romano Pontifici Eligendo*, see *L'Osservatore Romano* (English), November 20, 1975, pages 1-7, especially page 7.

4. Pope St. Pius X, Apostolic Constitution *Promulgandi*, September 29, 1906; in *Acta Apostolicae Sedis* I, 1909, page 5; cited by Bishop Leo Blais in the pamphlet listed in Note # 13, Question # 6, below.

5. St. Thomas Aquinas, *Summa Theologica*, II-II, Q. 104, A. 2.

6. The text of Pope Paul VI's May 24, 1976 Address to the Consistory of Cardinals is contained in *L'Osservatore Romano* (English edition), June 3, 1976, pages 1-4.

7. See Bouscaren and Ellis, *op. cit.*, Note # 11, Question # 4, above, page 42.

QUESTION # 6

1. The General Council of Trent, Fourth Session, Decree on Sacred Books and on Traditions to be Received (1546); the text quoted may be found in Neuner and Dupuis, *op. cit.*, Note # 14, Question # 2, above, page 73.

2. Pope Pius XII, Encyclical *Humani Generis*, August 12, 1950. In *The Church* (Papal Teachings), *op. cit.*, Note # 4, Question # 1, above, page 659.

3. Pope Pius IX, Letter *Inter Gravissimas*, October 28, 1870, to the Episcopal Assembly at Fulda. In *Ibid.*, pages 218-219.

4. Pope Gregory XVI, Encyclical *Quo Graviora*, October 4, 1833, to the Bishops of the Rhineland. In *Ibid.*, page 131.

5. Pope Pius VI, Apostolic Constitution *Auctorem Fidei*, August 28, 1794, in *Ibid.*, pages 94-95; page 343.

6. Pope Gregory XVI, Encyclical *Quo Graviora*, October 4, 1833, to the Bishops of the Rhineland. In *Ibid.*, page 132.

7. Pope Benedict XV, Encyclical *Ad Beatissimi*, November 1, 1914, in *Ibid.*, page 404.

8. On liturgical scholarship and the liturgical movement, see, for example: Quitslund, Sonya A., *Beauduin: A Prophet Vindicated*, Newman Press: New York, Paramus, New Jersey, and Toronto, Ontario, 1973; especially Chapters II and III; also, Bouyer, Louis, *Liturgical Piety*, University of Notre Dame Press, South Bend, Indiana, 1955, especially Chapters I, II, IV and V; also, Jungmann, Josef A., S.J., *The Mass: An Historical, Theological and Pastoral Survey*, translated by Julian Fernandes, S.J., and edited by Mary Ellen Evans, The Liturgical Press, Collegeville, Minnesota, 1975.

9. In *The Liturgy*, *op. cit.*, Note # 7, Question # 4, above, pages 217-221; 226-227.

10. Pope St. Pius X, Motu Proprio *Tra le Sollecutudini*, November 22, 1903. In *Ibid.*, page 178.

11. In *Ibid.*, pages 565-568.

12. Pope Pius XII, Instruction of the Congregation of Rites on Sacred Music and the Sacred Liturgy, September 3, 1958. Text in *The Pope Speaks*, Vol. 5, No. 2, Spring, 1959, pages 223 ff.

13. Figure quoted by Blais, Bishop Leo, *Les Messes de la Nouvelle Liturgie*, pamphlet published with the authorization of the Archbishop of Montreal, no date given, page 3.

14. See Martimort, Aimé-Georges, "But What Is the Mass of Pius V?" *L'Osservatore Romano* (English edition), September 16, 1976, page 11.

15. See "The Mass, Liturgy of the," in *op. cit.*, Note # 2, Question # 4, above, pages 793, 795.

16. Letter of the Holy Office to the Archbishop of Boston, 1949, text in Neuner and Dupuis, *op. cit.*, Note #14, Question #2, above, pages 235-237.

QUESTION #7

1. See Council of Trent, Twenty-second Session, Doctrine on the Most Holy Sacrifice of the Mass (1562), in Neuner and Dupuis, *op. cit.*, Note #14, Question #2, above, page 402.

2. See Blais, Bishop Leo, *op. cit.*, Note #13, Question #6, above, page 21; also *Documentation Catholique* #58, 1976, page 649.

3. The text of the Instruction on the Worship of the Eucharistic Mystery *Eucharisticum Mysterium*, 25 May 1967, is contained in Flannery, Gen. Ed., *op. cit.*, Note #2, Introduction, above, pages 100-136.

4. Most of the General Instruction on the Roman Missal may also be found in Flannery, *op. cit.*, Note #2, Introduction, above, pages 154-205; some detailed directives on the celebration of the Mass are omitted from this edition; the full text can be found in the front of many altar missals.

5. Quoted in Brodrick, James, S.J., *Saint Peter Canisius*, Loyola University Press, Chicago, 1962, page 35.

6. Quoted in *Note Doctrinale sur le Nouvel Ordo Missae, Capitulaire Doctrinale*, No. 2, *Sup. à Défense du Foyer*, No. 111, Février, 1970, page 44, Note 1.

7. Quoted in *La Croix* (Paris), June 15, 1977; our translation.

8. Pope Pius IX, Letter *Dolendum Profecto*, March 12, 1870, to Dom Gueranger, Abbott of Solesmes, in *The Church*, *op. cit.*, Note #4, Question #1, above, page 202.

9. See Dupuy, Abbé Jacques, *Le Missal Traditionel de Paul VI*, Editions Téqui, 82 Rue Bonaparte, 75006 Paris, France, 1977, pages 73-75.

QUESTION #8

1. See Note #10, Question #4, above.

2. See Newsletter, Bishops' Committee on the Liturgy, October-November, 1969; Vol. 5, No. 10-11.

3. *Ibid.*, Vol. 6, No. 2-3.

4. See *Ibid.*, September, 1967; Vol. 3, No. 9.

5. Pope Pius XII, "Priesthood and Government," Allocution to the Cardinals and Bishops, November 2, 1954, in *The Church* (Papal Teachings), *op. cit.*, Note #4, Question #1, above, page 719.

6. Pope Pius XII, Encyclical *Mediator Dei*, November 20, 1947, in *Ibid.*, page 634.

7. Pope Pius XI, Apostolic Letter *Singulare Illud*, June 13, 1926, to the General of the Jesuits, in *Ibid.*, page 445.

8. See Hardon, John, S.J., *The Catholic Catechism*, Doubleday and Company, Inc., Garden City, New York, 1975, pages 290-295, for a concise but very useful discussion of the role of conscience according to the traditional teaching of the Church.

9. Pope Pius XII, "The Church and Morality," Radio Message to Italian Families, March 23, 1952, in *The Church* (Papal Teachings) *op. cit.*, Note #4, Question #1, above, page 681.

10. Quoted in *Ibid.*, page 343.

11. Pope Gregory XVI, Encyclical *Mirari Vos*, August 15, 1832. In *Ibid.*, page 126.

12. St. Thomas Aquinas, *Summa Theologica*, II-II, Q. 104, A. 5.

13. Pope St. Pius X, Encyclical *Pascendi Dominici Gregis*, September 8, 1907, in *The Church*, Note # 4, Question # 1, above, page 377.

EXCURSUS

1. For background on the change from Latin to Vernacular, see Flannery, *op. cit.*, Note # 2, Introduction, above, pages 39, 1030.

2. *Jubilate Deo* is published by the Publications Office of the United States Catholic Conference, 1312 Massachusetts Avenue, Washington, D.C. 20005.

3. Hitchcock, James, *The Recovery of the Sacred*, The Seabury Press, New York, 1974.

QUESTION # 9

1. See Neuner and Dupuis, *op. cit.*, Note # 14, Question # 2, above, pages 538-539.

2. Council of Trent, Sixth Session, Decree on Justification (1547), Chapter III. In *Ibid.*, page 521.

3. See Ott, *op. cit.*, Note # 9, Question # 2, above, page 187.

4. *Ibid.*, page 186.

5. See in Neuner and Dupuis, *op. cit.*, Note # 14, Question # 2, above, page 130.

6. Benoit, Pierre, O.P., "The Accounts of the Institution and What They Imply," in *The Eucharist in the New Testament: A Symposium*, Helicon Press, Baltimore and Dublin, 1964, page 80.

7. Kilmartin, Edward J., S.J., "The Sacrificial Meal of the New Covenant," in Paulist Press Doctrinal Pamphlet series, 1965, page 4.

8. St. Thomas Aquinas, *Summa Theologica*, Q. 75, A. 2, Reply to Objection 2.

9. Gassner, Jerome, O.S.B., *The Canon of the Mass*, B. Herder Company, St. Louis and London, 1949, page 273.

10. Piault, Bernard, *What Is a Sacrament?* Twentieth Century Encyclopedia of Catholicism, New York, Hawthorne Books, 1963, Vol. 49, page 119.

11. This text has been reproduced from that found in Flannery, *op. cit.*, Note # 3, Introduction, pages 271-272.

QUESTION # 10

1. *Catechism of the Council of Trent for Parish Priests.* Issued by order of Pope Pius V. Translated into English with Notes by John A. McHugh, O.P., S.T.M., L.H.D. and Charles J. Callan, O.P., S.T.M., L.H.D., Marian Publications, South Bend, Indiana, no date, page 227.

2. Quoted from St. Thomas Aquinas, *Summa Theologica*. First complete American Edition in Three Volumes. Literally translated by Fathers of the English Dominican Province, Benziger Brothers, Inc., New York, Boston, Cincinnati, Chicago and San Francisco, 1947, Vol. II, page 2475; ST III, Q. 78, A. 3.

3. Quoted from *op. cit.*, Note # 1 to this Question, above, pages 226-227.

4. Quoted from *op. cit.*, Note # 2 to this Question above, page 2473; Reply to Obj. 2.

5. S. Thomae Aquinatis, *Summa Theologica, Tomus Quintus*, Taurini (Italia), *Ex Officina Libraria Marietti anno 1820 condita*, 1937, page 153.

6. St. Thomas Aquinas, *Quodlibetum* IX, q. 8, corp., *Questiones Quodlibetales*, Ed. R. Spiazzi, Rome, Marietti, 1949, page 94.

7. Attwater, Donald (Ed.), *A Catholic Dictionary*, Third Edition, New York, The Macmillan Company, 1961, page 117, Article "Consecration at Mass."

8. Wilmers, W., *Handbook of the Christian Religion*, Second Edition, 1891, page 336.

9. Capello, F. M., *Tractatus Canonico-Moralis de Sacramentis*, Vol. I., page 253, N. 288.

10. Davis, Henry, S.J., *Moral and Pastoral Theology*. In Four Volumes. Sheed and Ward, London, 1935, Volume Three, page 131.

11. In Ott, *op. cit.*, Note # 9, Question # 2, above, page 391.

12. Jungmann, Josef A., S.J., *The Mass: An Historical, Theological and Pastoral Survey*. Translated by Julian Fernandes, S.J.; edited by Mary Ellen Evans. The Liturgical Press, Collegeville, Minnesota, page 132.

13. See Attwater, *op. cit.*, Note # 7 to this Question, above, page 434.

14. Dom Leclercq, *Dictionnaire d'Archéologie Chrétienne et de Liturgie* (Col. 730-750).

15. In Jungmann, *op. cit.*, Note # 1, Question # 4, above, page 19.

16. From King, Archdale A., *Rites of Eastern Christendom*, Catholic Book Agency, Rome, 1947. In Vol. I, pages 621-622.

17. From Brightman, E., *Liturgies, Eastern and Western*, Oxford, 1896, Vol. I; also Day, Peter D., *Eastern Christian Liturgies*, 1972, page 141.

18. From Kucharek, Casimir, *The Byzantine Slavic Liturgy of St. John Chrysostom*, Alleluia Press, Allendale, New Jersey, 1971, pages 97-98.

19. For instance, see Hadji-Burmester, O.H.E., "A Comparative Study of the Forms of Words of Institution and the *Epiclesis* in the Anaphoras of the Ethiopic Church," *Eastern Churches Quarterly*, Vol. XIII, Spring, 1959, pages 13-42, who reproduces more than a dozen such eucharistic prayers, only two of which include the "for many."

20. *Ibid.*

QUESTION # 11

1. See Jungmann, *op. cit.*, Note # 1, Question # 4, above, pages 421-422.

2. St. Cyril of Alexandria, Commentary on the Gospel of St. Matthew. Quoted in Pope Paul VI's Encyclical *Mysterium Fidei*.

QUESTION # 12

1. See Coventry, John, S.J., *The Breaking of the Bread: A Short History of the Mass*, Sheed and Ward, London and New York, 1950, pages 37-43; 115-147; and Fortescue, Adrian, *The Mass: A Study of the Roman Liturgy*, Longmans, Green and Co., London, 1912, Chapter III, especially page 163.

2. Council of Trent, Thirteenth Session, Decree on the Most Holy Eucharist, in Neuner and Dupuis, *op. cit.*, Note # 14, Question # 2, above, especially page 392.

3. Jungmann, *op. cit.*, Note # 12, Question # 10, above, page 200.

4. Pleyber, Jean, in *Ecrits de Paris*, October, 1976.

QUESTION # 13

1. The relevant texts in the General Instruction on the Roman Missal can be found in Flannery, Gen. Ed., *op. cit.*, Note #3, Introduction above pages 154-205.

2. *Ibid.*, page 162.

3. *Ibid.*, page 174.
4. *Ibid.*, page 190.
5. *Ibid.*, page 154.
6. See the article on "The Mass, Liturgy of" in the old *Catholic Encyclopedia*, Note # 2, Question # 4, above, page 790. For a complete discussion of the origin of the name "Mass" to describe the eucharistic sacrifice, see also Jungmann, *op. cit.*, Note # 1, Question # 4, above, pages 129-133.
7. St. Cyril of Jerusalem, *Cat.* 18, 23-25: P. 6. 33, 1043-1047.
8. Quoted in Jungmann, *op. cit.*, Note # 12, Question # 10, above, page 25.

QUESTION # 14

1. In *Triumph*, December, 1969, special supplement.
2. Letter from His eminence Alfredo Cardinal Ottaviani to Dom Gérard Lafond, O.S.B., in *Documentation Catholique*, # 67, 1970, pages 215-216 and 343.
3. In *Cruzado Espagnol*, May 25, 1970.
4. From Leroy, Philippe, *"Pierre a Parlé,"* Chevaliers # 32, 1976.
5. "Cardinal Journet and the New Order of the Mass," in *Documentation Catholique* # 9, May 1, 1977, pages 444-445; our translation.
6. *Ibid.*, page 445; again our translation.

QUESTION # 15

1. Pope Pius XII, *Mediator Dei*, America Press, 1961. Notes and Commentary by Fr. Gerald Ellard.
2. Quoted in Ward, *op. cit.*, Note # 12, Question # 2, above, page 240.
3. Hughes, *op. cit.*, Note # 6, Question # 1, above, page 59.
4. Mich, Mario A., S.D.B., "Don Bosco: Apostle of the Papacy," in *American Ecclesiastical Review*, August, 1962, page 104.

QUESTION # 16

1. *Documentation Catholique*, # 58, 1976, page 42.
2. *Ibid.*
3. Pope Leo XIII, Letter *Epistola Tua* to Cardinal Guibert, Archbishop of Paris, June 17, 1885, in *The Church, op. cit.*, Note # 4, Question # 1, above, page 265.
4. Pope Pius XII, Allocution to the General Congregation of the Society of Jesus, September 10, 1957, in Ibid., page 759.
5. See Brodrick, *op. cit.*, Note # 5, Question # 7, above, page 70.
6. Quoted in Neuner and Dupuis, *op. cit.*, Note # 14, Question # 2, above, page 225.
7. Newman, *op. cit.*, Note # 7, Question # 3, above, page 133.
8. Pope St. Pius X, "Love for the Pope," Allocution to the members of the Apostolic Union, November 18, 1912, in *The Church, op. cit.*, Note # 4, Question # 1, above, pages 395-396.

QUESTION # 17

1. Wojtyla, Karol (Pope John Paul II), *Sign of Contradiction*, The Seabury Press, New York, 1979, page 155.
2. St. Thomas Aquinas, *Summa Theologica*, I-II, Q. 97. A. 2.

3. Newman, *op. cit.*, Note # 5, Question # 1, above, Preface, page lii.

4. St. Thomas Aquinas, *Summa Theologica*, I-II, Q. 97.

5. See Jungmann, *op. cit.*, Note # 1, Questions # 4, above, and Note # 12, Question # 10, above.

6. See Neuner and Dupuis, *op. cit.*, Note # 14, Question # 2, above, page 46.

7. See Note # 3, Introduction, above.

8. Pope Paul VI, "Obstacles to Liturgical Renewal," to the Commission for Implementing the Constitution on the Sacred Liturgy, in *The Pope Speaks*, Vol. 12, No. 2, April 19, 1967.

9. *The Cambridge Medieval History*, Edited by H. M. Gwatkin and J. P. Whitney, Volume 1, "The Christian Roman Empire and the Foundation of the Teutonic Kingdoms," Cambridge, at the University Press, 1967 (Second Edition), page 165.

10. See Newman, John Henry Cardinal, *On Consulting the Faithful in Matters of Doctrine.* Edited with an Introduction by John Coulson, Sheed and Ward, New York, 1961.

11. St. Athanasius, Apol. Contr. Arian. in *Historical Tracts of S. Athanasius, Archbishop of Alexandria*, Oxford: James Parker and Co., J.G.F. and J. Rivington, London, 1873, page 24.

12. For a brief account of the Council of Ephesus, see Hughes, *op. cit.*, Note # 6, Question # 1, above, pages 46-67.

13. See Neuner and Dupuis, *op. cit.*, Note # 13, Question # 2, above, page 147.

14. See Hughes, *op. cit.*, Note # 6, Question # 1, above, page 375; and for the reference to "apostasy" see Laux, John, *Church History*, Benziger Brothers, 1945, page 517.

15. See Ward, *op. cit.*, Note # 12, Question # 2, above, page 310.

16. St. Francis de Sales, *Treatise on the Love of God*, Book II, Chapter 14.

QUESTION # 18

1. Pope Leo XIII, Letter *Exima nos Laetitia* to the Bishop of Poitiers, July 19, 1893, in *The Church, op. cit.*, Note # 4, Question # 1, above, pages 291-293.

QUESTION # 19

1. See *National Catholic Register*, January 14, 1979 and July 15, 1979.

2. In the *New York Times*, August 16, 1979.

3. See, for example, the letter of the Bishop of Epinal in *Documentation Catholique*, 4 Mars, 1979, No. 1759, page 246; or the article in *Our Sunday Visitor*, August 19, 1979.

4. See Davis, Henry, S.J., *op. cit.*, Note # 10, Question # 10, above, pages 236 ff.

5. In *World Trends*, February, 1973.

6. See *Documentation Catholique*, No. 1759, 4 Mars, 1979, page 243.

7. See Hughes, *op. cit.*, Note # 6, Question # 1, above, page 42.

8. *Ibid.*, pages 37-45; on this whole period, see also Newman, John Henry Cardinal, *The Arians of the Fourth Century*, Christian Classics, Inc., Westminster, Maryland, 1968.

9. See Duchesne, Msgr. Louis, *Early History of the Christian Church: From Its Foundation to the End of the Fifth Century*, Volume II, New York, Longmans, Green and Company, 1922, pages 157 ff.; page 368; also page 310 ff.

10. Text of Pope Paul VI's June 27, 1977, Address to the Consistory of Cardinals is to be found in *L'Osservatore Romano* (English edition), July 7, 1977.

11. Story in *Timor Domini* (Switzerland), November 23, 1975.

12. Story in *Libre Belgique*, September 20, 1975 ("*L'Attitude Courageuse de Certains Eveques Italiens*"); see also the *New York Times*, September 5, 1976.

13. *L'Osservatore Romano* (English edition), March 13, 1975.

14. Story in *La Libre Belgique*, September 20, 1975, as in Note #12, Question #19, above.

15. Text of the Sacred Congregation for the Doctrine of the Faith's letter on Fr. McNeill's book is to be found in *Origins*, NC Documentary Service, March 16, 1978, Volume 7, No. 39.

16. See "Rome Scores Sexuality Study," *National Catholic Register*, August 19, 1979.

17. *Das Vaterland*, July, 1977.

18. "Tighter Ship Is Pope's Goal as He Steers Vatican II Course, Observers Say," *Our Sunday Visitor*, April 22, 1979.

19. The text of the Holy See's Declaration against Fr. Pohier, along with a commentary, can be found in *L'Homme Nouveau*, April 15, 1979.

20. For the statement of Fr. Schillebeeckx and other Dutch and Belgian theologians, see *Dossier sull' Humanae Vitae, a cura di Vittorio Varaia, Piero Gribandi Editore*, Torino (Italy), 1969, pages 86-88.

21. For the official documents concerning Fr. Hans Küng's censure, both by the Sacred Congregation for the Doctrine of the Faith, and by the German bishops, see *Origins*, NC Documentary Service, Vol. 9, No. 29, January 3, 1980.

22. For the principal documents on which our brief "history" of the Holy See's dealings with Professor Küng was based, see, in addition to the document cited Note #21 to this Question, *Origins*, NC Documentary Service, for the following dates: Vol. 7, No. 24, December 1, 1977; Vol. 3, No. 7, July 19, 1973; Vol. 1, No. 39, March 16, 1972. See also the Sacred Congregation for the Doctrine of the Faith, "Declaration on Two Books of Professor Hans Küng," February 15, 1975, in Kevane, Eugene, *Creed and Catechetics: A Catechetical Commentary on the Creed of the People of God*, Christian Classics, Westminster, Maryland, 1978, pages 239-241.

23. For the complete text of the Apostolic Constitution *Sapientia Christiana*, See *Origins*, NC Documentary Service, Vol. 9, No. 3, June 7, 1979.

24. "Rome Scrutinizes U.S. Theologians," *National Catholic Reporter*, December 7, 1979.

QUESTION # 20

1. Letter of the Holy Office to the Archbishop of Boston, 1949. In Neuner and Dupuis, *op. cit.*, Note #14, Question #2, above, pages 235-237.

2. First Vatican Council, Dogmatic Constitution on the Catholic Faith, *Dei Filius*, in *Ibid.*, page 45.

3. See Profession of Faith by Pope Pius IV, Bull *Injunctum Nobis*, 1564, in *Ibid.*, pages 21-24.

4. In *Ibid.*, page 267.

5. In *Ibid.*, page 267.

6. The full text of Pope Pius IX's encyclical *Quanta Cura* and of its attached Syllabus of Errors can be found in Fremantle, Anne, Ed., *The Papal Encyclicals in Their Historical Context*. Mentor Books, The New American Library, New York, 1956, pages 135-154.

7. Pope Leo XIII, encyclical *Libertas Praestantissimum*, June 20, 1888, in

Gilson, Etienne, Ed., *The Church Speaks to the Modern World: The Social Teachings of Leo XIII*, Image Books, Doubleday and Company, 1954, Garden City, New York, pages 56-85.

8. Text in *Ibid.*, pages 161-187.

9. See Maron, Edward, "A Friendly Separation of Church and State in Spain," *Our Sunday Visitor* magazine, May 20, 1979.

10. See the text of Canon 8 from the Second General Council of Nicaea in Neuner and Dupuis, *op. cit.*, Note #14, Question #2, above, page 262.

11. St. Thomas Aquinas, *Summa Theologica*, II-II, Q. 10, A. 8.

12. *Ibid.*, II-II, Q. 10, A. 12.

13. See Pope Pius XII, Allocution to the Tenth International Congress of Historical Sciences, September 7, 1955. In *The Church, op. cit.*, Note #4, Question #1, above, pages 725 ff.

14. The text of the address of Karol Cardinal Wojtyla to the Eucharistic Congress in Philadelphia can be found in *L'Osservatore Romano* (English edition), November 18, 1976.

15. Message of Pope John Paul II to the United Nations on the 30th Anniversary of the Universal Declaration of Human Rights, in *Origins*, NC Documentary Service, December 21, 1978, Vol. 8, No. 27, pages 417-420.

16. *L'Osservatore Romano* (English Edition), January 8, 1979.

17. *The New York Times*, June 11, 1979.

18. Pope Pius IX, Allocution *Singulari Quodam*, 1854, in Neuner and Dupuis, *op. cit.*, Note #14, Question #2, above, page 268.

19. In *Ibid.*, page 271.

20. In Wiltgen, *op. cit.*, Note #9, Question #4, above, page 252.

21. *Ibid.*, page 251.

22. Bishop Wilhelm Emmanuel von Kettler, "Freedom, Authority, and the Church," in *Social Justice Review*, June, 1976, page 73.

23. St. Athanasius, *op. cit.*, Note #11, Question #19, above, page 279.

QUESTION #21

1. Fr. Werenfried van Straaten, O. Praem., Aid to the Church in Need, Annual Report for 1977: Special Number of *The Mirror*, bimonthly periodical, No. 4, June, 1978, page 11.

QUESTION #22

1. For a brief account of the defection from Nicene orthodoxy in the Fourth Century, see Hughes, *op. cit.*, Note #6, Question #1, above, pages 37-45; for a longer account, see Duchesne, *op. cit.*, Note #9, Question #19, above, Chapters IV-XIII.

2. Vatican Council I, Dogmatic Constitution *Pastor Aeternus* on the Church of Christ, in Neuner and Dupuis, *op. cit.*, Note #14, Question #2, above, page 224.

3. In this account of the "case" of Pope Honorius I, we follow primarily Hughes, Philip, Msgr., *A History of the Church*, Vol. I, The World in Which the Church Was Founded, New York, Sheed and Ward, Revised Edition, 1949, pages 290-305.

4. *Ibid.*, page 294.

5. *Ibid.*, page 296.

6. *Ibid.*, page 295.

7. *Ibid.*, page 302.

8. See Jalland, T. G., *The Church and the Papacy*, SPCK, London, 1946, pages 363-367.

9. Daniel-Rops, Henri, *L'Eglise des Temps Barbares*, Librairie Arthème Fayard, Paris, 1950, page 384.

10. Hughes, *op. cit.*, Note # 3, above, page 302.

QUESTION # 23

1. St. Robert Bellarmine, *De Romano Pontifice*, Book II, Chapter 29. The Latin text can be found in *Roberti Bellarmini, Opera Omnia, Editio nova iuxta Venetam anni MDCCXXI, Dicata Eminentiss. Cardinali Xisto Riario Sforza, Archiepiscopo Neapolitano*, Naples, 1872, *Tomus Primus*, pages 117-118.

2. Pope Leo XIII, Letter *Est Sane Molestum*, December 17, 1888, to the Archbishop of Tours, in *The Church*, *op. cit.*, Note # 4, Question # 1, above, page 280.

3. Pope Pius XII, Allocution to Irish Pilgrims, October 8, 1957, *Ibid.*, page 766.

4. Pope Pius IX, Encyclical *Neminem Vestrum*, February 2, 1854, to the Armenian Catholics, in *Ibid.*, page 157.

5. Pope Leo XIII, Letter *Epistola Tua*, June 17, 1885, to Cardinal Guibert, Archbishop of Paris, in *Ibid.*, page 267 ff.

6. Pope Leo XIII, Letter *Est Sane Molestum*, December 17, 1888, to the Archbishop of Tours, in *Ibid.*, page 279.

7. Pope Pius IX, Encyclical *Quanta Cura* (1864), quoted in Neuner and Dupuis, *op. cit.*, Note # 14, Question # 2, above, pages 218-219.

8. Pope John XXIII, "Opening Speech to the Council," Note # 3, Question # 1, above, page 716.

9. See Note # 2 to this question, above.

10. Pope Leo XIII, Encyclical *Sapientiae Christianae*, in Gilson (Ed.), *op. cit.*, Note # 7, Question # 20, above, pages 267-268.

11. See Note # 2 to this question, above.

12. Vatican Council I, Dogmatic Constitution on the Church of Christ *Pastor Aeternus*, in Neuner and Dupuis, *op. cit.*, Note # 14, Question # 2, above, page 220.

13. Hamer, Jerome, O.P., "To Preach the Gospel: Reflections on the Episcopal Magisterium," in *L'Osservatore Romano* (English edition), January 29, 1979.

14. St. Thomas Aquinas, *Summa Theologica*, II-II, Q. 104, A. 5.

15. See Newman, John Henry Cardinal, *Letter to the Duke of Norfolk*, in *Difficulties of Anglicans*, Vol. II, Christian Classics, Inc., Westminister, Maryland, 1969, especially the chapters on "Divided Allegiance" and "Conscience."

16. See Note # 13 to this question, above.

QUESTION # 24

1. Pope St. Leo the Great, *Sermo II, de Ascensione* 1-4: PL 54, 397-399.

2. Quoted in Ward, *op. cit.*, Note # 12, Question # 2, above, Vol. II, page 313.

3. See Note # 2, Introduction, above, for the description of the best edition of the Council documents which has come out to date.

4. Newman, John Henry Cardinal, *Lectures on the Present Position of Catholics in England*, Longmans, Green and Company, New York and London, 1896, page 390.

5. Newman, John Henry Cardinal, *Discourses to Mixed Congregations.* Christian Classics, Inc., Westminster, Maryland, 1966, page 217.

6. See Note #8, Question #8, above.

7. Pope Pius IX, Encyclical *Mit Brennender Sorge*, March 14, 1937, in *The Church*, Note #4, Question #1, above, page 490.

INDEX